SPEAK CHINESE

by

M. Gardner Tewksbury

FAR EASTERN PUBLICATIONS
YALE UNIVERSITY
NEW HAVEN, CONNECTICUT

TABLE OF CONTENTS

PREFACE

Of the more than two-thirds billion people who speak Chinese, approximately eighty per-cent speak the most common form of Chinese, often loosely termed 'Mandarin,' while the rest speak other varieties of Chinese, including Cantonese, a dialect spoken widely in the many Chinatowns of the United States. In this book you will learn the national language of China or what the Chinese call PU-TUNG-HWA, the 'common language' or standard Mandarin. The Peking dialect is the basis of what is being promoted in China as the standard national language. Since 1949 the government of China has systematically encouraged the spread of 'the common language' all over the country. PU-TUNG-HWA is a standard language that is understood in all major cities, hotels, official travel spots in China and also on the island of Taiwan as well as among many Chinese abroad.

Chinese, like other major languages of the world, is steadily evolving and changing as it responds to the constant shifts in society and politics both within and without China. In particular the extensive changes that have taken place in China since 1949 have sparked considerable language change, especially in the written language. The Chinese government itself in its program to encourage a standard language has made deliberate attempts to alter and simplify the language. However, despite considerable change in the way Chinese looks when written and a very large increase in purely technical and scientific vocabulary, the basic features of the spoken language remain unchanged. In other words, the fundamental phonological patterns, the major grammatical structures and the basic vocabulary stock has not changed appreciably. What is important for the beginning student to keep in mind is that in learning Chinese he is faced with the same problems involved in learning any modern foreign language: master its pronunciation, absorb the major grammatical features thoroughly and acquire an active command of its basic vocabulary. This book, in use for many years at Yale University and, in fact all over the world has helped countless students successfully acquire these skills.

As the user of this book will shortly note, Chinese is represented in these lessons not by Chinese characters but by means of a transcription or romanization system, often called the 'Yale system' because it was first devised at Yale University chiefly by the eminent linguist, George Kennedy. Since then the 'Yale system' has been used at Yale and widely elsewhere. There are at least three transcription systems in common use for modern Chinese and, in reality they do not differ significantly from one another since they all employ English letters to represent Chinese sounds. But the 'Yale system' is the only modern system that was devised by linguists and language teachers especially to suit the needs of English-speaking learners of Chinese. It is perhaps for this reason that the 'Yale system' continues to receive wide approval from both students and teachers of

Chinese. Romanization is not a substitute for characters but is used as a simpler tool for learning spoken Chinese. In any case, the stu- should be warned against becoming romanized-conscious. He is urged, especially in the early stages of study, to get the lesson material primarily though the ear rather than the eye; to get it from class- room presentation and drill and from tapes, rather than from much reading of the text. Listen attentively, imitate accurately, do these things repeatedly, and use the text chiefly for recall purposes.

SPEAK CHINESE approaches the learning of spoken Chinese primar- ily from the angle of sentence structure. Within the brief compass of twenty-four lessons most of the basic sentence patterns of standard Mandarin as spoken in and around Peking are progressively presented. Only enough vocabulary is introduced to give these patterns, and to provide illustrative drill material. Each lesson commences with a dia- logue or narrative. This embodies the new sentence patterns and most of the new words and expressions. Idiomatic English equivalents are given for all of the Chinese text with literal translations added only where they help to clarify the sentence structure. Following the dia- logue or story is a list of the new words and expressions. These are grouped under their respective parts of speech, and in the order they are found in a Chinese sentence. This is important to keep in mind because much of Chinese grammar is related to word-order rather than to rules about inflection or tense.

The heart of our approach lies in the section giving the pattern sentences. These are introduced in logical sequence, starting with the simplest, and leading on to the more complex. The sentence desig- nated as 'pattern' under each heading should be practiced until it becomes not only perfect in pronunciation and rhythm, but automatic. These patterns and at least one of the illustrative sentences which follow should be memorized. The context of each sentence should also be kept in mind if it is not given in the text. In speaking one moves from one complete thought to another, not from one word to another. Hence in learning to speak a foreign language, one should from the very start master equivalents of complete thought not simply definitions of individual words. It has been rightly said that progress in the learn- ing of a spoken language is measured by one's growing familiarity with and facility in the use of basic sentence patterns, not in the number of new words one accumulates. Rapid accumulation of vocabulary is a task for the later stages of language learning.

Considerable care has been taken to keep all of the drill material idiomatic, with no forcing of sentences into particular molds. Among the hundreds of sentences presented, there are none which have to be unlearned as one progresses in the language, although obviously very few of the sentences, particularly those in the earlier lessons, repre- sent the only way a certain idea can be expressed, or even the common- est. A living language is a flexible thing, never stereotyped.

No attempt is made in these lessons to indicate just how a partic- ular sentence is spoken. Although tone marks are given, stress within the sentence or the accent of an individual word or phrase, both of which are of utmost importance, cannot be learned except by much atten- tive listening and accurate imitating of native speakers, or from tapes of their voices. The presence of a tone mark on a syllable does not imply that it receives special stress in speaking. In the first ten lessons tone marks appear on all syllables except those which have no stress or tonal quality whatever. From Lesson XI on, tone marks for many partially stressed syllables are left off. Tape recordings recorded by native speakers are available for the entire book. Students are urged to make constant use of tapes.

A number of notes come at the close of each lesson. These deal with the function of various words, particles and expressions, and describe the structure of different types of sentences as they are introduced. Illustrative sentences accompany all notes. Particular attention is given to the position of words, phrases, clauses, etc., in the sentence, since the author believes that it is more useful, for example, for the student to know that a noun is a word which can be preceded by a measure, than to know that it is the name of a person, place or thing; that a verb is a word distinguised by its ability to take a negative prefix; that everything which modifies a noun precedes it; that Chinese adverbs precede verbs which they quality, etc. Observations such as these describe how Chinese is spoken. They are not offered as rules to be followed.

Students who wish to concentrate entirely on the spoken language should after completing this text, turn to the second volume in this series, a text called CHINESE DIALOGUES, which continues the basic approach of emphasizing grammar-pattern control and strictly limiting vocabaulary. Those students who desire to learn to read Chinese may begin the text called READ CHINESE after completing twelve lessons of SPEAK CHINESE. For those course programs that require a heftier vocabulary and additional drill materials for the spoken language,the text, SPEAK CHINESE: SUPPLEMENTARY MATERIALS, is available. The student or teacher should write to the publisher, Far Eastern Publications, for further information and advice regarding the extensive books and supplementary aids that make up the 'Mirror Series.'

It would be impossible to mention by name each person who has had a share in the making of SPEAK CHINESE. However, special thanks are due to Dr. George Kennedy, past Director of the Institute of Far Eastern Languages at Yale, who was responsible for the main outlines of this approach. to Prof. Gerald P. Kok, Associate Director, for the introductory notes on pronunciation; to Henry C. Fenn, formerly of the Yale faculty for encouragement in the initial stages, and incidentally for the name of this text; to Fred Fangyu Wang, member of the Yale faculty, who has given so much of his time and though to checking the Chinese text; and to many, many others. Although all of the text has been gone over by a number of co-workers and friends and has been 'classroom-tested' at Yale for several years, the author alone takes responsibility for the work as it stands. We issue SPEAK CHINESE in this more permanent form, not because the need for revision is past but in order that it may without further delay become available to a wider group of students and teachers. It is hope that they will share with us their impressions and suggestions for improvement.

M. Gardner Tewksbury with
John Montanaro, General
Editor, Mirror Series

DESCRIPTION OF THE SOUNDS OF CHINESE

Tones   In learning to speak Chinese the initial problems seem more difficult than they really are. This is particularly true of pronunciation. The Chinese have very few sounds which cannot be found in the English language. One of the chief differences between the two languages is the characteristic tone, or movement of pitch, attached to each syllable of Chinese. For instance, in English, the word 'fan' is intelligible whether spoken with a rising inflection as in the question 'Do you have a fan?', or with a falling inflection in the statement 'Let me use your fan.' In Chinese the word 'fan' pronounced with a rising inflection means "to be bored, fed up"; with a falling inflection it means "food or cooked rice." A Chinese word or syllable that will convey a certain meaning when pronounced with a certain tone will yield either a different meaning or no meaning at all if pronounced with a different tone.

In the Peking dialect there are four tones. These tones vary relatively to the range of the speaker's voice. In combination of syllables, the tones may vary slightly but are related to the tone which each syllable has in isolation. The four tones are as follows:

No.	Description	Symbol	Example
1	high and level	‾	gāu
2	high and rising	´	máng
3	(a) by itself or at the end of a phrase low and rising	ˇ	hǎu
	(b) before another syllable with third tone - the syllable is pronounced in the second tone		hěn hǎu → hén hǎu
	(c) before syllables other than third tone - low with no rise		nǐ gāu nǐ máng nǐ lèi
4	falling from high to low		lèi

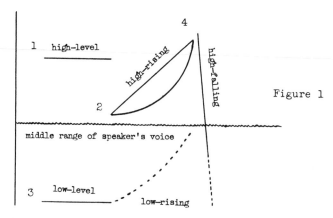

Figure 1

Vertical line indicates the range of the speaker's voice
which may total between a sixth and an octave.

Chinese one-syllable words when they are pronounced by them-
selves have one of the tones described above, but when they are
pronounced in series with other syllables they may be more or less
unstressed. When this occurs, the first, second and fourth tones may
be pitched slightly lower than when receiving stress or all four tones
may be very short and often cut off sharply at the end. In certain
cases syllables have so little stress that they lose their original
tone entirely; such syllables are toneless and will be written without
any marks. The pitch of the toneless syllable depends on the tone of
the syllable before it. The following chart shows the approximate
position of the pitch of the toneless syllable after one of the four
tones in two-syllable combinations.

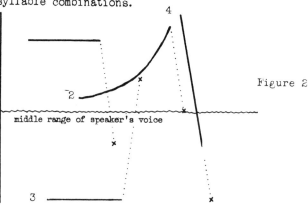

Figure 2

Finals   The number of elements of a Chinese syllable cannot be higher than three: (1) an initial, or the beginning sound, (2) a final, the ending of a syllable, (3) a tone, which may be regarded as characterizing the whole syllable. Tones have already been described. Next we will take up the finals. A final may be a vowel, a consonant, or combination of vowel-plus-vowel or vowel-plus-consonant. Finals alone may constitute complete syllables. The following is a list of finals:

Symbol	Description	Example	Meaning
a	as in *father,* or *ma,* with the mouth wide open	mǎ	horse
am	like the *alm* in *calm*	tām	they
an	between the *o* in *John* and the *a* in *an,* but closer to the *o.*	màn	be slow
ang	like the *a* in *father* plus *ng* in *song*	máng	be busy
ai	as in *aisle*	mài	sell
au	as in *how*	māu	cat
ar	as in *ar* in *car*	wár	to play
e	like the *o* in *done*	dé	obtain
	after *y* like the *e* in *yet*	yě	also
o	like the *o* in *worn* (appears only after *w* or before *u*)	wǒ	I
em	like the *um* in *hum*	dzěm	how
en	like the *un* in *under*	kěn	be willing to
eng	like the *ung* in *lung*	leng	be cold
ei	as in *eight*	lèi	be tired
ou	as in *low*	lóu	building
(w)om	like the *ome* in *come*	wǒm	we
er	like the *er* in *her*	èr	two
i	as in *machine*	pǐ	skin
im	as in *him*	nǐm	you (pl)
in	as in *pin*	pīn	spell out
ing	as in *sing*	pǐng	be level
u	like *u* in *super*	kū	cry

ung	like the *oo* in *book*	lúng	dragon
yu	a sound which is made with the tongue in the position of *i* (as in machine) but with the lips rounded. Like French *u* or German *ü*.	nyŭ	female
yun	the same sound described above plus an *n*	yùn	to ship

Initials. An initial may be a single consonant or a consonant cluster

p	as in *pun*, but with a strong puff of breath	pén	basin
b	like the *p* in *spun*, without any breath after it	bĕn	volume
t	as in *tongue*, but with a strong puff of breath	téng	ache
d	like the *t* in *stung*, without any breath after it	dēng	lamp
k	as in *cool*, but with a strong puff of breath	kū	to cry
g	like the *c* in *scoop*, without any breath after it	gù	to hire
m	as in *month*	mén	door
n	as in *none*	néng	be able to
f	as in *fun*	fēn	to divide
l	as in *lung*	lĕng	be cold
h	as a strong *h* sound in *hot* when said emphatically (like the German *ch* as in *ach*)	hú	lake
y	as in *yet*	yĕ	also
w	as in *weigh*	wèi	to feed
ch	pronounced with a strong puff of breath	chū	emerge
	(1) the tip of the tongue held in the position it occupies in pronouncing the *r* in *true*.		

	(2) the initial pronounced with the tip of the tongue placed as described in (1) and held there until the tone has been completed.	chr̄	to eat
	(3) when followed by *i, y, yu* or *yw* the tip of the tongue is held against the back of the lower teeth.	chī	seven
		chyán	money
		chyù	to go
		chywán	altogether
j	like the *ch* above but without a puff of breath	jù	to dwell
	(1) tongue position same as in (1) under *ch*		
	(2) same as in (2) under *ch*	jř	paper
	(3) same as in (3) under *ch*	jī	chicken
		jyàn	cheap
		jyù	sentence
		jywé	consider
sh	(1) tongue position same as in (1) under the *ch* group	shū	book
	(2) same as in (2) under the *ch* group	shř	ten
r	(1) tongue position same as in (1) under the *ch* group	rén	man
	(2) same as in (2) under the *ch* group	ř	sun
ts	(1) like the *ts* in *it's high,* but with a strong puff of breath	tsài	vegetable
	(2) the initial pronounced with the tip of the tongue held in the position of an *s* until the tone has been completed.	tsž	occasion
dz	(1) like the *ts* in *it's I,* without any breath	dzài	again
	(2) same as in (2) under the *ts* group	dž	character

s	(1) as in *sight*	sài	to compete
	(2) same as in (2) under the *ts* group	sż	four
	(3) when followed by *y, yu,* or *yw* the tip of the tongue is held against the back of the lower teeth.	syî syǔ sywe	west to permit to learn

Consonant clusters. The only consonant clusters found are clusters formed of the initials above, plus *w, y,* or *yw,* for example:

chwán	boat	jyāu	to teach
dzwèi	most	sywé	to learn
lyòu	six	chywán	altogether
syǎng	to think		

Tonal Modifications. The first and second tone (high-level and high-rising) under certain conditions may alter the pronunciation of the diphthongs *au, ou,* and *ei.*

(1) when *y* appears initially or between an initial and the final *ou,* the *ou* is pronounced like the *u* in *super.* The Chinese syllable *you* pronounced with the first and second tones is like the English word *you,* while pronounced with the third and fourth tones it is like the *yeo* in *yeoman.*

(2) when *y* appears initially or between an initial and the final *au,* the *au* is pronounced with a sound between the *ow* in *know* and the *ow* in *now.*

(3) when *w* appears between an initial and the final *ei,* the *ei* is pronounced like the *ei* in *seize.*

ABBREVIATIONS USED IN THE TEXT AND NOTES

N	Noun	NU	Number
A	Adverb	MA	Movable Adverb
SV	Stative Verb	SP	Specifier
P	Particle	M	Measure
Neg	Negative	EV	Equational Verb
V	Verb	IE	Idiomatic Expression
S	Subject	VO	Verb Object
O	Object	CV	Co-verb
AV	Auxiliary Verb	PV	Potential Verb form

LESSON I

STATIVE VERBS – QUESTIONS

HOW DO YOU DO?

A: Nǐ hǎu ma?　　　　　　　　　How do you do?
B: Hǎu. Nǐ hǎu ma?　　　　　　I'm fine. How are you?
A: Hěn hǎu.　　　　　　　　　　Excellent.
B: Nǐ máng bùmáng?　　　　　　Are you busy?
A: Bùmáng. Nǐ máng ma?　　　No, I'm not. Are you?
B: Wǒ hěn máng.　　　　　　　　Yes, I'm quite busy.
A: Nǐ búlèi ma?　　　　　　　　Aren't you tired?
B: Wǒ hěn lèi. Nǐ lèi búlèi?　I'm very tired. Are you?
A: Bùhěn lèi.　　　　　　　　　　Not very.

VOCABULARY

Pronouns (N)

wǒ	I, me
nǐ	you (sing)
tā	he, she, him, her
wǒmen	we, us
nǐmen	you (pl)
tāmen	they, them

Adverbs (A)

hěn	very; quite

Stative Verbs (SV)

gāu	be tall, high
máng	be busy, hurried
hǎu	be good, well
lèi	be tired

Particles (P)

bù–	(negative prefix to verbs and adverbs)
ma	(sentence suffix to simple questions)

PATTERN SENTENCES

I. SIMPLE SENTENCES WITH STATIVE VERBS

　　　　　　　　　n (neg)SV
Pattern: *Wǒ máng.*　I am busy.
　　　　　Wǒ búlèi.　I am not tired.

N	SV		N	neg–	SV
wǒ	*gāu*		*wǒ*	*bù–*	*gāu*
nǐ	*máng*		*nǐ*	*bù–*	*máng*
tā	*hǎu*		*tā*	*bù–*	*hǎu*
wǒmen	*lèi*		*wǒmen*	*bú–*	*lèi*
nǐmen			*nǐmen*		
tāmen			*tāmen*		

II. SIMPLE SENTENCES WITH ADVERBIAL MODIFIER

                N   (neg)A   SV

Pattern: *Tā*   *hěn* *gāu.* He is quite tall.

           Nǐ   *bùhěn* *gāu.* You are not very tall.

N	A	SV		N	neg–	A	SV
wǒ	*hěn*	*gāu*		*wǒ*	*bù–*	*hěn*	*gāu*
nǐ		*máng*		*nǐ*			*máng*
tā		*hǎu*		*tā*			*hǎu*
wǒmen		*lèi*		*wǒmen*			*lèi*
nǐmen				*nǐmen*			
tāmen				*tāmen*			

III. QUESTIONS AND ANSWERS

a) Simple type of question

             N   SV   P

Pattern: *Nǐ* *hǎu* *ma?* *Wǒ hěn hǎu.* How are you? I'm fine.

1. Wǒ gāu ma? Nǐ hěn gāu.   Am I tall? Yes, you're very tall.
2. Nǐ máng ma? Wǒ bùmáng.   Are you busy? No, I'm not busy.
3. Nǐmen hǎu ma? Wǒmen hěn hǎu.   How are you (pl)? We're fine.
4. Nǐ lèi ma? Wǒ bùhěn lèi.   Are you tired? No, not very.

b) Choice type of question

        N   SV   neg-SV

Pattern: *Nǐ máng bùmáng? Wǒ bùmáng.* Are you busy or not? No, I'm not.

1. Tāmen gāu bùgāu? Tāmen bùhěn   Are they tall? They're not so
    gāu.   tall.

2. Nǐmen máng bùmáng? Wǒmen hěn
   máng.

   Are you busy? Yes, we're quite
   busy.

3. Tā hǎu bùhǎu? Tā hěn hǎu.

   Is he (a) good (man) or not? Yes,
   he's (a) very good (man). Or:
   How is he? He's very well.

4. Nǐ lèi búlèi? Wǒ búlèi.

   Are you tired? No, I'm not.

c) Negative form of simple question

                    N   neg-SV   P
Pattern: *Nǐ   búlèi   ma? Wǒ bùhěn lèi.*

Aren't you tired? No, I'm not so tired.

1. Wǒ bùgāu ma? Nǐ bùhěn gāu.

   Am I not tall? You're not very
   tall.

2. Nǐ bùmáng ma? Wǒ bùmáng.

   Aren't you busy? No, I'm not busy.

3. Tā bùhǎu ma? Tā hěn bùhǎu.

   Isn't he (any) good? No, he's
   very bad.

4. Nǐmen búlèi ma? Wǒmen bùhěn lèi.

   Aren't you (pl) tired? Not very.

NOTES

1. VERBS (V) are words which may take the negative prefix *bù-*. Chinese
   verbs are not inflected. Hence the Chinese say 'I is', 'you is',
   'he is', 'we is', etc. One verb form suffices, regardless of
   person, number or tense.

2. STATIVE VERBS (SV) are verbs which describe a quality or condition,
   as: *máng,* be busy; *lèi,* be tired; etc.

   Note that in English the adjective 'busy' is preceded by the verb
   'to be'. When translating this type of sentence from English into
   Chinese, the verb 'to be' is omitted, since it is embedded in
   the stative verb.

3. ADVERBS (A): The function of adverbs in Chinese, as in English,
   is to modify verbs or other adverbs. In every case adverbs precede
   verbs.

4. PRONOUNS (N) behave like nouns, and are classified as nouns.

5. PARTICLES (P) are elements which may be added to a word, phrase or
   sentence to indicate some particular function or aspect. For
   example, the particle *-men* is added to pronouns, and a few nouns

denoting persons, to form a plural; *bù-* is prefixed to verbs to
negate the action of the verb; *ma* is added to the end of a sentence
to form the simplest type of question, etc. (Compare the English
endings -s and -es to indicate plural.)

6. QUESTIONS whose answer in English is yes or no are formed in
   several ways:
   a. The simplest and commonest type of question is made by adding
      the particle *ma* to a statement. The order of the sentence is
      not changed:

      Statement: *Tā hěn lèi.*   He is very tired.
      Question: *Tā hěn lèi ma?* Is he very tired?

   b. Another common type of question is the choice type, formed by
      coupling the positive and negative forms of a verb. The stress
      always comes on the first or positive half of this type of
      question:

      Nǐ lèi búlèi? Are you tired (or not)?

   c. A question may take the negative form of the simple type:

      Statement: *Tā búlèi.*   He is not tired.
      Question: *Tā búlèi ma?* Is he not tired?

7. ANSWERS: A question is commonly answered by repeating the verb of
   the question in its positive or negative form:

   Question: *Tā gāu bùgāu?* Is he tall (or not?)
   Answers: *Tā hěn gāu.*   Yes, he's very tall.
            Tā bùgāu.   No, he isn't tall.

   As in English, it is not necessary to repeat the entire question
   in the answer, if it is perfectly obvious what is meant:

   Question: *Nǐ máng ma?* Are you busy?
   Answers: *Máng.*   Yes, I am.
            Bùmáng.   No, I'm not.

   Note that there is no literal equivalent for 'yes' or 'no' in
   Chinese.

8. TONES ON *BU-* The negative particle *bù-* is pronounced with a falling
   tone, except when it is followed by another falling tone, in which
   case it changes to a rising tone. For example: *bùgāu, bùmáng,*
   bùhǎu, but *búlèi.*

9. GREETING IN CHINESE: In addition to the common form
Nǐ hǎu ma?, How are you?, introduced in Lesson One, another very common greeting is *Nǐ hǎu!* Hello! The res-
onse to *Nǐ hǎu* is also *Nǐ hǎu. Nǐ hǎu* may be used at
any time of the day but *Dzǎu,* Good Morning, is a common
early morning (before ten) greeting.

LESSON II

DIRECT OBJECT – ADVERB *DOU*

BUYING A PEN

A: Nǐ yàu mǎi bàu ma?	Do you want to buy a paper?
B: Wǒ búyàu mǎi bàu.	No, I don't want to buy a paper.
A: Nǐ búkàn bàu ma?	Don't you read papers?
B: Búkàn. Wǒ kàn shū.	No, I don't. I read books.
A: Nǐ mǎi shū ma?	Are you buying a book?
B: Bùmǎi. Shū tài gwèi.	No, I'm not. Books are too expensive.
A: Nǐ mǎi bǐ bùmǎi?	Are you buying a pen?
B: Měigwo bǐ gwèi búgwèi?	Are American pens expensive?
A: Měigwo bǐ bùdōu gwèi.	Not all American pens are expensive.
B: Dōu hǎukàn ma?	Are they all goodlooking?
A: Dōu hěn hǎukàn. Nǐ yàu bùyàu?	Yes, they're all very good looking. Do you want one?
B: Wǒ yàu.	Yes, I do.
A: Nǐ bùmǎi Jūnggwo bǐ ma?	Aren't you buying a Chinese pen?
B: Bùmǎi.	No, I'm not.

VOCABULARY

Nouns (N)		Stative Verbs (SV)	
shū	book	*hǎukàn*	be goodlooking
bàu	newspaper	*gwèi*	be expensive
bǐ	pen, pencil; any writing instrument		
		Verbs (V)	
Jūnggwo	China	*yàu*	want; want to
Měigwo	America (U.S.A.)	*mǎi*	buy
		kàn	look; look at; read
Adverbs (A)			
tài	too, excessively		
dōu	all, both; in all cases		

PATTERN SENTENCES

I. SUBJECT-VERB-OBJECT SENTENCES

             S   V   O

Pattern: *Nǐmen mǎi bàu ma? Wǒmen bùmǎi bàu.*

             Are you buying papers? No, we're not.

N	(neg)	V	N	(P)
wǒ	(*bú-*)	*yàu*	*shū*	(*ma?*)
nǐ	(*bù-*)	*mǎi*	*bàu*	
tā	(*bú-*)	*kàn*	*bǐ*	
wǒmen	(*bú-*)	*yàu mǎi*	*Jūnggwo shū*	
nǐmen	(*bú-*)	*yàu kàn*	*Měigwo bàu*	
tāmen				

1. Nǐ mǎi shū ma? Wǒ bùmǎi shū.

   Are you buying a book? No, I'm not.

2. Nǐmen yàu bǐ búyàu? Wǒmen yàu bǐ.

   Do you want pens? Yes, we do.

3. Nǐ kàn búkàn Jūnggwo bàu? Wǒ búkàn Jūnggwo bàu. Wǒ kàn Měigwo bàu.

   Do you read Chinese papers? No, I don't. I read American papers.

4. Tāmen yàu mǎi bàu, búyàu mǎi shū.

   They want to buy papers, not books.

5. Nǐmen bùmǎi Měigwo bǐ ma? Wǒmen bùmǎi Měigwo bǐ. Měigwo bǐ tài gwèi.

   Aren't you buying an American pen? No, we're not. They're too expensive.

6. Nǐ yàu mǎi bǐ ma? Wǒ yàu mǎi bǐ.

   Do you wish to buy a pen? Yes, I do.

II. USE OF THE ADVERB *dou*

Patterns: (1-4) *Wǒmen dōu mǎi bàu* All of us are buying papers.

                (5-8) *Wǒmen bùdōu mǎi bàu.* Not all of us are buying papers.

                (9-10) *Wǒmen dōu bùmǎi bàu.* None of us are buying papers.

1. Nǐmen dōu hǎu ma?   How are you (all)?
2. Wǒmen dōu hěn máng.   We are all quite busy.
3. **Nǐmen dōu yàu mǎi shū ma?**   Do all of you want to buy books?

4. Měigwo bǐ dōu hěn gwèi.	All American pens are very expensive.
5. Tāmen bùdōu gāu.	Not all of them are tall.
6. Nǐmen bùdōu kàn bàu ma?	Don't you all read newspapers?
7. Tāmen bùdōu kàn shū.	They don't all read books.
8. Měigwo shū bùdōu hěn gwèi ma?	Aren't all American books very expensive?
9. Wǒmen dōu bùhěn lèi.	None of us are very tired.
10. Wǒmen dōu búkàn bàu.	None of us read the paper.

NOTES

1. SENTENCE ORDER: Normal sentence order is essentially the same as in English, namely, Subject-Verb-Object (SVO):

    Wǒ   kàn shū. I read books.

    Tā yàu mǎi   bǐ. He wants to buy a pencil.

2. SUCCESSIVE NOUNS: When one noun follows another noun, the first is subordinated to and modifies the second, unless the two nouns are conventionally coordinated. For example:

    Měigwo shū American books　　But: *shū bàu* books and papers

    Jūnggwo bǐ Chinese pens　　　　 *nǐ wǒ* you and I

3. ADVERBS IN SERIES: The order of a series of adverbs before a verb depends on the sense of the sentence, and the intention of the speaker:

    Tāmen dōu hěn gāu. They are all very tall.

    Tāmen bùdōu gāu. Not all of them are tall.

    　　　　(lit. They are not-all tall)

    Tāmen dōu bùgāu. None of them are tall.

    　　　　(lit. They are all not-tall)

    Tāmen dōu bùhěn gāu. None of them are very tall.

    　　　　(lit. They are all not-very tall)

    Note that the particle *bù-* is here treated as an adverb.

4. THE VERB *YAU* may serve as the main verb in a sentence, or it may stand immediately before the main verb to supplement and assist it. Other such auxiliary verbs will be introduced later:

    Nǐ yàu bǐ ma? Do you want a pen?

    Nǐ yàu mǎi bǐ ma? Do you want to buy a pen?

5. CHOICE TYPE OF QUESTION WITH OBJECT may be expressed in two ways:

a. The object may stand between the positive and negative forms
   of the verb. This is the commoner pattern:

   Nǐ mǎi bàu bùmǎi? Are you buying a newspaper?

b. The object may follow both verb forms:

   Nǐ mǎi bùmǎi bàu? Are you buying a newspaper?

LESSON III

INDIRECT OBJECT – INVERTED SENTENCES

WHO WANTS A CLOCK?

Wǒmen yǒu byǎu. Tā méiyǒu. Tā yǒu jūng. Wǒmen méiyǒu.

We have watches. He doesn't. He has a clock. We don't.

Tā syǐhwan byǎu, bùsyǐhwan jūng. Wǒmen yě bùsyǐhwan jūng.

He likes watches, he doesn't like clocks. We don't like clocks either.

Tā chǐng wǒmen gěi tā byǎu. Wǒmen gěi tā bùgěi tā? Wǒmen bùgěi tā.

He asks us to give him a watch. Will we give him one? No, we won't.

Tā yàu gěi wǒmen chyán. Wǒmen búyàu chyán. Wǒmen yǒu chyán.

He wants to give us money. We don't want money; we have money.

Tā yàu gěi wǒmen jūng. Wǒmen búyàu jūng. Wǒmen bùsyǐhwan jūng.

He wants to give us the clock. We don't want the clock. We don't like clocks.

Jūng bùhǎu. Jūng tài gwèi, yě bùhǎukàn.

Clocks are no good. Clocks are too expensive, and they are not goodlooking either.

Byǎu hǎu. Wǒmen dōu syǐhwan byǎu. Byǎu hǎukàn, yě bùhěn gwèi.

Watches are better. We all like watches. Watches are goodlooking, and not so expensive either.

VOCABULARY

Cardinal Numbers (NU)				
yī	one		shŕyī	eleven
èr	two		shŕèr	twelve
sān	three			etc.
sè	four		èrshŕ	twenty
wǔ	five		èrshryī	twenty-one
lyòu	six			etc.
chī	seven			
bā	eight		Nouns (N)	
jyǒu	nine		chyán	money
shŕ	ten		jūng	clock
			byǎu	watch

	Adverbs (A)	*yǒu*	have, has
yě	also, too; (with negative	*méiyǒu, méiyou*	don't have, hasn't
	statements) either	*syǐhwan*	like, be pleased with
	Verbs (V)	*chǐng*	invite, request; please
gěi	give	*syèsye*	thanks, thank you

PATTERN SENTENCES

I. SENTENCES WITH BOTH INDIRECT AND DIRECT OBJECTS

	S	V	indO	dirO	
Pattern:	*Wǒ*	*gěi*	*nǐ*	*shū.*	I give you a book.
	Chǐng nǐ gěi		*wǒ*	*bǐ.*	Please give me a pencil.

S	(neg)	V	indO	dirO
wǒ	(*bù–*)	*gěi*	*nǐ*	*chyán*
wǒmen		*yàu gěi*	*nǐmen*	*shū*
			tā	*Jūnggwo bǐ*
			tāmen	*Měigwo bàu*
tā	(*bù–*)	*gěi*	*wǒ*	*jūng*
tāmen		*yàu gěi*	*wǒmen*	*byǎu*
chǐng nǐ		*gěi*	*wǒ*	*bǐ*
nǐmen			*tā*	*byǎu*
			wǒmen	*chyán*
			tāmen	*shū*

1. Tā gěi wǒ bǐ. Wǒ syèsye tā.   He gives me a pen. I thank him.
2. Tā méiyou chyán. Wǒ yàu gěi tā chyán.   He has no money. I want to give him money.
3. Nǐmen gěi tā chyán bùgěi?   Are you (pl) giving him money?
4. Tā yàu Měigwo bǐ. Wǒ gěi tā Jūnggwo bǐ.   He wants an American pen. I give him a Chinese pen.
   Wǒ yàu gěi tā jūng. Tā búyàu jūng, tā yàu byǎu.   I want to give him a clock. He doesn't want a clock, he wants a watch.
6. Chǐng nǐ gěi wǒmen bǐ, yě gěi wǒmen byǎu.   Please give us pens and watches.
7. Wǒ gěi tā jūng, bùgěi nǐ jūng.   I give a clock to him, not to you.
8. Tā gěi wǒ shū, bùgěi wǒ bǐ.   He gives me a book, not a pencil.

II. INVERTED SVO SENTENCES

Pattern:

     O   S   V

Shū, bàu, wǒ dōu kàn.   I read both books and papers.

1. Jūnggwo shū, Měigwo shū, wǒ dōu kàn.

   I read both Chinese and American books.

2. Měigwo bǐ, Jūnggwo bǐ, wǒ dōu bùmǎi.

   I'm not purchasing either American or Chinese pens.

3. Shū, bàu, wǒ dōu yàu mǎi. Bǐ, wǒ yě yàu mǎi.

   I'm going to buy both books and papers. I'm going to buy a pen, too.

4. Byǎu wǒ yàu, jūng wǒ búyàu.

   I want a watch, not a clock.

5. Jūnggwo bàu, nǐ kàn búkàn?

   Do you read Chinese newspapers?

6. Jūng, byǎu, wǒ dōu méiyǒu.

   I have neither clock nor watch.

7. Bǐ, nǐmen dōu yǒu ma?

   Do you all have pencils?

8. Jūnggwo shū, nǐmen dōu yàu kàn ma?

   Do you all want to read Chinese books?

NOTES

1. INDIRECT OBJECT: An indirect object precedes a direct object, following the pattern of the English sentence, 'I give you the book.' *Wǒ gěi nǐ shū.*

2. SEVERAL OBJECTS: When there are two or more objects to the same verb, the verb is usually repeated with each object, and a connective such as *yě* used to introduce each subsequent predicate:

   Wǒ kàn shū, yě kàn bàu.   I read books and papers (too).

   Wǒ bùsyǐhwan jūng, yě bùsyǐhwan byǎu, yě bùsyǐhwan bǐ.   I don't like clocks, watches or pens.

   Tā yàu mǎi Měigwo bǐ, yě yàu mǎi Jūnggwo bǐ.   He wants to buy an American pen and (also) a Chinese pen.

3. TRANSPOSED OBJECTS: The object of a sentence may be transposed to the beginning of the sentence, in front of the subject, where it becomes the topic of the sentence. A plural object or a series of objects thus transposed are usually summarized by the adverb *dōu* just before the verb:

   Shū wǒ kàn, kěshr bàu wǒ búkàn.   I read books, but not papers.

Shū, bàu, wǒ dōu kàn.	I read both books and papers. (lit. as to books I read them, but as to papers I don't).
Jūng, byǎu, bǐ, wǒ dōu bùsyǐ-hwan.	I dislike clocks, watches and pens.
Měigwo bǐ, Jūnggwo bǐ, wǒmen dōu yàu mǎi.	We want to buy both American and Chinese pens.

4. THE ADVERB *DOU*: It was seen in Lesson II (Note 3) that the adverb *dōu* always refers back to someone or something already mentioned. In the case of sentences involving both transposed object and the subject of the sentence, if the subject is singular, *dōu* refers back to the transposed object:

Shū, bàu, wǒ dōu kàn.	I read both books and papers.

Where the subject is plural, only context will show whether transposed object or subject or both is referred to:

Shū, bàu, wǒmen dōu kàn.	We read both books and papers, or: We both read books and papers, or: We both read both books and papers.

5. NUMBERS FROM 11 TO 99:

   a. Numbers from 11 to 19 are built on the pattern:
      ten one (eleven) *shŕyī*
      ten two (twelve) *shŕèr*

   b. Tens from 20 to 90 follow the English pattern:
      two-tens (twenty) *èrshŕ*
      three-tens (thirty) *sànshŕ*

   c. The other numbers from 21 to 99 also follow the English pattern:
      four-tens one (forty-one) *sàshr-yī*
      five-tens six (fifty-six) *wǔshr-lyòu*

   In pronouncing three-syllable numeral compounds, the stress is always on the last syllable.

6. *MEI*- is a special negative particle used before *yǒu*. *Bù* is never used with *yǒu*.

LESSON IV

SPECIFIED, NUMBERED, AND MEASURED NOUNS

A DEBATE ON WATCHES

Rénrén dōu syǐhwan byǎu, kěshr rénrén bùdōu yǒu byǎu.	Everyone likes watches, but not everyone has a watch.
Yǒude rén yǒu byǎu, yǒude rén méiyǒu.	Some people have watches, some people don't.
Yǒude rén syǐhwan dà byǎu, yǒude rén syǐhwan syǎu byǎu.	Some people like big watches, some like small ones.
Wǒ yǒu lyǎngge hǎu péngyou. Tāmen lyǎngge rén dōu yǒu byǎu.	I have two good friends. Both of them have watches.
Jèige péngyou yǒu yíge dà byǎu. Tā shwō dà byǎu hǎu.	This friend has a big watch. He says big watches are better.
Nèige péngyou yǒu yíge syǎu byǎu. Tā shwō syǎu byǎu hǎu.	The other friend has a small watch. He says small watches are better.
Wǒ shwō dà byǎu syǎu byǎu dōu hǎu.	I say, big watches and small watches are both good.
Nǐ shwō něige hǎu?	Which do you say are better?

VOCABULARY

	Movable Adverbs (MA)		Measures (M)	
kěshr	but, however	−ge	single person or thing	
		−běn	volume (books)	
	Specifiers (SP)			
jèi−	this (here)		Nouns (N)	
nèi−	that (there); the other	rén	man, person	
něi−	which?	péngyou	friend	
		jwōdz	table	
	Numbers (NU)	yǐdz	chair	
lyǎng−	two or couple of	yǒude	some, some of, certain (used only in subject)	
jǐ−	how many? (answer usually implies only a few)	rénrén	everyone (subject only)	

	Verbs (V)	*dwèi*	SV: be right, correct
dà	SV: be big, large	*shwō*	V: say (that)
syǎu	SV: be little, small	*dǔng*	V: understand

PATTERN SENTENCES

I. SPECIFIED NOUNS

SP-M	N	SP-M	N
jèi-ge	*rén*	*jèi-ge*	*jwōdz*
nèi-ge	*péngyou*	*nèi-ge*	*yǐdz*
něi-ge (?)	*bǐ*	*něi-ge* (?)	
	chyár		
	jūng	*jèi-běn*	*shū*
	byǎu	*nèi-běn*	
	bàu	*něi-běn* (?)	

Pattern: *Jèige rén yǒu chyán.*   This man has money.
　　　　Tā yàu mǎi nèige jwōdz. He wants to buy that table.

1. Jèige jwōdz tài syǎu. Nǐ yǒu dà jwōdz méiyǒu?

   This table is too small. Have you any large tables?

2. Wǒ yǒu lyǎngge péngyou. Jèige yǒu chyán, nèige méiyou chyán.

   I have two friends. This one is wealthy, the other isn't.

3. Nèiběn shū bùhǎu, kěshr jèiběn hěn hǎu.

   That book is no good, but this one is very good.

4. Chǐng nǐ gěi wǒ nèige jūng. Wǒ búyàu jèige. Jèige jūng bùhǎukàn.

   Please give me that clock. I don't want this one. This one is ugly.

5. Jèige rén yǒu byǎu. Nèige rén yě yǒu byǎu. Rénrén dōu yǒu byǎu.

   This man has a watch. That man has a watch, too. Everyone has a watch.

6. Yǒude rén syǐhwan jèige, yǒude rén syǐhwan nèige. Nǐ shwō nǐ syǐhwan něige?

   Some like this one, some like that one. You say which one you like better.

II. NUMBERED NOUNS

NU	-M	N	NU	-M	N
yǐ	-ge	rén	jyǒu	-ge	rén, etc.
lyǎng	-ge	péngyou	shŕ	-ge	
sān	-ge	bǐ	shryí	-ge	
sż	-ge	jūng	jǐ	-ge (?)	
wǔ	-ge	byǎu			
lyòu	-ge	jwōdz	yì	-běn	shū
chǐ	-ge	yǐdz	lyǎng	-běn	
bá	-ge		jǐ	-běn (?)	

Pattern: *Wǒ yǒu yíge péngyou.* I have a friend.
Tā yǒu lyǎngběn shū. He has two books.

1. Wǒ yǒu sānge jūng. Nǐ yàu yíge búyàu?

   I have three clocks. Do you want one?

2. Tā shwō tā yàu mǎi yíge dà jwōdz. Nǐmen yǒu méiyǒu?

   He says he wants to buy a large table. Do you have any?

3. Wǒ yǒu byǎu. Tā yě yǒu byǎu. Wǒmen lyǎngge rén dōu yǒu byǎu.

   I have a watch. He has a watch too. We both have watches.

4. Tā yàu gěi wǒmen sżge yǐdz, yíge syǎu jwōdz.

   He wants to give us four chairs and a small table.

5. Tā shwō tā yǒu sżge byǎu. Wǒ yàu chǐng tā gěi wǒ yíge.

   He says he has four watches. I want to ask him to give me one.

6. Wǒ yàu mǎi yíge Měigwo byǎu, kěshr wǒ méiyou chyán.

   I want to buy an American watch, but I haven't any money.

III. SPECIFIED AND NUMBERED NOUNS

SP	NU	-M	N	SP	NU	-M	N
jèi	yǐ	-ge	rén	jèi	yì	-běn	shū
nèi	lyǎng	-ge	péngyou	nèi	lyǎng	-běn	
něi	sān	-ge	bǐ	něi	sān	-běn	
	sż	-ge	jūng		sż	-běn	
	etc.		byǎu		etc.		
			jwōdz				
			yǐdz				

Pattern: *Jèi lyǎngge rén dōu yǒu chyán.* These two men are both rich.
Tāmen yàu mǎi nèi sānge jwōdz. They want to buy those three
tables.

1. Nèi lyǎngge Měigwo rén, yíge   Those two Americans, one has
   yǒu chyán, yíge méiyou chyán.   money, one hasn't.
2. Nèi lyǎngge jūng, wǒ yàu yíge, I want one of those two clocks,
   tā yàu yíge.   and he wants one.
3. Jèi sānběn shū hěn hǎu, kěshr   These three books are fine, but
   dōu tài gwèi.   they're all too expensive.
4. Jèi shŕge rén dōu yàu kàn Jūng- All ten of these persons want to
   gwo shū.   read Chinese books.
5. Wǒ hěn syǐhwan nèi lyǎngge rén, I like those two persons very much,
   kěshr wǒ péngyou bùsyǐhwan tāmen. but my friend doesn't like them.
6. Jèi lyǎngge yǐdz, wǒ bùmǎi. Wǒ I don't want to buy these two
   yàu mǎi nèi lyǎngge.   chairs, I want to buy those two.

FLUENCY DRILL

Tā mǎi shū.

Tā yàu mǎi shū.

Tā yàu mǎi Jūnggwo shū.

Tā yàu mǎi lyǎngběn Jūnggwo shū.

Tā yàu mǎi jèi lyǎngběn Jūnggwo shū.

Tā yàu kàn jèi lyǎngběn Jūnggwo shū.

Tā hěn syǐhwan jèi lyǎngběn Jūnggwo shū.

Wǒ yě syǐhwan jèi lyǎngběn Jūnggwo shū.

Wǒ yě yàu mǎi jèi lyǎngběn Jūnggwo shū.

Rénrén dōu syǐhwan jèi lyǎngběn Jūnggwo shū.

Rénrén dōu yàu kàn jèi lyǎngběn Jūnggwo shū.

Rénrén yě dōu yàu mǎi jèi lyǎngběn Jūnggwo shū.

NOTES

1. A NOUN (N) is a word which may be preceded by a measure. As in
   English, the chief function of a noun is as subject or object of a
   verb. All Chinese nouns stand for generalized concepts such as
   paper, grain or tea. In English one says: Paper is made of wood
   pulp; Tea is imported from China, etc.

2. NUMBERED NOUNS: Since Chinese nouns are usually not inflected for number or quantity, when it is desired to indicate these aspects, a noun is always preceded by both a number and a measure, as in the following:

>*Wǒ yǒu sānge byǎu.*   I have three watches.
>
>*Tā yàu mǎi lyǎngběn shū.* He wants to buy a couple of books.

3. A MEASURE (M) is a word which may be preceded by a number, or a specifier, or both, and is followed by a noun, in fact or understood. English expressions with a similar function are: a flock of sheep, this pair of shoes, three pieces of pie, etc.

4. THE COMMONEST MEASURE: The general measure, applicable to most nouns, is *-ge*. Even when a more appropriate measure is available, *-ge* is usually permissible:

>*yíge rén*   a person (lit. one 'single' man)
>
>*shŕèrge bǐ* twelve pencils (lit. twelve 'pieces' pencils)

5. MORE SPECIFIC MEASURES: There are a number of nouns which require more specific and appropriate measures. *Shū* is one of these, and *-běn* is the accepted measure:

>*Nǐ yàu mǎi jǐběn shū?* How many (vols.) books do you want to buy?
>
>*Wǒ yàu mǎi sānběn.*   I want to buy three (vols.).

Compare the following English sentences: Give me two sheets of paper; He drank three cups of tea.

6. A SPECIFIER (SP) serves to designate or point out the person or thing referred to. It may stand before a measure and its noun, or before a numbered noun:

>*Nǐ yàu něige yǐdz?*   Which chair do you want?
>
>*Tā yàu jèi sānge bǐ.* He wants these three pens.

7. QUESTION WORDS: A question word occupies in the sentence the same position as the word or words which replace it in the answer:

>*Nǐ yàu něige bǐ?*   Which pen do you want?
>
>*Wǒ yàu jèige bǐ.*   I want this pen?
>
>*Nǐ mǎi jǐběn shū?*   How many books are you buying?
>
>*Wǒ mǎi sānběn shū.* I am buying three books.

Note that sentences containing question words never take the final particle *ma.*

8. NOUNS UNDERSTOOD: Where it is clear from the context what is indicated, the noun numbered or specified may be understood:

Nǐ mǎi něige bǐ? Wǒ mǎi jèige.   Which pen are you buying? This one.
Nǐ yàu jǐge bǐ? Wǒ yàu wǔge.   How many pens do you want? Five.

9. STATIVE VERBS: In addition to their basic verbal use, stative verbs function also as adjectives. Note the following expressions: *dà jwōdz, syǎu yǐdz, hǎu rén, hǎu péngyou,* and *máng rén.*

10. MOVABLE ADVERBS (MA): The Adverbs introduced thus far have all been fixed adverbs (A), in that they always immediately precede the verb or another adverb (*hěn, tài, dōu, yě*). In this lesson, the first of a large group known as movable adverbs is introduced (*kěshr*). These are 'adverbs' in that they always precede the verb, and 'movable' in that they may stand before the subject of the verb, as well as immediately before the verb:

> *Wǒ yǒu chyán, kěshr tā méiyou chyán.*
> *Wǒ yǒu chyán, tā kěshr méiyou chyán.*

11. PRONOUNS BEFORE CERTAIN NOUNS: Pronouns may stand immediately before certain nouns such as *péngyou* (friend) to modify them, where there is a close personal relationship between the two words:

> *wǒ péngyou,* my friend; *tāmen péngyou,* their friends.

12. TONES ON *YI*: The numeral *yī* (one), when used as a cardinal in counting, has the high, level tone. When followed by a measure, however, it behaves exactly like the negative particle *bù-* (see Lesson I, Note 7). Hence *yíge* (*-ge* being intrinsically a falling tone), but *yìběn.* This change is most evident when the number is stressed.

13. *YIGE* AS AN ARTICLE: *Yī* with a measure often corresponds to the English article 'a' or 'an', rather than 'one'. In this sense it never receives stress in speaking:

> *Wǒ yǒu yíge hǎu péngyou.*   I have a good friend.
> *Tā yàu mǎi yìběn shū.*   He wants to buy a book.
> *Wǒ yàu mǎi ge Jūnggwo bǐ.* I want to buy a Chinese pen.

Note that in this use of *yige* as 'a', *yi* is often dropped, leaving *ge* to stay for 'a'.

14. TONES ON *CHI* AND *BA*: These two numerals keep the level tone, except when followed by a falling tone, when they (like *yī*) tend to rise: *chīběn shū,* but *chíge rén.*

As in the case of *bù-* and *yī*, this tone change is most noticeable when the numeral is stressed.

LESSON V

EQUATIONAL SENTENCES

MAY I ASK YOUR NAME?

A: Nín gwèisyìng? — What is your name, sir?

B: Wǒ syìng Wáng. Nín gwèisyìng? — My name is Wang, and yours?

A: Wǒ syìng Jāng. Nèige rén syìng shémma? — My name is Chang. What is that man's name?

B: Tā syìng Yáng. — His name is Yang.

A: Tā shr̀ Dégwo rén búshr̀? — Is he a German?

B: Búshr̀, tā shr̀ Yīnggwo rén. — No, he is an Englishman.

A: Wáng Syānsheng, nín yě shr̀ Yīng-gwo rén ma? — Mr. Wang, are you an Englishman too?

B: Búshr̀, wǒ shr̀ Fàgwo rén. — No, I'm a Frenchman.

A: Nǐmen yǒu syǎu háidz méiyǒu? — Do you have any children?

B: Wǒmen yǒu sānge syǎu háidz: lyǎngge nánháidz, yíge nyǔháidz. — We have three children: two boys and a girl.

A: Nǐmen syáujye jyàu shémma? — What is your daughter's name?

B: Tā jyàu Měishēng. — She is called Meisheng.

A: Wáng Tàitai hǎu ma? — How is Mrs. Wang?

B: Hěn hǎu, syèsye. — Fine, thanks.

A: Háidzmen dōu hǎu ma? — Are the children well?

B: Dōu hǎu. — Yes, they're all well.

VOCABULARY

syānsheng	N: Mr., sir, gentle-man; teacher; polite for husband; you, sir!	(*syǎu*)*háidz*	N: child
		syìng	N: surname
		shéi	N: who?
		shém(*ma*)	N: what?
tàitai	N: Mrs., madam; polite for wife	*dūngsyi*	N: thing
		gwó	N: country, nation
syáujye	N: Miss; polite for daughter	*nán–*	N: male (of persons)
		nyǔ–	N: female (of persons)
nín	N: polite for *nǐ*	*shr̀*	EV: is, are (equals)

jyàu	EV: is called, named	*jŕdau*	V: know, know of or
syìng	EV: is surnamed		about
wèn	V: ask, inquire of or about	*gwèisyìng*	IE: what is your (sur)name?

PATTERN SENTENCES

I. EQUATIONAL SENTENCES

N   EV   N

Pattern: *Tā   shŕ shéi?*   Who is he?

         Jèi(ge) shŕ shémma? What is this?

         Tā syìng shémma?   What is his (sur)name?

         Nèi(ge) jyàu shémma? What is the name of that?

1. Nín gwèisyìng? Wǒ syìng Yáng.   What is your (sur)name? My name is Yang.

2. Nèige rén shŕ shéi? Tā shŕ Yáng Syānsheng.   Who is that man (or woman)? He is Mr. Yang.

3. Něige rén shŕ nǐ péngyou? Nèige rén shŕ wǒ péngyou.   Which one is your friend? That man is my friend.

4. Nèige rén shŕ shémma rén? Tā shŕ Jāng Syānsheng.   Who is that? He is Mr. Chang.

5. Tā syìng shémma? Tā syìng Lǐ.   What is his (sur)name? His name is Lee.

6. Tā shŕ Měigwo rén. Shŕ ma? Shŕ.   He is an American. Is he? Yes, he is.

7. Tā búshŕ Fàgwo rén ma? Tā búshŕ Fàgwo rén.   Isn't he a Frenchman? No, he isn't a Frenchman.

8. Nín háidz jyàu shémma? Tā jyàu Měishēng.   What is your child's name? Her name is Meisheng.

9. Jèi jyàu shémma? Nèi jyàu yǐdz.   What do you call this? That is a chair.

10. Nèige dūngsyi shŕ shémma? Nèige shŕ yíge jūng.   What is that thing? That's a clock.

II. SPECIFIED NOUNS FURTHER MODIFIED BY PRONOUNS

N   SP-M   N

Pattern: *Nǐ nèige péngyou syìng shémma?* What is your friend's name?

                                     (lit. that friend of yours)

1. Wǒ nèige péngyou syìng Lǐ.   My friend's name is Lee.
2. Tā nèige byǎu hěn hǎukàn.   His watch is very goodlooking.
3. Wǒmen jèige háidz hěn syǐhwan kàn shū.   Our child loves to read books.
4. Wǒ bùsyǐhwan wǒ jèige bǐ.   I don't like this pen of mine.
5. Nǐ yàu búyàu kàn wǒ jèiběn shū?   Would you like to see this book of mine?
6. Wǒmen jèige jwōdz tài syǎu.   Our table is too small.
7. Nǐmen jèi lyǎngge yǐdz hěn hǎukàn. Gwèi búgwèi?   These two chairs of yours are very goodlooking. Are they expensive?

FLUENCY DRILLS

Jèi shr̀ shémma?
Jèige shr̀ shémma?
Jèige dūngsyi shr̀ shémma?
Shr̀ bǐ.
Jèi shr̀ bǐ.
Jèi shr̀ Jūnggwo bǐ.
Jèige shr̀ Jūnggwo bǐ.
Jèige dūngsyi shr̀ Jūnggwo bǐ.
Jèige dūngsyi shr̀ Jūnggwo bǐ ma?
Shr̀.

Tā shr̀ shéi?
Nèige rén shr̀ shéi?
Shr̀ Jāng Syānsheng.
Tā shr̀ Jāng Syānsheng.
Tā shr̀ něigwó rén?
Tā shr̀ Jūnggwo rén.
Tā búshr̀ Rběn rén ma?
Jāng Syānsheng búshr̀ Rběn rén ma?
Jāng Syānsheng shr̀ Jūnggwo rén.

Nèi jyàu shémma?
Nèige jyàu shémma?
Nèige dūngsyi jyàu shémma?
Nèige syǎu dūngsyi jyàu shémma?
Jyàu chyán.
Nèi jyàu chyán.
Nèige jyàu chván.
Nèige dūngsyi jyàu chyán.
Nèige syǎu dūngsyi jyàu chyán.
Nèige syǎu dūngsyi jyàu chyán ma?
Dwèile!

Tā jyàu shémma?
Háidz jyàu shémma?
Syǎu háidz jyàu shémma?
Nèige syǎu háidz jyàu shémma?
Nǐmen nèige syǎu háidz jyàu shémma?
Jyàu Měishēng.
Tā jyàu Měishēng.
Háidz jyàu Měishēng.
Syǎu háidz jyàu Měishēng.
Jèige syǎu háidz jyàu Měishēng.
Wǒmen jèige syǎu háidz jyàu Měishēng.

NOTES

1. EQUATIONAL VERBS (EV) state the equality of the two nouns between which they stand. They function like the English verb 'is' in the sentence 'this man is a Chinese':

N	EV	N	
Jèi (ge)	*shř*	*bǐ.*	This is a pen.
Nèi (ge)	*jyàu*	*shémma?*	What do you call that?
Wǒ		*syìng Jāng.*	My (sur)name is Chang.
nèi (ge) rén shř		*Egwo rén.*	That man is a Russian.

   Note that the specifiers *jèi*, *nèi* and *něi*, before *shř* and *jyàu*, may function as nouns, and stand alone without measures.

2. PRONOUNS BEFORE PERSONALIZED AND SPECIFIED NOUNS FURTHER SPECIFIED: Nouns specified and certain personalized nouns may be further specified by the addition of pronouns:

tā tàitai	his wife
wǒ péngyou	my friend
wǒ jèige bǐ	my pen (here), lit. this pen of mine here
tāmen nèi lyǎngge syáujye.	their two daughters, lit. those two daughters of theirs' there.

3. *GWÈISYING* AND *NIN*: *Gwèisying* is the polite form for *Nǐ sying shémma? Nín gwèisying?*, *Syānsheng gwèisying?*, are common variations. *Nǐ jyàu shémma?* is used in asking children their given names, and wherever etiquette does not require a more formal form. *Nín* is a polite form of *nǐ*, very common in North China.

4. SURNAMES precede titles in Chinese, instead of following them as in English. In speaking, the stress always comes on the surname: *Wáng Syānsheng* (Mr. Wang), *Yáng Tàitai* (Mrs. Yang), *Jāng Syáujye* (Miss Chang).

5. NAMES OF COUNTRIES are commonly constructed out of a sound syllable taken from the native name of that country, plus the ending –*gwó* (country):

America	*Měigwo*	(*měi*	beautiful)
England	*Yīnggwo*	(*yīng*	brave)
Russia	*Egwo*	(*è*	suddenly)
France	*Fàgwo*	(*fà*	law, order)
Germany (Deutschland)	*Dégwo*	(*dé*	virtuous)
Italy	*Yìdàlì*	(*yì*	righteous)

   China (*Jūnggwo*) is composed of *jūng* (middle) and *gwó* (country).
   Japan (*Rběn*) is composed of *r̀* (sun) and *běn* (root).

6. TITLES such as Mr., *syānsheng*, Mrs., *tàitai*, and Miss, *syáujye*, while retaining their popularity outside China and in Taiwan, have declined in use in China being replaced by the neutral and non-elitist term, Comrade, *túngjr̀*, used for both males and females.

LESSON VI

MONEY AND COUNTING

BARGAINING FOR A PICTURE

Jāng: Wáng Syānsheng, nǐ yǒu chyán méiyǒu? — Mr. Wang, do you have any money?

Wáng: Yǒu. Nǐ yàu dwōshau? Lyǎngkwai chyán gòu búgòu? — Yes, how much do you want? Would $2.00 be enough?

Jāng: Nǐ yǒu wǔkwài méiyǒu? Wǒ yàu mǎi yìjāng hwàr. — Do you have $5.00? I want to buy a picture.

Wáng: Gěi nǐ shŕkwai chyán. Chǐng nǐ mǎi lyǎngjāng. Wǒ yě yàu yìjāng. — Here is $10.00. Please buy two copies. I want a copy, too.

(MR. CHANG AT LEE'S STORE)

Jāng: Lǐ Syānsheng, nǐmen mài hwàr búmài? — Mr. Lee, do you sell pictures?

Lǐ: Mài. Nín yàu shémma hwàr? — Yes, we do. What kind of pictures do you want?

Jāng: Nǐmen yǒu shémma hwàr? — What do you have?

Lǐ: Jūnggwo hwàr, Měigwo hwàr, wǒmen dōu yǒu. Jèijāng hǎu bùhǎu? — We have both Chinese and American pictures. How about this one?

Jāng: Dwōshau chyán? — How much is it?

Lǐ: Lyòukwai chyán. — $6.00.

Jāng: Lyòukwai chyán tài gwèi. — $6.00 is too high.

Lǐ: Nín gěi dwōshau chyán? — How much will you give?

Jāng: Wǒ yàu lyǎngjāng. Lyǎngjāng wǒ gěi nǐ jyòukwài. — I want two. I'll give you $9.00 for the two.

Lǐ: Shŕkwai chyán, nǐ yàu búyàu? — How about $10.00?

Jāng: Hǎu, gěi nǐ shŕkwai chyán. — All right, here is $10.00.

Lǐ: Dzàijyàn! — Goodbye!

Jāng: Dzàijyàn! — See you again!

VOCABULARY

yígùng	MA:	altogether, in all	*jř*	N:	paper
-bǎi	NU:	hundred	*hwàr*	N:	picture (drawing or
-chyān	NU:	thousand			painting)
-wàn	NU:	ten-thousand	*yìdyǎr*	N:	a little, a bit; some
lǐng	NU:	zero (see note 2)	*jyòu*	A:	only, just
bàn-, -bàn	NU:	half	*gòu*	SV:	be sufficient,
dwōshau	NU:	how much? how many?			enough
-kwài	M:	dollar	*mài*	V:	sell; sell for
-máu	M:	dime	*dzàijyàn*	IE:	goodbye! (lit. see
-fēn	M:	cent			you again)
-jāng	M:	(measure for paper,	*hǎu bùhǎu*	IE:	how about (it)?
		pictures, tables, etc.)			

PATTERN SENTENCES

I. SUMS OF MONEY UP TO $100

Dollars			Dimes			Cents		
NU	M	N	NU	M	N	NU	M	N
yì	-kwai	chyán	yì	-máu	chyán	yì	-fēn	chyán
lyǎng	-kwai	chyán	lyǎng	-máu	chyán	lyǎng	-fēn	chyán
sān	-kwai	chyán	sān	-máu	chyán	sān	-fēn	chyán
sż	-kwai	chyán	sż	-máu	chyán	sż	-fēn	chyán
wǔ	-kwai	chyán	wǔ	-máu	chyán	wǔ	-fēn	chyán
lyòu	-kwai	chyán	lyòu	-máu	chyán	lyòu	-fēn	chyán
chī	-kwai	chyán	chī	-máu	chyán	chī	-fēn	chyán
bá	-kwai	chyán	bā	-máu	chyán	bā	-fēn	chyán
jyǒu	-kwai	chyán	jyǒu	-máu	chyán	jyǒu	-fēn	chyán
shŕ	-kwai	chyán	yì	-kwai	chyán	yì	-máu	chyán
jǐ	-kwai	chyán?	jǐ	-máu	chyán?	jǐ	-fēn	chyán?

bàn	-kwài					$ .50
yì	-kwai	lǐng-		wǔ	-fēn	1.05
yì	-kwai	yì	-máu			1.10
lyǎng	-kwai	èr	-máu			2.20
sān	-kwai	sān	-máu	chyán		3.30
sż	-kwai	sż	-máu	lyòu	-fēn	4.46
wǔ	-kwai	wǔ	-máu	chī	-fēn	5.57

lyòu -kwai	lyòu -máu	bā -fēn	chyán	$ 6.68
chǐ -kwai	chī -máu	jyǒu -fēn		7.79
bá -kwai	bā -máu	sż		8.84
jyǒu -kwai	jyǒu -máu	chyán		9.90
shŕ -kwai	bàn			10.50
shryǐ -kwài				11.00
shrèr -kwai	lǐng-	wǔ -fēn		12.05
èrshryǐ -kwai	lyǎng-máu	èr -fēn	chyán	21.22
sānshrchǐ -kwai	wǔ -máu		chyán	37.50
wǔshrbá -kwai	lǐng-	chī -fēn	chyán	58.07
bāshrjyǒu -kwai	jyǒu -máu	bā		89.98
jyǒushrwǔ -kwai	-bàn			95.50
yìbǎi -kwài				100.00

II. NUMBERS FROM 100 UP

yìbǎi-yī (shŕ)	110	yíwàn	10,000
èrbǎi (or lyǎngbǎi)	200	lyǎngwàn (or èrwàn)	20,000
sānbǎi-chī (shŕ)	370	shŕwàn	100,000
sżbǎi-lǐng-sān	403	èrshr-wǔwàn	250,000
yìchyān	1,000	yìbǎiwàn	1,000,000
lyǎngchyān-èr (bǎi)	2,200	lyǎngchyānwàn	20,000,000
sānchyān-lǐng-wǔ (shŕ)	3,050	yíwànwàn	100,000,000
wǔchyān-lǐng-yī	5,001	(Telephone numbers)	
lyòuchyān-bābǎi-wǔshrchī	6,857	chī-bā-sż-lyòu-bā	7-8468
bāchyān-sānbǎi-bā (shŕ)	8,380	yī-lǐng-lǐng-lǐng-wǔ	1-0005

III. SUMS OF MONEY FROM $100 UP

10,000s (-wàn)	1,000s (-chyān)	100s (-bǎi)	10s (-shŕ)	1s	M	N	
		yìbǎi	lǐng	wǔ	-kwai	chyán	$ 105
		èrbǎi	yìshr		-kwài		210
		sānbǎi	èrshr	bá	-kwai	chyán	328
	sżchyān				-kwai	chyán	4,000
	wǔchyān	lǐng	sānshr		-kwai	chyán	5,030
	lyòuchyān	sżbǎi	lǐng	lyòu	-kwài		6,406
yíwàn					-kwài		10,000
lyǎngwàn	chīchyān	wǔbǎi	sżshr		-kwai	chyán	27,540

IV. USE OF QUESTION WORDS *ji-* AND *dwoshau*

Pattern: *Jèijang hwàr dwōshau chyán?*   How much is this picture?
     Sānkwai-wǔ (máu chyán). $3.50.
     Nèiběn shū mài jǐkwai chyán?   What does that book sell for?
     Sānkwai èrmáu-wǔ. $3.25.

1. Jèige Měigwo bǐ dwōshau chyán?   How much is this American pen?
   Bákwai-chīmauwǔ. $8.75.
2. Nǐ yàu dwōshau yǐdz? Wǒ jyòu   How many chairs do you want? I
   yàu èrshrge.   want only twenty.
3. Nín gěi dwōshau chyán? Wǒ gěi   How much will you give? I'll give
   lyòukwài. $6.00.
4. Yígùng jǐkwai chyán? Yígùng   How much is it altogether? It
   chīkwai-bàn.   comes to $7.50.
5. Jwōdz yǐdz yígùng dwōshau chyán?   How much altogether for table and
   Yìbǎi-líng-wǔkwai chyán.   chairs? $105.00
6. Nèige dà jwōdz shr̀ jǐshrkwài?   How much is that big table? $68.00.
   Lyòushr-bákwài.
7. Jèiběn shū mài jǐmáu chyán?   How much does this book sell for?
   Sānmáu-wǔ yìběn. $.35 a copy.
8. Nǐ yàu mǎi dwōshaujāng jr̆? Wǒ   How many sheets do you want to
   yàu mǎi wǔbǎijāng.   buy? I want to buy 500 sheets.
9. Nǐmen yǒu jǐge háidz? Wǒmen   How many children do you have?
   jyòu yǒu yíge.   Only one.

NOTES

1. NUMBERS ABOVE 100: In fractional numbers above 100, the last
   measure of a series is often dropped:
       yìbǎi-yī (shr̆)   110
       lyǎngchyān-wǔ (bǎi)   2,500
       lyòuwàn-bā (chyān)   68,000
2. LING: Where one or more zeros stand between numbers, the word *líng*
   is inserted:
       yìbǎi-líng-wǔ   105
       yìchyān-líng-wǔ   1,005
       yìchyān-líng-wǔshr̆   1,050
       yíwàn-líng-wǔshr̆   10,050

In giving numbers 'telephone-style', cardinal numbers without measures are used, and *líng* is repeated for each zero:

yī-líng	10
yī-líng-èr	102
yī-èr-líng	120
bā-líng-líng-lyòu-líng	8-0030

3. MONEY EXPRESSIONS: The commonest units for indicating sums of money are the three measures *-kwài* (dollar), *-máu* (dime), and *-fēn* (cent). These are preceded by appropriate numbers, and followed by the noun *chyán* (money):

wŭfēn chyán	$ .05
sānmáu chyán	.30
wŭkwai chyán	5.00

In fractional money sums, the larger units precede the smaller, as in English, and *chyán* follows the entire expression:

yìmáu-wŭfēn chyán	$ .15
shrèrkwai-lyòumáu chyán	12.60

Note that money sums in Chinese become fractional from eleven cents up:

yìmáu-sānfēn chyán $ .13 (not *shŕsānfēn chyán*)

yìkwai-wŭmáu chyán 1.50 (not *yìkwai-wŭshrfēn chyán*)

4. ABBREVIATED FORMS OF MONEY EXPRESSIONS: Money sums are frequently abbreviated, dropping such words as are easily understood from the context. This is specially true of fractional sums. Compare English expressions such as two seventy-five, three pound ten and six:

yìmáu(chyán), èrmáuwŭ(-fēn chyán), sānkwài(chyán),

lyòukwai-chīmáuwŭ(-fēn chyán), yìbăikwài(chyán),

wŭchyán-wŭbăi-lyòushrkwài(chyán)

Note that where abbreviated forms end in a measure, the measure is stressed.

5. *JI-* AND *DWOSHAU*: The question word *jĭ-* (how many?) expects only a small number in reply, usually less than ten. *Dwōshau* (how many? how much? what quantity?) on the contrary, imposes no limit on the number or quantity expected in the answer:

Nĭ yŏu jĭge byău? How many watches do you have?

Wŏ yŏu lyăngge. I have two.

Nǐ mǎi jǐbǎijāng jř?   How many hundred sheets of paper
  Yìchyān-wǔbǎijāng.   are you buying? 1,500 sheets.
Jèige mài dwōshau chyán? What does this sell for?
  Sānkwai-bàn.   Three and a half.
Nǐ yàu dwōshau bǐ?   How many pencils do you want?
  Wǒ yàu sānshrge bǐ.   I want 30 pencils.

Note that *jř-* always takes a measure, whereas *dwōshau,* although
it is a number, seldom requires a measure.

6. ASKING PRICES: In asking and giving prices no verb is necessary,
simply *chyán* (money) preceded by a question expression of quantity.
However, sometimes a verb such as *shř* (is) or *mài* (sell for)
is used:

              Duōshau chyán?   How much?
           Bǐ shr jǐfen chyán? How much for the pencil?
                                (lit. how many cents?)
       Jèige syǎu juōdz mài What does this small table sell
           jǐkwai chyán?   for? (lit. how many dollars?)

7. *ER* AND *LYANG-* COMPARED: In counting, the cardinal number *èr* is
used for the 2s, 20s, and 200s:

       èr, shrèr, yìbǎi-lǐng-èr, etc.
       èrshř, èrbǎi-èrshř, èrshrwàn, èrbǎiwàn, etc.

Either *èr* or *lyǎng-* may be used in the following higher numbers:
èrchyān or *lyǎngchyān, èrwàn* or *lyǎngwàn,* etc.

When two of anything or anyone is indicated, *lyǎng* with an
appropriate measure is used:

       lyǎngge rén   *shrèrge rén*
       lyǎngběn shū   *yìbǎiběn shū*
       lyǎngjāng jř   *èrbǎi-èrshrjāng jř*
       lyǎngkwai chyán   *lyǎngwàn(ge) rén*

Lyǎng- never stands at the end of a number expression: *yǐkwai-*
lyǎngmáu chyán becomes *yǐkwaièr* for the abbreviated form, etc.

In fractional sums, *lyǎng-* is commonly used for the larger units,
and *èr* for the subdivisions:

       lyǎngchyān-èrbǎi, lyǎngwàn-èrchyān-sān,
       lyǎngkwai-èr, lyǎngmáu-èr, etc.

8. TWO OR THREE: Indefinite expressions like 'two or three', in
Chinese, use the pattern 'two-three':

yì-lyǎngge rén	one or two persons
lyǎng-sānběn shū	two or three volumes
sè-wǔmdu chyán	40 or 50 cents
bā-jyǒubǎikwai chyán	$800 or $900
yì-lyǎngchyān(ge) háidz	one or two thousand children

9. THE *WAN* AND *WANWAN* GROUPS: The next units above the *chyān* (1,000) group are not millions and billions as in English, but *wàn* (10,000) and *wànwàn* (100,000,000). This makes the transfer of larger sums into Chinese quite difficult for the Westerner. One way to make this transfer is to point off these higher sums into groups of four digits, rather than the familiar three:

100,000 would be	10,0000	(*shŕwàn*)
1,000,000 would be	100,0000	(*yìbǎiwàn*)
10,000,000 would be	1000,0000	(*yìchyānwàn*)
140,000,000 would be	1,4000,0000	(*yìwànwàn-sèchyānwàn*)
450,000,000 would be	4,5000,0000	(*sèwànwàn-wǔchyānwàn*)

10. APIECE: Expressions such as '5¢ apiece', '$1.00 a volume', etc., are said in Chinese as follows: *wǔfēn chyán yíge, yíkwai chyán yìběn*, etc. The stress usually comes on the last measure, as in English.

Expressions such as "one apiece", "$10.00 a person", etc., are said as follows: *yíge rén yíge, yíge rén shŕkwai chyán*, etc.

LESSON VII

AUXILIARY VERBS – VERB-OBJECT COMPOUNDS

WHAT DO YOU LIKE TO DO?

Lǐ: Gāu Syānsheng, nín ài chr̄ Jūnggwo fàn ma?

Mr. Kao, do you like to eat Chinese food?

Gāu: Wǒ hěn ài chr̄. Wǒmen háidz yě dōu ài chr̄.

I love to eat it. Our children all love to eat it, too.

Lǐ: Nín tàitai hwèi dzwò Jūnggwo fàn búhwèi?

Does your wife know how to cook Chinese food?

Gāu: Hwèi yidyǎr.

A little.

Lǐ: Nín háidz yě hwèi dzwòfàn ma?

Can your children cook, too?

Gāu: Háidz búhwèi dzwòfàn. Tāmen jyòu hwèi chr̄fàn!

The children can't cook. They only know how to eat!

Lǐ: Nǐmen dōu hwèi shwō Jūnggwo hwà ma?

Do you all know how to speak Chinese?

Gāu: Háidz hwèi shwō. Wǒ tàitai yě hwèi shwō. Wǒ jyòu hwèi shwō yìdyǎr.

The children know how to. My wife does, too. But I can only speak it a little.

Lǐ: Nín tài kèchi! Jūnggwo dz̀ nín néng syě ma?

You're being too polite! Can you write Chinese characters?

Gāu: Bùnéng. Ou, wǒ néng syě 'yī, èr, sān' sānge dz̀!

No, I can't. Oh, I can write the three characters 'one, two, three.'

Lǐ: Nǐmen ài chànggēr ma?

Do you folks like to sing?

Gāu: Wǒmen hěn ài chàng.

We love to sing.

Lǐ: Wǒmen syàndzài chàng yìdyǎr, hǎu bùhǎu?

How about singing a little now?

Gāu: Nǐmen ywànyi chàng shémma gēr?

What kind of songs would you like to sing?

Lǐ: Nǐmen hwèi chàng Jūnggwo gēr ma?

Do you know how to sing Chinese songs?

Gāu: Hwèi.

Yes, we do.

Lǐ: Hǎu, wǒmen kéyi chàng lyǎngge Jūnggwo gēr.

Good, we might sing a couple of Chinese songs.

VOCABULARY

syàndzài	MA:	now, at present	*néng*	AV:	can, be able to
fàn	N:	food (cooked rice)	*hwèi*	AV:	can, know how to
táng	N:	sugar, candy	*kéyi*	AV:	may, can, be per-
hwà	N:	speech (spoken			mitted to
		words); language	*ywànyi*	AV:	wish to, be willing
dz̀	N:	word (written char-			to
		acter)	*ài*	V:	love
shr̀(ching)	N:	affair; undertaking		AV:	like or love to
mǎimai	N:	business (buy-sell)	*chr̄*	V:	eat
gē(r)	N:	song	*syě*	V:	write
dàrén	N:	adult, grownup	*dzwò*	V:	do, make; act part
jēn	A:	truly, really			of
kèchi	SV:	be polite, stand on	*chàng*	V:	sing
		ceremony			

PATTERN SENTENCES

I. AUXILIARY VERBS USED WITH VO COMPOUNDS

shwōhwà	talk (speak-language)	*chr̄fàn*	eat (eat-food)
kànshū	read (look at-books)	*dzwòfàn*	cook (make-food)
syědz̀	write (write-words)	*chànggēr*	sing (sing-songs)

S AV — VO

Pattern: *Nǐ ài chànggēr ma? Wǒ hěn ài chànggēr.*

Do you like to sing? I love to sing.

1. Syǎu háidz dōu ài chànggēr. Dàrén yě ài chànggēr. Shéi búài chànggēr?

   All children like to sing. Grown-ups like to sing too. Who doesn't like to sing?

2. Jāng Syānsheng hěn ài kànshū. Tā yě hěn ài syědz̀. Kěshr tā búài shwōhwà.

   Mr. Chang loves to read. He also loves to write. But he doesn't like to talk.

3. Wáng Syáujye jyòu ài kànshū. Tā hěn búywànyi dzwòshr̀.

   Miss Wang only likes to read. She's very unwilling to work.

4. Rénrén dōu hwèi shwōhwà, kěshr bùdōu hwèi kànshū.

   Everybody can talk, but not everybody can read.

5. Yǒude rén hwèi dzwòfàn. Yǒude

   Some people know how to cook, some

	rén búhwèi. Kěshr rénrén dōu hwèi chr̄fàn!	don't. But everyone knows how to eat!
6.	Jūnggwo rén hěn néng dzwòshr̀.	Chinese are very capable.
7.	Nèige rén jēn hwèi shwōhwà!	That man certainly knows how to talk!
8.	Wǒmen syàndzài kéyi chr̄fàn ma?	May we eat now?

II. VO COMPOUNDS WITH MODIFIED OBJECTS

          S   V   Mod   O
Pattern: *Nǐ ài chàng shémma gēr? Wǒ ài chàng Fàgwo gēr.*
What kind of songs do you like to sing? French songs.

1.	Nǐ ywànyi chr̄ shémma fàn?	What kind of food do you wish to eat?
2.	Nǐ yàu búyàu chr̄ yidyǎr Ègwo fàn?	Do you want to eat a little Russian food?
3.	Nǐ hwèi dzwò Ègwo fàn ma?	Do you know how to cook Russian food?
4.	Nǐ hwèi shwō R̀běn hwà búhwèi?	Can you speak Japanese?
5.	Nǐ hwèi syě Jūnggwo dz̀ búhwèi?	Do you know how to write Chinese?
6.	Syàndzài nǐ néng kàn Jūnggwo bàu ma?	Can you read Chinese newspapers now?
7.	Nǐ néng dzwò jèige bùnéng?	Can you do this?
8.	Jèige hwà kéyi shwō ma?	Can one say this?

III. *hau* AS AN ADVERBIAL PREFIX

Pattern: *Jūnggwo fàn hǎuchr̄, kěshr bùhǎudzwò.*
Chinese food is good to eat, but not easy to make.

1.	Jūnggwo hwà hěn hǎushwō, kěshr Jūnggwo dz̀ bùhǎusyě.	Chinese is very easy to speak, but Chinese characters are not easy to write.
2.	Jèige shr̀(ching) jēn bùhǎudzwò.	This affair is surely hard to carry through.
3.	Tā nèige mǎimai bùhǎudzwò.	That business of his is not easy to carry on.
4.	Tāde hwà hěn hǎudǔng.	He is very easy to understand.

5. Tā shwō jèibĕn shū hĕn hăumài.   He says this book is very easy tu
                                      sell.

6. Nĭmen nèi lyăngge háidz jēn   Those two children of yours are
   hăukàn!   certainly attractive looking!

7. Yŏude Mĕigwo gēr bùhăuchàng.   Some American songs are not easy
                                      to sing.

8. Syàndzài yŏude dūngsyi bùhău-   Some things are difficult to buy
   măi.   now.

NOTES

1. AUXILIARY VERBS (AV): An auxiliary verb immediately precedes
   the verb which it aids. (See Lesson II, Note 4). When the context makes the meaning clear, the main verb is often omitted, as
   in English:

   > *Nĭ hwèi shwō Jūnggwo hwà ma?* Can you speak Chinese?
   > *Wŏ hwèi shwō yìdyăr.*   Yes, a little.

2. *NENG, HWEI,* AND *KEYI*: The English auxiliary verb 'can' is freely
   used in common speech to cover the meanings 'can', 'may' and
   'know how to'. Similar looseness in use is common in Chinese.
   Essentially, *néng* implies physical ability or possibility, *hwèi*
   acquired ability or 'know how', while *kéyi* implies permissi-
   bility.

3. VERB-OBJECT COMPOUNDS (VO): Some verbs in Chinese are commonly
   associated with generalized objects, which together form single
   concepts in the Western mind, and translate into single English
   intransitive verbs. Such are called VO compounds.

   In English these generalized objects are more often implied,
   whereas in Chinese they are always expressed, unless they have just
   appeared in the immediate context. For example, in English one
   says: I want to eat, but in Chinese it becomes: I want to eat food.
   (*Wŏ yàu chīfàn*).

   When a specific object is indicated, it replaces the generalized
   object, and is never used together with it. For instance, one says:
   Wŏ yàu chī táng, for 'I want to eat candy', NEVER *Wŏ yàu chīfàn
   táng.*

   Like any verb and its object, the object within a VO compound
   may be modified:

Wǒ ài chànggēr.	I like to sing.
Wǒ ài chàng Yīnggwo gēr.	I like to sing English songs.
NEVER *Wǒ ài chànggēr Yīnggwo gēr.*	

4. APPOSITION: Two or more nouns may stand in apposition to one
   another:

Wǒmen Měigwo rén dōu ài chr̄ táng.	We Americans like to eat candy.
Tāmen lyǎngge rén dōu yǒu chyǎn.	Both of them have money.
Lǐ Syānsheng jèige rén shr̀ yǐge hǎu rén.	Mr. Lee (just mentioned) is a good man.
'Yī, èr, sān' sānge dž hěn hǎu-syě.	The three characters *'yī, èr, sān'* are very easy to write.
Jèige, Jūnggwo hwà jyàu shémma?	What is this called in Chinese?

5. ADVERBIAL FUNCTION OF STATIVE VERBS: In additi)n to their verbal
   and adjectival uses, many stative verbs function as adverbs, as
   in the following sentences:

Nǐmen syǎu háidz jēn hǎukàn!	Your child is really pretty?
Nèige gēr bùhǎuchàng.	That song is not easy to sing.
Jūnggwo fàn búdà hǎudzwò.	Chinese food is not so easy to make.
Fàn gòu chr̄ ma?	Is there enough to eat?

LESSON VIII

MODIFICATION OF NOUNS: BY NOUNS AND STATIVE VERBS

OLD CHAO, THE HATMAKER

Wǒ yǒu yíge lǎu péngyou, syìng Jàu. Rénrén dōu syǐhwan tā, shwō tā shr̀ yíge hǎu rén.

I have an old friend named Chao. Everybody likes him, and says he is a good man.

Lǎu Jàu jeige rén hěn yǒuyìsz. Tā yě hěn néng dzwòshr̀.

'Old Chao' is a most interesting person; and he is very capable, too.

Tā yǒu yíge hěn dàde mǎimai. Tā dōu mài shémma? Tā jyòu mài màudz. Tā mài nánrénde màudz, tā yě mài nyǔrénde màudz.

He has a big business. What all does he sell? He only sells hats. He sells men's hats, and he also sells women's hats.

Lǎu Jàu yě hwèi dzwò màudz. Dàrénde, syǎu háidzde, tā dōu hwèi dzwò.

Old Chao also knows how to make hats, both for adults and for children.

Tā yǒu yíge gēge, lyǎngge dìdi. Tāmen yě dōu hwèi dzwò màudz.

He has an older brother, and two younger brothers. They all know how to make hats, too.

Rénrén dōu syǐhwan dài tāde màudz. Tāmen shwō Lǎu Jàude màudz hǎu, yě pyányi.

Everyone likes to wear his hats. They say Old Chao's hats are good, and inexpensive, too.

Tāde màudz dōu mài dwōshau chyán? Dàde syǎude dōu mài wǔkwai chyán yígè.

What do his hats sell for? Big ones and little ones sell for $5.00 apiece.

Wǔkwai chyán jēn pyányi!

Five dollars is really cheap!

VOCABULARY

yìsz	N: idea, meaning		*fùmǔ*	N: parents
syāngsya	N: country (rural)		*gēge*	N: elder brother
màudz	N: hat		*dìdi*	N: younger brother
fùchin	N: father		*jyějye*	N: elder sister
mǔchin	N: mother		*mèimei*	N: younger sister

sywésheng	N: student (learner)	*méiyìsz*	SV: be dull, flat
dwō	SV: be much, many	*dài*	V: wear, put on (hat,
shǎu	SV: be little in quanti-		watch, etc.)
	ty, few	*yǒu*	V: there is or are
pyányi	SV: be inexpensive	*sywé*	V: study; learn
lǎu	SV: be old (in years)		AV: learn to, study how to
syīn	SV: be new	*syǐhwan*	AV: like to, enjoy
jyòu	SV: be old (not new)	*-de*	P: (N and V suffix indi-
yǒuyìsz	SV: be interesting		cating modification)

PATTERN SENTENCES

I. NOUNS MODIFIED BY OTHER NOUNS

(a) more often without *-de*

N - N

Pattern: *Wǒ fùchin hěn ài dzwòshr̀.* My father loves to work.

1. Syāngsya rén dōu méichyán ma? Are all country people poor?
2. Wǒmen dzwò yìdyǎr Jūnggwo fàn, How about our making a little Chi-
   hǎu bùhǎu? nese food?
3. Nǐ fùchin yǒu Jūnggwo syìng Does your father have a Chinese
   méiyǒu? surname?
4. Jèi shr̀ shémma jǐ? Shr̀ Dégwo jǐ. What kind of paper is this? German
   paper.
5. Tā gēge dìdi dōu yàu sywé His elder and younger brothers
   (shwō) Jūnggwo hwà. want to learn (to speak) Chinese.

(b) usually with *-de*

Nde - N

Patterns: *Wǒ mǔchinde màudz hěn hǎukàn.* My mother's hat is very pretty.
Nyǔrénde màudz dōu hǎukàn ma? Are all women's hats pretty?
Wǒ yàu yìmáu chyánde táng. I want a dime's worth of candy.

1. Nǐde yìsz hěn dwèi. You have the right idea.
2. Wǒ bùdǔng nǐnde hwà. I don't understand what you are
   saying.
3. Jèi shr̀ shéide yìsz, nǐ jr̄dau ma? Whose idea is this, do you know?

4. Nèige sywéshengde jyějye hwèi   That student's big sister knows
   chànggēr, kěshr tāde mèimei   how to sing, but his little
   bùhwèi.   sister doesn't.

5. Jūnggwode syāngsya rén dài   Do the country people of China
   màudz búdài?   wear hats?

6. Yǐkwai chyánde táng gòu ma?   Will a dollar's worth of sugar be
                                     enough?

(c) same with modified nouns understood

Patterns: *Jèige shr shéide? Shr nǐde ma? Búshr.*
          Who does this belong to? To you? No, it isn't mine.
          Něige shr wǒde? Jèige shr nǐde.
          Which one is mine? This one is yours.

1. Jèige bǐ shr shéide? Shr yíge   To whom does this pen belong? It
   sywéshengde, búshr syānshengde.   belongs to a student, not to the
                                     teacher.

2. Nèi lyǎngjāng hwàr shr shémma   To whom do those two pictures be-
   rénde? Wǒ bùjrdàu.   long? I don't know.

3. Něige shr nǐde? Jèige shr wǒde, Which is yours? This is mine, that
   nèige shr nǐde.   is yours.

4. Jèige bùyě shr nǐde ma?   Isn't this yours also?

5. Nǐ mǎi jǐkwai chyánde jr? Wǒ   How many dollar's worth of paper
   mǎi sānkwai chyánde.   are you getting? I'm getting
                                     $3.00 worth.

II. NOUNS MODIFIED BY STATIVE VERBS

(a) more often without -de (Simple and Unqualified SVs)

SV - N

Pattern: *Wǒ yǒu yíge hǎu péngyou.* I have a good friend.

1. Wǒ mèimei syǐhwan dài syīn   My younger sister likes to wear
   màudz.   new hats.

2. Wǒ dìdi syǐhwan mǎi jyòu shū.   My younger brother likes to buy
                                    used books.

3. Nyŭrén bùnéng dài dà byău.   Women can't wear big watches.
4. Nĭmen yŏu hău jĭ mĕiyŏu?   Do you have any good paper?
5. Hău rén bùdwō. Jèige hwà dwèi   Good people are not numerous. Is
   búdwèi?   this correct?
6. Tā jyĕjye shŕ ge hău sywésheng.   His elder sister is a good stu-
                                        dent.

(b) usually with -de

SV   de - N

Pattern: *Méichyánde rén dōu syĭhwan tā.* Poor people all like him.

1. Égwo shŕ yíge hĕndàde gwó.   Russia is a very large country.
2. Tā tàitai jyòu syĭhwan dài hău-   His wife only likes to wear pretty
   kànde màudz.   hats.
3. Búdwèide shŕ tā búdzwò.   He doesn't do improper things.
4. Jèige hĕnsyăude dūngsyi jyàu   What is this tiny thing called? I
   shémma? Wŏ bùjrdàu.   don't know.
5. Jūnggwo méiyou hĕndwō (de) Rbĕn   There are not very many Japanese
   rén. (see note 5)   in China.
6. Mĕigwo yŏu bùshău (de) Jūnggwo   There are quite a few Chinese in
   rén. (see note 5)   America.

(c) same with modified nouns understood

SVde(N)   Nde(N)

Pattern: *Jèige syăude shŕ wŏde, nèige dàde shŕ tāde.*
This small one is mine, that large one is his.

1. Nĭ yàu măi dàde, yàu măi syău-   Do you want to buy a big one, or a
   de?   little one?
2. Dàde pyányi, syăude gwèi.   The large one is cheap, the small
                                       one expensive.
3. Jèige hăukànde shŕ tāde, bùhău- This goodlooking one is his, and
   kànde yĕ shŕ tāde!   the ugly one is his also!
4. Syău byău hău, kĕshr syăude   A small watch is better, but a
   gwèi.   small one is more expensive.
5. Jèijāng hwàr shŕ syīnde, nèi-   This painting is a new one, that
   jāng shŕ jyòude.   is an old one.

NOTES

1. MODIFICATION: One of the basic principles of Chinese word order is that the modifier precedes the modified. This holds true whether one or both are single words, phrases or clauses. Position alone is sufficient to indicate the relationship of modification.

The suffix -*de* plays an essential part in modification. Practically any modifying element can take -*de*, but not all do, as will be seen below. In general, modifying elements of more than one syllable usually take -*de*.

2. NOUNS MODIFIED BY OTHER NOUNS:

(a) without -*de*: Certain nouns between which there is a particularly close personal relation often omit -*de*:

wǒ péngyou, nín tàitai, wǒmen háidz, Lǐ Syānsheng fùmǔ, etc.

Modifying nouns of place usually omit -*de*:

Měigwo rén, Jūnggwo hwàr, Yīnggwo péngyou, etc.

Two nouns which through usage have become fused into a single word omit -*de*. In English one says 'footstep', never 'foot's step', and seldom step of the foot. Innumerable nouns exist in Chinese which were formed in this way, as for example:

fànchyan (food money), *kèren* (guest), *fànjwō* (dining table), *gwógē* (national anthem), etc.

(b) with -*de*: Nouns modifying inanimate objects usually take -*de*:

wǒde byǎu, tāde shū, shéide chyán? Lǐ Syānshengde bǐ, etc.

Modifying expressioss of value usually take -*de*:

wǔmáu chyánde táng, yìbǎikwai chyánde shū, etc.

3. NOUNS MODIFIED BY STATIVE VERBS: Stative verbs in their adjectival function are used before nouns to modify them.

(a) without -*de*: Simple unqualified stative verbs, in their adjectival function, seldom take -*de*:

dà gwó, syīn màudz, syǎu byǎu, hǎu rén,
lǎu rén, lǎu tàitai, máng rén, etc.

Through association and usage, some stative verbs have become attached to certain nouns, so that they practically function as one word:

dàrén (adult), *syǎurén* (rascal, bad character), *syǎuháidz* (child), *dàgē* (eldest brother), *dàjyě* (eldest sister), etc.

(b) with *-de*: When a stative verb is preceded by some qualifying
element, *-de* is always added:

> *hěn lǎude rén, bùhǎude háidz,*
> *hǎukànde hwàr, méiyìszde shū, etc.*

4. MODIFIED NOUNS UNDERSTOOD: When the context makes it perfectly
clear what is meant, the noun modified may be understood, as in
English:

> *Jèi shr̀ shéide? Shr̀ wǒde.* Whose is this? It's mine.
> *Jūnggwo shr̀ Jūnggwo rénde.* China belongs to the Chinese.

5. *DWO* AND *SHAU*: These two words behave somewhat differently from
other stative verbs. First of all, in their adjectival function,
they never appear without an adverbial modifier. Then again, in
their qualified form they may or may not take *-de*:

> *hěndwō (de) rén, bùshǎu (de) dūngsyi,* etc., NEVER *dwō*
> *rén, shǎu dūngsyi,* and NEVER *dwōde rén* or *shǎude dūngsyi.*

6. IMPERSONAL USE OF *YOU*: When no subject is expressed before *yǒu*
(have), it becomes impersonal, and is equivalent to 'there is' or
'there are'. The same holds true when a place word stands before
yǒu:

> *Yǒu yíge rén.*   There is (or was) a man.
> *Jūnggwo yě yǒu hǎu byǎu.* There are good watches in China, too.

7. *MEI* SHORT FOR *MEIYOU*: The negative prefix to *yǒu* (have) is often
used instead of the full form *méiyou*:

> *Wǒ méi chyán.*   I don't have (any) money.
> *Tāde hwà méiyìsz.* There is no point to what he says.

LESSON IX

MODIFICATION OF NOUNS: BY CLAUSES

MR. CHANG'S TWO DAUGHTERS

Wǒ yǒu lyǎngge Jūnggwo péngyou. Yíge syìng Jāng, yíge syìng Chén. Syìng Jāngde nèige péngyou yǒu lyǎngge nyǔer. Tāmen dōu hěn tsūngming.

Jāng Syansheng hěn hwèi hwàhwàr. Tā hwàde hwàr rénrén dōu syǐhwan. Dàsyaujye yě syǎng sywé hwàhwàr. Tā shwō: "Bàba, hwàhwàr dzwèi yǒuyìsz. Wǒ syǎng sywé yidyǎr. Nín néng jyāu wǒ ma?" Tā fùchin shwō: "Wǒ hwàde bùhǎu. Yǒu yíwèi Chén Syansheng, tā hwàde hěn hǎu. Nǐ chǐng tā jyāu nǐ, bùhǎu ma?"

Èrsyáujye shwō Jūnggwo sywésheng dzwèi ài sywéde shr̀ Yīngwén. Tā syǎng jyāu tāmen, kěshr tāde Yīngwén bútài hǎu. Tā chǐng tā mǔchin jyāu tā. Tā mǔchin shwō: "Wǒde Yīngwén yě bútài hǎu. Dzwèi hǎu, nǐ chǐng jyāu Yīngwénde nèiwei wàigwo syānsheng jyāu nǐ".

I have two Chinese friends. One is named Chang and one Chen. The friend who is named Chang has two daughters. They are both very bright.

Mr. Chang knows how to paint. Everyone likes the pictures he paints. The elder daughter wanted to learn how to paint, too. She said "Papa, painting is most interesting. I'd like to study it a little. Could you teach me?" Her father said: "I don't paint well. There is a Mr. Chen who paints very well. How about asking him to teach you?"

The second daughter says what Chinese students like most to study is English. She wants to teach them, but her English is not too good. She asked her mother to teach her. Her mother said: My English is not too good, either. The best thing for you to do is to ask the foreign gentleman who teaches English to teach you.

VOCABULARY

-syē	M:	quantity of; several	tsūngming	SV:	be intelligent,
-wèi	M:	(polite for persons)			clever
érdz	N:	son	hǎutīng	SV:	be good to listen
nyǔer	N:	daughter			to, pretty
wàigwo	N:	foreign country	syǎng	V:	think, think about;
Yīngwén	N:	English language			desire
chá	N:	tea		AV:	consider, plan to;
shwěi	N:	water			want to
jyǒu	N:	wine or liquor	nyàn	V:	read aloud; study
dzwèi	A:	the most, -est	jyāu	V:	teach
cháng(cháng)	A:	often, usually, al-	hwà	V:	draw or paint
		ways	hē	V:	drink
nán	SV:	be difficult, hard	nyànshū	VO:	study; go to school
rúngyi	SV:	be simple, easy	jyāushū	VO:	teach

PATTERN SENTENCES

I. CLAUSES IN SENTENCES OF A GENERAL NATURE (OFTEN WITH *dou*)

Patterns: (1-5) *Néng kànshūde rén yě dōu néng syědz ma?*
Are all who can read able to write too?
(lit. can read*de* people also all can write?)
(6-10) *Tā shwōde hwà dzwèi yǒuyìsz.*
What he says is extremely interesting.
(lit. he-says*de* things most have meaning)

1. Hwèi shwō Jūnggwo hwà de Měigwo rén bùshǎu, kěshr hwèi syě
Jūnggwo dz de bùdwō.
    Quite a few Americans know how to
speak Chinese, but not many can
write Chinese.

2. Ài hējyǒu de rén chángcháng
méichyán.
    Those who like to drink are often
without money.

3. Nyànshūde dōu shr sywésheng ma?   Are all who study students?

4. Dzwòmǎimaide dōu yǒuchyán ma?   Are all business people rich?

5. Syǐhwan tā nyǔer de rén bùshǎu.   Quite a few people like his
daughter.

6. Tā shwōde hwà nǐ dōu dǔng ma?   Do you understand all he says?

7. Wǒ hěn ài kàn tā dzwòde shū.   I love to read the books he writes.

8. Nǐmen nyànde shū nán bunán?   Is what you are studying difficult?
9. Wǒ shwōde dwèi búdwèi?   Is what I say (or said) correct?
10. Tāmen chàngde shr̀ shémma gēr?   What song are they singing?

II. CLAUSES IN SENTENCES OF A SPECIFIC NATURE (ALWAYS WITH SPECIFIER)

Patterns: (1-4) *Chànggērde neige rén syìng Lǐ.*
    The person who is singing is named Lee.
    (lit. sing-songsde the-person is named Lee)
  (5-8) *Tā chàngde neisye gēr jēn hǎutīng!*
    The songs he is singing are certainly pretty!
    (lit. he-singsde the-several-songs are truly pretty)
  (9-10) *Nèige màitángde shr syāngsya rén.*
    The (or that) candydealer is a countryman.
    (lit. that sell-candyde is country person)

1. Mài jūngbyǎu de neige lǎu syānsheng hěn tsūngmíng.   The old gentleman who sells clocks and watches is very intelligent.

2. Jyāu Yīngwén de neiwei syáujye syìng Chén.   The lady who teaches English is named Chen.

3. Chǐng nǐ chrfàn de neiwei syānsheng shr̀ bushr Jāng Syansheng?   Is the gentleman who invited you to a meal Mr. Chang?

4. Chànggērde neisye háidz dōu shr wǒde sywésheng.   All of the children (there) who are singing are my students.

5. Wǒ yàu kànkan nǐ mǎide neige syīn bǐ.   I want to have a look at the new pen you bought.

6. Wǒ syàndzài dàide jeige màudz tài nánkàn!   The hat I am wearing now is terrible looking!

7. Tā shwōde neisye hwà búdwèi.   What he is saying is not correct.

8. Nǐnde nyǔer syěde neisye dz̀ jēn hǎu!   The characters your daughter wrote are certainly fine!

9. Nèige màibàude syàndzài hěn yǒu chyán.   The (or that) newsdealer is now very rich.

10. Nèi lyǎngge dzwòfànde, yíge jyàu Lǎu Jāng, yíge jyàu Lǎu Lǐ.   Of the (or those) two cooks, one is called Old Chang; and one Old Lee.

FLUENCY DRILLS

Háidz hěn tsūngming.

Syău háidz hěn tsūngming.

Nèige syău háidz hěn tsūngming.

Nyànshūde neige syău háidz hěn tsūngming.

Nyàn Jūnggwo shū de neige syău háidz hěn tsūngming.

Nyàn Jūnggwo shū de nei lyǎngge syǎu háidz hěn tsūngming.

Nyàn Jūnggwo shū de nei lyǎngge syǎu háidz jēn tsūngming.

Tāde Yīngwén hǎu.

Tāde Yīngwén hěn hǎu.

Wáng Syānshengde Yīngwén hěn hǎu.

Nèiwei Wáng Syānshengde Yīngwén hěn hǎu.

Jyāushūde neiwei Wáng Syānshengde Yīngwén hěn hǎu.

Jyāu Yīngwén de neiwei Wáng Syānshengde Yīngwén hěn hǎu.

Jyāu Yīngwén de neiwei Wáng Syānshengde Yīngwén dzwèi hǎu.

NOTES

1. MODIFYING CLAUSES, like nouns and stative verbs, precede the
   nouns which they modify, and always take the suffix -de. There
   are no Chinese equivalents for the relative pronouns 'who', 'which',
   and 'that'. For example, in English one says: 'the house that
   Jack built', whereas in Chinese it is 'the Jack-built-house'.
   (Compare English expressions such as 'a self-made man', 'home-
   cooked meals', etc.):

   shwōhwàde rén the person who is talking (lit. say-thingsde person)
   tā shwōde hwà the things which he says (lit. he-saysde things)

2. RELATION OF CLAUSES TO OTHER QUALIFYING ELEMENTS: When a noun is
   already specified, or both specified and numbered (see Lesson IV),
   the modifying clause usually stands in front of these specifying
   elements. Compare the following expressions:

   (1) nèige rén   that man
       shwōhwàde neige rén   the man who is speaking
                              (say-thingsde the-man)
   (2) nèiwei syānsheng   that gentleman (or teacher)
       jyāu Yūngwén de neiwei the gentleman who teaches English
       syānsheng   (teach-Englishde the-gentleman)

(3) *jèi lyǎngge háidz*   these two children

    nyànshūde jei lyǎngge   the two children who are studying

      háidz   (study-books*de* the-two-children)

(4) *nèisye sywésheng*   those students

    chànggērde neisye sywé-   the students who are singing

      sheng   \ (sing-songs*de* the-several-students)

(5) *jèige byǎu*   this watch

    wǒ jeige byǎu   this watch of mine

    wǒ mǎide jèige byǎu   the watch (here) that I bought

                            (I-bought*de* the-watch)

(6) *nèijang hwàr*   that painting

    nǐ neijang hwàr   that painting of yours

    nǐ hwàde neijang hwàr   the picture that you painted

                            (you-painted*de* the-picture)

(7) *nèi lyǎngkwai chyán*   those two dollars

    nǐ gěi wǒ de nèi lyǎng-   the two dollars that you gave me

      kwai chyán   (you-gave-me*de* the-two-dollars)

(8) *nèisye shr̀(chǐng)*   those affairs (or matters)

    nǐ wèn wǒ de neisye shr̀   the several things you asked me about

                            (you-ask-me*de* the-several matters)

Note that the specifiers in the above expressions have more the force of the English 'the', than the stronger 'that' or 'those'. They receive no stress in speaking.

3. CLAUSES BECOME NOUNS: A few modifying clauses, which describe a more or less permanent condition or aspect, have become fused into single words which function as nouns. These correspond to certain English nouns ending in -er, etc.:

màishūde	bookseller	*dzwòmǎimaide*	business man
màibàude	newsdealer	*dzwòfànde*	cook
màitángde	candy seller	*yàufànde*	beggar

Since these expressions are equivalent to nouns, they may be specified and/or numbered in the same manner as other nouns:

Nèige màibàude syìng Jāng. The (or that) newsdealer is named Chang.

Tāmen yǒu lyǎngge dzwòfànde. They have two cooks.

There are more formal terms for many of these descriptive expressions, as for example: *chúdz* for *dzwòfànde*, *shāngren* for *dzwòmǎi-maide*, etc.

4. REDUPLICATION OF VERBS: Verbs are sometimes reduplicated. This
   often gives a casual touch to the sense. Sometimes *yi* (one, a) is
   inserted between the two verbs:

   kànkan   have or take a look   *syǎngyisyǎng*   think it over

   wènwen   make an inquiry   *sywéyisywé*   put a little study
                                                        on it

LESSON X

EXISTENCE AND LOCATION

WHERE MR. LEE LIVES AND WORKS

A: Lǐ Syansheng, nín jyā dzai nǎr? — Mr. Lee, where is your home?

B: Dzai Nánjīng. — In Nanking.

A: Dzai chéng lǐtou ma? — Inside the city?

B: Bù, dzai chéng wàitou. — No, outside.

A: Chéng wàitou shémma dìfang? — Whereabouts outside the city?

B: Chéng wàitou yǒu yige sywésyàu. Wǒmen jyā jyòu dzai nèige sywésyàu hòutou. — There is a school outside the city. Our home is just outside the school.

A: Nín dzai nèige sywésyàuli jyāushū ma? — Do you teach in that school?

B: Bù. Wǒ shr̀ ge dzwòmǎimaide. — No, I am a business man.

A: Nǐmende pùdz dzai nǎr? — Where is your shop?

B: Dzai chéng lǐtou. Wǒmende pùdz hěn syǎu. — Inside the city. Our shop is very small.

A: Nín tài kèchi! Nín cháng dzai jyā chr̄fàn ma? — You're being too polite! Do you usually eat at home?

B: Wǒ búdzai jyā chr̄. — No, I don't eat at home.

A: Wèishémma? — Why not?

B: Yīnwei pùdzlide shr̀ tài dwō. — Because there's too much work at the shop.

A: Nín dzai nǎr chr̄fàn? — Where do you eat?

B: Wǒmen pùdz chyántou yǒu yige syǎu fàngwǎr. Wǒ cháng dzai nèr chr̄fàn. — There is a small restaurant in front of our shop. I often eat there.

VOCABULARY

wèishém(ma)	MA: why? (for what reason)	wàitou	N: outside
yīnwei	MA: because (of), for	chyántou	N: front
shàngtou	N: above, top	hòutou	N: back
syàtou	N: below, bottom	dìsya	N: underneath
lǐtou	N: inside	jèr	N: here

nèr	N:	there		*tùdz*	N:	store
nǎr	N:	where?		*-pù*	N:	-store, -shop
jyā	N:	home; family		*fàngwǎr*	N:	restaurant (food-eat-
fángdz	N:	house, building				ing-place
lóu	N:	storied building		*dzài*	V:	be at, in, or on
lóushang	N:	upstairs			CV:	at, in, or on
wūdz	N:	room		*ne*	P:	(sentence suffix indi-
difang	N:	place				cating continuance of
chéng	N:	city				action in positive
sywésyàu	N:	school				statements)

PATTERN SENTENCES

I. POSITIONAL NOUNS BEFORE *you* TO INDICATE EXISTENCE

            PosN   yǒu   N
Pattern: *Jwōdzshang yǒu shū.*   There are books on the table.
         Jèr yǒu fàngwǎr meiyou? Is there a restaurant here?

1. Chéng wàitou méiyou fàngwǎr.   There are no restaurants outside
                                         the city.
2. Jwōdz dǐsya yǒu bushǎu dūngsyi.   There are quite a few things under
                                         the table.
3. Jyāli yǒu rén méiyǒu?   Is there anybody home?
4. Nǐmen jyāli yǒu dwōshau rén?   How many are there in your family?
5. Nǐmen sywésyàu yǒu jǐwèi syān-   How many teachers are there in
   sheng? Yǒu dwōshau sywésheng?   your school? How many students?
6. Jūnggwode syāngsya yǒu sywé-   Are there any schools in the
   syàu méiyǒu?   country districts of China?
7. Nǎr yǒu fàngwǎr?   Where is there a restaurant?

II. *dzai* WITH POSITIONAL NOUNS TO INDICATE LOCATION

            N   dzài PosN
Pattern: *Wǒmen jyā dzai chéng wàitou.* Our home is outside the city.
         Nǐmende pùdz dzai nǎr?   Where is your store?

1. Wǒmen syǎng mǎide neige fángdz   The house we are thinking of buy-
   dzai syāngsya.   ing is in the country.
2. Háidz dōu dzai wàitou ne.   The children are all outside.

3. Jāng Syansheng búdzai jèr, tā dzai wàigwo.

   Mr. Chang is not here, he is abroad.

4. Tāmen dōu dzai lóushang ne. Syàtou méiyou rén.

   They are all upstairs. There is no one down below.

5. Syānsheng dzàijyā ma? Dzàijyā.

   Is the 'mister' at home? Yes.

6. Wǒde bǐ dzai nǎr? Dzai jèr ne.

   Where is my pen? It's here.

7. Shéi dzai chyántoude wūdzli?

   Who is in the front room?

III. *dzai* AS A CO-VERB AS SETTING FOR MAIN ACTION

CV – PosN   V(O)

Pattern: *Wǒ bucháng dzai fàngwǎrli chīfàn.*

I don't often eat in a restaurant.

1. Tāmen dzai nèige wūdzli chīfàn ne.

   They are in that room eating.

2. Háidzmen dōu dzai chéng lǐtou nyànshū.

   The children all go to school inside the city (downtown).

3. Nín dzai nǎr dzwòshr̀? Dzai Nánjīng.

   Where do you work? In Nanking.

4. Nín dzai Nánjīng dzwò shémma? Wǒ dzai nèr jyāushū.

   What do you do in Nanking? I teach there.

5. Chǐng nín dzai wǒmen jyāli chī yidyǎr dūngsyi.

   Have a little something to eat in our home.

6. Nǐ syàndzài dzai něige pùdz dzwòshr̀?

   Which shop are you working at now?

IV. ADDITIONAL SENTENCES WITH POSITIONAL NOUNS

1. Bàushang shwō shémma?

   What does the paper say?

2. Nín shr nǎrde rén?

   Where are you from?

3. Jwōdz dǐsyade dūngsyi dōu shr shéide?

   Whose are all the things under the table?

4. Pùdz chyántoude neiwei syānsheng sying Jàu.

   The gentleman in (the) front of the store is named Chao.

5. Wǒmen jeige sywésyàulide sywésheng, yibàn shr nyǔde.

   Half of the students in our school are women.

6. Jèrde rén bucháng kàn bàu.

   The people here don't often read the paper.

7. Fángdz hòutoude neige chìchē shr nǐde ma? Shr̀.

   Is the car at the back of the house yours? Yes.

FLUENCY DRILL

Wŏde byău dzai năr?

Wŏ neige byău dzai năr?

Wŏde neige byău dzai năr?

Dzai yĭdzshang.

Nínde byău dzai yĭdzshang.

Nín neige byău dzai yĭdzshang.

Nínde neige byău dzai yĭdzshang.

Dzai něige yĭdzshang?

Dzai neige dà yĭdzshang.

Dzai něige dà yĭdzshang?

Dzai hòutou neige dà yĭdzshang.

Dzai wūdz hòutoude neige dà yĭdzshang.

Nínde byău dzai wūdz hòutoude ncige dà yĭdzshang.

Nín nèige byău dzai wūdz hòutoude neige dà yĭdzshang.

Nínde nèige byău dzai wūdz hòutoude neige dà yĭdzshang.

Syèsye!

NOTES

1. POSITIONAL NOUNS: This lesson introduces a number of nouns which indicate position, such as *lĭtou* (inside), *chyántou* (in front), *jèr* (here), etc. These words may be used alone like any other noun:

Shàngtou yŏu shū.	There are books on top. (lit. topside has books)
Háidz dōu dzai wàitou.	The children are all outside.
Chyántoude neisye rén dōu shr shéi?	Who are all those people in front? (lit. front*de* the-several-people all are who?)

2. POSITIONAL SUFFIXES: Positional nouns may also be suffixed to other nouns. When the resulting position is a familiar one, *-tou* is often dropped. This is more often the case with *shàngtou* and *lĭtou* than with some of the others:

Nèiběn shū dzai jwōdzshang.	That book is on the table. (lit. is on table-top
Yĭdzshangde jeige màudz shr shéide?	Whose hat is this on the chair? (lit. chair-top*de* the-hat is whose?)

3. EXISTENCE WITH *YOU*: When a positional noun precedes the verb *yŏu* (used

in its impersonal sense of 'there is'), it signifies that 'at x there is y':

Wūdz hòutou yǒu bushǎu yǐdz.	There are quite a few chairs at the back of the room.
Wūdzli yǒu sānge rén.	There are three people in the room.
Wǒmen jyāli méiyou syǎu háidz.	There are no children in our home.
Jūnggwo syàndzài méiyou hěndwō Rběn rén.	There aren't very many Japanese in China now.

4. LOCATION WITH *DZAI*: When a positional noun follows the verb *dzài* (be located at, in or on), it signifies that 'y is located at x':

Nǐnde shū dzai yǐdzshang.	Your book is on the chair.
Háidz dzai nǎr? Dzai wàitou ne.	Where are the children? Outside.
Nǐnde byǎu dzai wǒ jyāli.	Your watch is at my house.
Wǒ fùmǔ dōu dzai Yīnggwo ne.	My parents are in England.

5. CO-VERBS (CV): A co-verb indicates a relationship between a noun and the main verb. It functions like an English preposition, and never receives stress in speaking. The co-verb and its object always precede the main verb, and form a setting for the action of the main verb:

Tā dzai Jūnggwo jyāushū.	He teaches in China. (lit. he in-China teaches)
Wǒmen dzai jèr sywé Jūnggwo hwà.	We are studying Chinese here. (lit. at-here studying Chinese)
Chén Taitai dzai jyāli dzwò-fàn ne.	Mrs. Chen is at home cooking.

6. CONTINUANCE WITH *NE*: When it is desired to stress the fact that the action of the verb is going on at the moment of speaking, the particle *ne* is added to the end of the sentence:

Tāmen syàndzài chīfàn ne.	They are eating now.
Lǐ Syansheng dzai sywésyàuli jyāushū ne.	Mr. Lee is at the school teaching.
Nǐ dzwò shémma ne? Hwàhwàr ne.	What are you doing? Drawing.

7. NAMES OF CITIES OR COUNTRIES AFTER *DZAI* never take the positional

suffix *lǐtou* or *-li*. For example, one says *dzai Jūnggwo*, NEVER *dzai Jūnggwo lǐtou*, or *dzai Jūnggwoli*.

Certain other particularized nouns after *dzài* sometimes drop the positional suffix *-li*:

Syānsheng búdzai jyā.	The 'man of the house' is not at home.
Ḥáidz dzai sywésyàu ne.	The child is at school.
Wǒmen dzai něige fàngwǎr chr̄fàn?	At which restaurant shall we eat?

LESSON XI

MOTION AND DIRECTION – CONVEYANCE AND PURPOSE

A PROJECTED TRIP TO NEW YORK

A: Nǐmen dau nǎr chyu?

Where are you going?

B: Wǒmen dau Nyǒuywe chyu.

We're going to New York.

A: Nǐmen dzwo hwǒchē chyù ma?

Are you going by train?

B: Bù, wǒmen dzwo chìchē.

No, we're going by car.

A: Wèi shémma búdzwo fēijī?

Why don't you go by plane?

B: Tsúng jèr dau Nyǒuywe méiyou fēijī.

There are no planes from here to New York.

A: Nǐmen dau nèr chyù dzwò shémma?

What are you going to do there?

B: Wǒmen chyù kàn lyǎngge péngyou. Wǒmen yě syǎng mǎi yidyǎr dūngsyi.

We are going to see a couple of friends. We are also thinking of buying a few things.

A: Nǐmen péngyou dzai Nyǒuywe shémma dìfang?

Whereabouts in New York are your friends?

B: Dzai chéng lǐtou, Yibǎi-yīshr Jyē.

In the city, on 110th Street.

A: Nǐmen háidz yě dōu chyù ma?

Are all your children going, too?

B: Dzwèi syǎude buchyù. Dàde dōu chyù.

The littlest is not going. All of the older ones are going.

A: Nǐmen wèishémma buchǐng nǐmen péngyou dau jèr lái?

Why don't you invite your friends to come here?

B: Tāmen hěn syǐhwan lái. Kěshr tāmende shr̀ching tài dwō, háidz yě tài syǎu, swóyi syàndzài bunéng lái.

They would like very much to come. But they have too much to do, and the children are too small, so they can't come now.

VOCABULARY

swóyi	MA: therefore, so	*fēijī*	N: airplane (flying machine)
chē	N: any wheeled vehicle	*jyē*	N: street
chìchē	N: automobile, car	*yídìng*	A: certainly, definitely
hwǒchē	N: train	*bùyídìng*	A: not necessarily; uncertain
chwán	N: boat, ship	*dzěm(ma)*	A: how? in what way?

sying	SV:	be satisfactory, all right, 'can do'			shall, will
			lái	V:	come (here)
tsúng	CV:	from	chyù	V:	go (there)
dàu	CV:	to (towards)	kàn	V:	see, visit
dzwò	V:	ride on (sit on)	jànchilai	V:	stand up
	CV:	go by	dzwòsya	V:	sit down
yàu	AV:	going to, expect to;	chǐng dzwò!	IE:	please sit down!

PATTERN SENTENCES

I. CO-VERBS OF MOTION AND DIRECTION (*tsung* AND *dau*)

CV – PosN V

Pattern: *Nǐ tsúng nǎr lái? Wǒ tsúng jyāli lái.*
Where did you come from? I came from home.
Nǐ dau nǎr chyù? Wǒ dau chéng lǐtou chyu.
Where are you going? I am going into the city.

Nǐ tsúng shémma dìfang lái. Wǒ tsúng pùdzli lái.

Where did you come from? I came from the store.

Tā tsúng nǎr lái? Tā tsúng sywé-syàu lái.

Where did he come from? He came from school.

Nèisye rén yě dōu tsúng sywésyàu lái ma? Bù, tāmen tsúng chéng wàitou lái.

Did all those people come from school, too? No, they came from outside the city.

Nǐ dau shémma dìfang chyu? Wǒ dau syāngsya chyu.

Where are you going? I'm going to the country.

Nǐ tsúng jyāli chyù ma? Bù, wǒ tsúng pùdzli chyù.

Are you going from home? No, from the shop.

Nǐ búdau Nyǒuywe chyu ma? Buchyù.

Aren't you going to New York? No, I'm not.

Wǒmen dōu syǎng chyù. Nǐ wèishémma buchyù? Wǒ tài máng, bunéng chyù.

We're all thinking of going. Why aren't you going? I'm too busy, I can't go.

II. CO-VERB OF CONVEYANCE (*dzwo*)

CV MeansN V

Pattern: *Nǐ dau Jūnggwo chyu, dzěmma chyù? Nǐ dzwò chwán chyù ma?*
How are you going to China? Are you going by boat?

Nǐ dau Yīnggwo chyu, dzwò chwán ma? Bù, wǒ syǎng dzwò fēijī.	Are you going by boat to England? No, I'm thinking of taking a plane.
Dzwò fēijī bugwèi ma? Buhěn gwèi.	Isn't it expensive by plane? No, not very expensive.
Dzwò hwǒchē chyù syǐng busyíng? Busyíng, méiyou hwǒchē.	Can one go by train? No, it isn't possible. There are no trains.
Wèishémma búdzwo chwán? Dzwo dà chwán tài gwèi. Wǒ yě busyǐhwan dzwò syǎu chwán.	Why don't you go by boat? It is too expensive by a large boat, and I don't enjoy small boats.

III. PURPOSE OF COMING OR GOING

Patterns: *Nǐ dau jèr lái dzwò shémma? Wǒ dàu jèr lái nyànshū.*
What did you come here to do? I came here to study.
Nǐ dau Jūnggwo dzwò shémma chyu? Wǒ syǎng jyāu yi-
dyǎr shū chyu.
Nǐ dau Jūnggwo chyù dzwò shémma chyu? Wǒ syǎng
chyù jyāu yidyǎr shū chyu.
What are you going to China to do? I want to do a
little teaching.

1. Nǐ dau jyēshang chyu mǎi shémma? Wǒ yau mǎi yige màudz.	What are you going upstreet to buy? I want to buy a hat.
2. Nǐmen dau jèige sywésyàu lái sywé shémma? Sywé Jūnggwo hwà.	What do you come to this school to learn? Spoken Chinese.
3. Chǐng nǐ dau wǒmen jyā lái dzwòdzwo.	Please come to our home and pay us a little visit.
4. Nǐ dau chéng lǐtou chyù kàn shéi? Wǒ yau kàn neiwei syìng Lǐ de.	Whom are you going to see downtown? I want to see the man named Lee.
5. Tā dau Rběn dzwò mǎimai chyu ma? Bù, tā jyāushū chyù.	Is he going to Japan to carry on business? No, he's going to teach.
6. Nǐ dau nǎr chyu nyànshū? Wǒ ywànyi dau Nyǒuywe, kěshr wǒ fùmǔ buywànyi wǒ dzai Nyǒuywe nyànshū.	Where are you going to study? I'd like to go to New York, but my parents don't want me to study in New York.
7. Nǐ wèishémma búdau wàigwo chyù dzwòshr̀ chyu? Méichyán!	Why don't you go abroad to work? No money!

CLASSROOM ACTIVITY

A: requests a certain action
B: says what he is going to do, just before he starts to do it`

A: Chǐng nǐ jànchilai.	Please stand up.
B: Wǒ yau jànchilai.	I'm going to stand up.
Chǐng nǐ dau wǒ jèr lái.	Please come here to me.
Wǒ yau dau nǐ nèr chyu.	I'm going to you there.
Wǒ yau nǐ dau wūdz hòutou chyu.	I want you to go to the rear.
Wǒ yau dau wūdz hòutou chyu.	I'm going to the rear.
Nǐ syàndzài dzai nǎr?	Where are you now?
Wǒ dzai wūdz hòutou ne.	I'm at the back of the room.
Nǐ syǐhwan dzai hòutou ma?	Do you like it at the back?
Bùsyǐhwan.	No, I don't.
Nǐ ywànyi dau chyántou lái ma?	Do you wish to come to the front?
Wǒ hěn ywànyi lái.	I'd like very much to come.
Hǎu, nǐ kéyi dau chyántou lái.	All right, you may come to the front.
Wǒ jyòu yau dau chyántou lái.	I'm just about to come to the front.
Nǐ ywànyi dzwòsya ma?	Do you wish to sit down?
Wǒ hěn ywànyi dzwòsya.	I'd like very much to sit down.
Hǎu, nǐ kéyi dzwòsya.	Good, you may sit down!

FLUENCY DRILL

Wǒ dau Jūnggwo chyu.

Wǒ yau dau Jūnggwo chyu.

Nǐ wèishémma yau dau Jūnggwo chyu?

Wǒ yau dau Jūnggwo chyu dzwòshr̀.

Nǐ yau dau Jūnggwo chyu dzwò shémma shr̀?

Wǒ yau dau Jūnggwo chyu jyāushū.

Nǐ yau dau Jūnggwo chyu jyāu shémma shū?

Wǒ yau dau Jūnggwo chyu jyāu Yīngwén.

Wǒ yau dau Jūnggwo chyu jyāu yidyǎr Yīngwén.

Nǐ búyau dau Jūnggwo chyu jyāu yidyǎr Yīngwén ma?

Hǎu, wǒ yě yau dau Jūnggwo chyu jyāu yidyǎr Yīngwén.

Wǒmen dōu kéyi dau Jūnggwo chyu jyāu yidyǎr Yīngwén.

Wǒmen dōu kéyi dau Jūnggwo chyu jyāu yidyǎr Yīngwén chyu.

NOTES

1. MOTION AND DIRECTION WITH *LAI* AND *CHYU*: The two verbs *lái* and *chyù* express both motion and direction, *lái* (come) indicating motion toward the speaker, or his point of reference, and *chyù* (go) motion toward a point other than the speaker.

2. CO-VERBS OF MOTION AND DIRECTION *TSUNG* AND *DAU*: These two co-verbs, with appropriate positional objects, serve to indicate the particular origin and the specific objective of the action of the main verbs *lái* and *chyù* which they precede. *Tsúng* (from) indicates motion out from or away from some point, and *dàu* (to) motion towards some point. When the negative is indicated, the negative particle precedes the entire expression:

tsúng Jūnggwo lái	come from China
dàu Měigwo chyù	go to America
búdau nèr chyù	not go (to) there
tsúng sywésyàu chyù	go from school

3. CO-VERBS *DZAI*, *TSUNG*, AND *DAU* COMPARED: *Dzài* signifies 'being at' a point in space or time, and may be represented by a dot. *Tsúng* and *dàu* on the other hand, involve motion. *Dàu* shows 'motion to or toward' some point, and may be represented by an arrow. *Tsúng* signifies 'motion starting from or leading out of' some point, and may be represented by an inverted arrow.

4. CO-VERB OF CONVEYANCE (*DZWO*): The co-verb *dzwò* (go by, lit. sit on) and its object indicate the means of conveyance adopted to get from one point to another:

dzwò chwán lái	come by boat
búdzwò fēijī chyù	not go by plane

   Note that since *dzwò* literally means 'to sit', it is only used with respect to conveyances which provide places to sit down.

5. PURPOSE OF COMING OR GOING: The purpose of coming from or going to a place is indicated by placing the purpose expression either immediately before or immediately after the main verb *lái* or *chyù*. Sometimes *lái* or *chyù* appear both before and after the purpose expression:

dàu jèr lái nyànshū	come here to study
búdau Fàgwo dzwòshr̀ chyù	not go to France to work
dàu jyēshang chyù mǎi dūngsyi chyu	go downtown to make purchases

6. PRONOUNS BEFORE POSITIONAL NOUNS: Expressions such as 'with us here', 'at his place', 'here to me', etc., are formed by placing pronouns before the positional words *jèr* and *nèr* (compare Lesson V, Note 2):

Chǐng nǐ dàu wǒ jèr lái.	Please come here to me.
Wǒ buywànyi dau tā nèr chyù.	I don't wish to go to his place.
Chǐng nǐ dzai wǒmen jèr chr̄ yidyǎr fàn.	Please have a bite to eat here with us.

LESSON XII

COMPLETED ACTION WITH -LE

REPORT ON THE TRIP TO NEW YORK

A: Nǐmen jīntyan dzǎushang dau nǎr chyule?

Where did you go this morning?

B: Dau Nyǒuywe chyule.

We went to New York.

A: Dau chéng lǐtou chyùle meiyou?

Did you go into the city?

B: Chyùle. Wǒmen dau Yibǎi-yīshr Jyē, yige péngyou jyāli chyule.

Yes, we went to a friend's home on 110th Street.

A: Péngyou jr̄dau nǐmen yau lái ma?

Did the friends know you were coming?

B: Bùjrdàu.

No, they didn't.

A: Tāmen dzai jyā budzai jyā?

Were they at home?

B: Syānsheng dzai jyā, kěshr tàitai dau jyēshang mǎi dūngsyi chyule.

The husband was home, but the wife had gone out to shop.

A: Nǐmen dzai tāmen jyāli chr̄fàn-le ma?

Did you eat at their house?

B: Méiyou. Yīnwei tàitai búdzai-jyā, swóyi wǒmen dau fàngwǎr chyù chr̄fàn chyule.

No, since the wife was not at home, we went to a restaurant to eat.

A: Nǐmen méichyu kàn byéde péngyou ma?

Didn't you go see any other friends?

B: Méiyou.

No, we didn't.

A: Nǐmen wǎnfàn chr̄le meiyou?

Have you had your supper?

B: Hái méichr̄ ne.

Not yet.

A: Dzai wǒmen jèr chr̄ yidyǎr dūngsyi, hǎu buhǎu?

How about having a bite to eat here with us?

B: Syèsye, syèsye. Nǐmen tài kèchi!

Thanks, you are being courteous!

A: Méi shémma!

Don't mention it!

VOCABULARY

dzwótyan	(MA)N:	yesterday	*hái*	A:	still, yet, again
jīntyan	(MA)N:	today	*dzŏu*	V:	walk; go, leave
míngtyan	(MA)N:	tomorrow	*hwéilai*	V:	come back, return here
dzăushang	(MA)N:	morning	*shwō gùshr*	VO:	tell a story
wănshang	(MA)N:	evening	*tīng gùshr*	VO:	listen to a story
dzăufàn	N:	breakfast (early meal)	*-le*	P:	(verb and sentence suffix, indicating completion of action)
jūngfàn	N:	lunch (middle meal)			
wănfàn	N:	supper, dinner (late meal)	*méi(you)*	P:	(verb prefix, negating completion of action)
gùshr	N:	story	*ne*	P:	(sentence suffix, indicating suspense in negative statements)
byéde	N:	(an)other (person or thing)			
byéren	N:	other people	*méi shémma!*	IE:	don't mention it! it's nothing at all!
yĭjing	·A:	already			

PATTERN SENTENCES

I. VERBS OF MOTION AND DIRECTION WITH *-le*

```
         S   Vle
```
Pattern: *Tā láile ma? Láile.*

Did he come or has he come? Yes, he came or has come.

Tāmen dzŏule meiyou? Méidzŏu(ne).

Tāmen dzŏule meidzŏu? Méidzŏu(ne).

Have they left? No, they haven't (yet).

1. Nĭde péngyou láile meiyou? Tā yĭjing láile.

   Has your friend come? Yes, he's already come.

2. Lĭ Syansheng dzŏule ma? Méidzŏu ne.

   Did Mr. Lee leave? No, not yet.

3. Tāmen dzwótyan chyùle meichyu? Méichyù. Tāmen jīntyan chyù.

   Did they go yesterday? No, they didn't. They go today.

4. Nèige rén hwéilaile ma? Hái méi ne.

   Has that man returned? Not yet.

5. Shéi láile? Nĭde péngyou Jāng Syansheng láile.

   Who came (or who's come)? Your friend, Mr. Chang.

6. Nǐ méichyù ma? Méichyù.

    Didn't you go? No, I didn't.

7. Nín syānsheng hái méihwéilai ma? Hái méihwéilai ne.

    Hasn't your husband returned yet? Not yet.

8. Rén dōu dzǒule ma?

    Dōu dzǒule.

    Méidōu dzǒu.

    Dōu méidzǒu.

    Wǒ bùjrdàu tāmen dzǒule méi-dzǒu.

    Has everybody left?

    Yes, everybody's gone.

    No, not everybody.

    Nobody has gone.

    I don't know whether they have left or not.

9. Wáng Syansheng dau nǎr chyule? Tā dau fàngwǎr chrfàn chyule.

    Where has Mr. Wang gone? He has gone to the restaurant to eat.

10. Tā dau Jūnggwo chyù dzwò shémma chyule? Tā chyù jyāushū chyule.

    What has he gone to China to do? He has gone to teach.

II. VERBS WITH SIMPLE OBJECTS AND *-le*

      S   V(le)Ole

Pattern: *Nín chrfànle ma? Chrle, syèsye.*

    Have you eaten? Yes, thank you.

    Nǐ wènle syānsheng le meiyou? Wǒ wènle tā le. Tā shwō kéyi.

    Did you ask the teacher? Yes, I asked him and he said all right.

1. Nǐmen chrle dzǎufàn le meiyou? Wǒmen yǐjing chrle.

    Have you had breakfast? We have already eaten.

2. Nǐ kànle jīntyande bàu le ma? Hái méikàn ne.

    Have you read today's paper? Not yet.

3. Tā gěi nǐ neige chyán le ma? Méiyou.

    Has he given you the money? No, he hasn't.

4. Nǐ chǐng tāmen le meiyou? Chǐngle.

    Have you invited them? Yes, I have.

5. Nǐ méichyu kàn ta ma? Wǒ chyù kàn ta le.

    Didn't you go to see him? I did go to see him.

6. Dūngsyi dōu mǎile ma?

    Méidōu mǎi ne.

    Dōu méimǎi ne.

    Has everything been bought?

    Not everything yet.

    Nothing yet.

7. Nǐde chìchē màile meiyou? Méi ne. Méi rén yàu!

    Have you sold your car? Not yet. Nobody wants it!

III. STRESSING PLACE, CONVEYANCE, AND PURPOSE WITH *shr...de*

Patterns: (1-2) *Wŏde Jŭnggwo hwà shr dzai Mĕigwo sywéde.*
My Chinese was learned in America.

(3-4) *Tā shr tsúng Fàgwo ldide, búshr ma? Shr̀.*
He came from France, didn't he? Yes.

(5-6) *Tā shr dzwo chwán ldide. Tā méidzwo fēijī.*
He came by boat. He didn't come by plane.

(7-8) *Tā shr nyànshū láide* (or *lái nyànshū de*).
He came to study.

1. Nĭnde Yīngwén shwōde jēn hău! Dzai năr sywéde?
You speak English wonderfully! Where did you learn it?

2. Nĭ neige bĭ shr dzai nĕige pùdzli măide? Shr dzai chénglĭ neige dzwèi dàde pùdzli măide.
At which store did you buy that pen of yours? At the largest store in the city.

3. Jèiwei syáujye shr tsúng Dégwo láide.
This lady came from Germany.

4. Wŏmen dōu shr tsúng wŏmen jyāli chyùde, kĕshr Lĭ Syansheng shr tsúng sywésyàu chyùde.
We all went from our homes, but Mr. Lee went from the school.

5. Nín shr̀ bushr dzwo chwán láide? Búshr, wŏ shr dzwo chìchē láide.
Did you come by boat? No, I came by car.

6. Tā shr dzĕmma chyùde? Tā shr dzwo péngyoude chìchē chyùde.
How did he go? He went in a friend's car.

7. Tā shr wèishémma láide? Tā shr kàn yige péngyou láide.
Why was it that he came? He came to see a friend.

8. Tā dau nèr chyù shr dzwo shémma chyùde? Shr dzwo măimai chyùde.
What did he go there to do? He went to carry on business.

CLASSROOM ACTIVITY

     A: asks B to do something
     B: does it and then reports on what he has done
     C: the class says what they just saw him do

A: Chĭng nĭ jànchilai.
     Please stand up.

B: Wŏ jànchilaile.
       I have stood up.

C: Tā jànchilaile.
       He has stood up.

A: Chǐng nǐ dau jèr lái.   Please come here.
  B: Wǒ dau jèr láile.   I have come here.
  C: Tā dau nèr chyule.   He has gone there.
Chǐng nǐ dau hòutou chyu.   Please go to the rear.
  Wǒ dau hòutou láile.   I have come to the rear.
  Tā dau hòutou chyule.   He has gone to the rear.
Chǐng nǐ dau chyántou lái.   Please come to the front.
  Wǒ dau chyántou láile.   I have come to the front.
  Tā dau chyántou chyule.   He has gone to the front.
Nǐ kéyi dzwòsya.   You may sit down.
  Wǒ dzwòsyale.   I have sat down.
  Tā dzwòsyale.   He has sat down.

FLUENCY DRILL

Chīfàn.

Méichīfàn.

Wǒ méichīfàn.

Wǒmen méichīfàn.

Wǒmen méi dzai tā nèr chīfàn.

Swóyi wǒmen méi dzai tā nèr chīfàn.

Tā dau jyēshang chyule, swóyi wǒmen méi dzai tā nèr chīfàn.

Tāmen dau jyēshang chyule, swóyi wǒmen méi dzai tāmen nèr chīfàn.

Tāmen dōu dau jyēshang chyule, swóyi wǒmen méi dzai tāmen nèr chīfàn.

Tāmen dōu dau jyēshang chyule, swóyi wǒmen méi dzai tāmen nèr chī jūngfàn.

NOTES

1. COMPLETED ACTION WITH -*LE*: The particle -*le*, either as a suffix
   to verbs, or as a sentence final, indicates the completion of the
   action of the verb, or of the entire predicate:

   Jāng Syansheng láile.   Mr. Chang came (or has come).
   Wǒ yǐjing chǐng tāmen le.   I have already invited them.
   Tā gěi wǒ chyán le.   He gave (or has given) me money.

   In the case of verbs with simple objects, in addition to the -*le*
   at the end of the sentence, one often finds another -*le* attached to
   the main verb:

   Nín chīle fàn le ma?   Have you eaten?
   Wǒ gěile ta neige byǎu le.   I've given him that watch (already).

2. NEGATION OF COMPLETED ACTION WITH *MEI*: The negative particle
méi- (or *méiyou-*), when prefixed to verbs, negates all idea of
completion of the action of that verb, or of the entire predicate:

Tā méilái (or *méiyou lái*).	He didn't (or hasn't) come.
Wǒmen dōu méichyù.	None of us went.
Wǒ méikàn bàu.	I didn't (or haven't) read the paper.

3. SUSPENSE WITH NE: It was shown in Lesson X (see Note 6) that the
sentence suffix *ne* in positive statements (in contrast to *-le*)
carries forward the action of the verb. In the case of negated
statements with *méi-*, the addition of *ne* suggests the idea of
suspense, or a holding over of the action, with the probability
of an early completion:

Tā méilái ne.	He hasn't come yet.
Byǎu hái méimǎi ne.	I still haven't bought the watch yet.
Tā méigěi wǒ neige chyán ne.	He hasn't given me the money yet.

4. QUESTIONS AND COMPLETED ACTION: Note the following forms of questions as to action already completed:

Tā láile ma?	Did or has he come?
Tā láile meilai?	do.
Tā láile meiyou?	do.
Tā méilái ma?	Didn't or hasn't he come?

Where simple objects are involved, the following forms are most
commonly used:

Nín chr̄(le) fàn le ma?	Did you eat or have you eaten?
Nín chr̄(le) fàn le meiyou?	do.
Nín méichr̄fàn ma?	Didn't you eat or haven't you eaten?

With transposed objects, *-le* is attached to the verb only:

Jīntyande bàu, nín kànle ma?	Have you read today's paper?
Jīntyande bàu, nín kànle mei-kan?	do.
Jīntyande bàu, nín kànle mei-you?	do.
Jīntyande bàu, nín méikàn ma?	Haven't you read today's paper?

5. PURPOSE AND COMPLETED ACTION: In the last lesson (see Note 5), three variant forms of the same pattern for expressing the purpose of coming or going were shown. When completed action is indicated, -*le* is preferably attached to either of the two forms ending in *lái* or *chyù*, and to the end of the sentence only:

Tā dau Jūnggwo jyāushū chyùle.   He has gone to China to teach.

Tā dau chéng wàitou chyù kàn   He has gone outside the city to
péngyou chyule.   see a friend.

6. STRESSING PLACE, CONVEYANCE, AND PURPOSE: Circumstances connected with the action of the main verb, such as the place where the action occurred (with *dzài*), or started from (with *tsúng*), or what conveyance was used (with *dzwò*), or the purpose of coming or going, are all singled out for special stress in the same way that the person who instigated the action was stressed in Lesson IX (see Note 4), with the *shr...de* clausal construction:

Nínde màudz (shr) dzai nǎr   Where did you buy your hat?
mǎide?

Tā (shr) tsúng nǎr láide?   Where did he come from?

Nǐ (shr) dzwò hwǒchē hwéilaide   Did you come back by train?
ma?

Wǒ (shr) dau jèr lái nyànshū   I came here to study.
de (or nyànshū 'láide).

Note that the *shr* in this construction is often omitted and understood.

LESSON XIII

TIME WHEN EXPRESSIONS – PROBABILITY WITH *BA*

HOW MANY MONTHS IN A YEAR?

A: Yìnyán yǒu jǐge ywè?

How many months are there in a year?

B: Yìnyán yǒu shrèrge ywè.

There are 12 months in a year.

A: Yǒu dwōshautyan?

How many days?

B: Sānbǎi-lyòushr-wǔtyan.

365 days.

A: Yíge ywè yǒu dwōshautyan?

How many days in a month?

B: Yǒude yǒu sānshrtyan, yǒude yǒu sānshr-yītyan.

Some have 30 days, some have 31 days.

A: Èrywe méiyou sānshrtyān ba?

February doesn't have 30 days, does it?

B: Méiyou. Èrywe jyòu yǒu èrshr-bātyan.

No, it doesn't. February has only 28 days.

A: Diyíge ywè, Jūnggwo hwà jyàu shémma?

What is the first month called in Chinese?

B: Jyàu Yíywe.

It is called First Month.

A: Dièrge ywè jyòu jyàu Èrywe ba?

The second month is just called Second Month, isn't it?

B: Dwèile!

You're right!

A: Ou, nà bunán! Yíge ywè yǒu jǐge syīngchī? *

Oh, that's not difficult! How many weeks in a month?

B: Sžge syīngchī. Yìnyán you wǔshrèrge syīngchī, yíge syīngchī yǒu chītyan.

Four weeks. A year has 52 weeks, a week has 7 days.

A: 'Sunday' Jūnggwo hwà jyàu shémma?

What is Sunday called in Chinese?

B: 'Sunday' jyàu Syīngchītyān, 'Monday' jyàu Syīngchīyī.

Sunday is called 'Syingchi-tyan', Monday Syingchiyi.

A: Nà yě bùnán!

That's not difficult either!

B: Swóyi wǒ shwō: Jūnggwo hwà hěn rúngyi sywé!

Therefore I say that Chinese is very easy to learn!

*Repeat the dialog substituting lǐbài for syīngchī. Do this exercise throughout this lesson and in succeeding sections.

VOCABULARY

yǒu(de)shŕhou	MA:	sometimes	*hwǒchejàn*	N:	railroad station
chyùnyán	(MA)N:	last year	*chĭchejàn*	N:	bus station or stop
jīnnyán	(MA)N:	this year	*tyāntyān*	A:	every day
míngnyán	(MA)N:	next year	*nyánnyán*	A:	year by year
nà	SP:	that (in general)	*yàujĭn*	SV:	be important
(dì)jĭ-	SP:	which? (of series)	*dàu*	V:	arrive at, reach
-tyān	M:	day	*syīwang*	V:	hope that, hope for,
-nyán	M:	year			expect that
-hàu	M:	day (of month);	*dì-*	P:	(ordinalizing prefix
		number (of house,			to numbers)
		room, etc.)	*ba*	P:	(sentence suffix,
ywè	N:	month			implying probability)
syīngchī	N:	week	*(nà) bú-*	IE:	that's nothing!
lĭbài	N:	week	*yaujĭn!*		never mind!
shŕhou	N:	time	*dwèile!*	IE:	that's right! (in-
syīwang	N:	hope, expectation			dicates agreement)
chējàn	N:	station			

THE YEAR			THE MONTH		THE DAY	
Yìchyān-jyǒubǎinyán	1900	*Yīywe*[1]	January	*yīhau*	first
Yìchyān-bābǎi-	1863	*Èrywe*	February	*èrhau*	second
lyòushr-sānnyán		*Sānywe*	March	*sānhau*	third
Yìchyān-jyǒubǎi-	1947	*Sèywe*	April	*sèhau*	fourth
sèshr-chīnyán		*Wǔywe*	May	*wǔhau*	fifth
		Lyòuywe	June	*lyòuhau*	sixth
(telephone-style)		*Chīywe*	July	*chīhau*	seventh
Yī-sè-jyǒu-èr-nyán	1492	*Báywe*	August	*báhau*	eighth
Yī-líng-sān-yī-nyán	1031	*Jyǒuywe*	September	*jyǒuhau*	ninth
Yī-bā-líng-líng-nyán	1800	*Shŕywe*	October	*shŕhau*	tenth
Yī-bā-yī-líng-nyán	1810	*Shryīywe*	November	*shryī(hau)*	eleventh
		Shrèrywe	December	etc.	
shémma nyán	what year?	*jĭywe*	which month?	*jĭhau*	which day?
			(of the 12)		(of the 31)
chyùnyán	last year	*shàngywe*[2]	last month	*dzwótyan*	yesterday
jīnnyán	this year	*jèiywe*	this month	*jīntyan*	today
míngnyán	next year	*syàywe*	next month	*míngtyan*	tomorrow
něinyán	which year?	*něiywe*	which month?	*něityan*	which day?

THE WEEK

shàngsyīngchī²	last week	Syīngchīyī	Monday
jèisyīngchī	this week	Syīngchīèr	Tuesday
syàsyīngchī	next week	Syīngchīsān	Wednesday
nèisyīngchī	which week?	Syīngchīsż	Thursday
shàngsyīngchī-sān	last week Wednesday	Syīngchīwǔ	Friday
		Syīngchīlyòu	Saturday
jèisyīngchī-sān	this week Wednesday	Syīngchītyān	Sunday
		Syīngchīrì	Sunday
syàsyīngchī-sān ⌣	next week Wednesday		
nèisyīngchī-sān	which Wednesday?	syīngchījǐ	Which day? (of the week)

Note: *two words for Sunday in Chinese; lǐbài may replace syīngchī; students should drill both forms. Unlike Western week, the Chinese week begins with Monday.*

¹Distinguish between *Yíywè* (January) and *yíge ywè* (one month).

²The measure *-ge* may be inserted in these two columns, as for example: *shànggeywè, nèige ywè?, shànggelǐbài, nèige lǐbài?*, etc.

ORDINAL NUMBERS

diyītyān	the 1st day
dièrtyān	the 2nd day, next day
disānnyán	the 3rd year
disàge	the 4th one (person or thing)
diwǔwèi	the 5th person (polite for teachers, etc.)
dilyòuběn	the 6th volume (books)
dichījāng	the 7th sheet (paper)
dijǐběn	which volume? (of a series)

PATTERN SENTENCES

I. TIME WHEN EXPRESSIONS (PRECEDE VERB)

Time When   CV - N   V

Pattern: **Nǐ shémma shŕhou dau Jūnggwo chyu? Wǒ mìngnyán chyù.**
When are you going to China? I'm going next year.

1. Nǐ dzwótyan wǎnshang chyùle ma?   Did you go last evening? No, I
   Méichyù.   didn't.
2. Jāng Syansheng mìngtyan lái   Is Mr. Chang coming tomorrow? No,
   bulái? Mǐngtyan bulái.   he's not.

3. Tā Lǐbaièr hwéilaile meiyou?   Did he return Tuesday? Yes, he
   Hwéilaile.   did.

4. Shànglǐbài nǐ dzai nǎr? Shàng- Where were you last week? Last week
   lǐbài wǒ dzai Nyǒuywe.   I was in New York.

5. Nǐ syàywe búdau Yīnggwo chyu   Aren't you going to England next
   ma? Buchyù. Nǐ dzěmma jřdau wǒ   month? No. How did you know I
   buchyù?   wasn't going?

6. Chyùnyán láide neige rén dau   Where has the man who came last
   nǎr chyule?   year gone?

7. Wǒ syīwang nǐ mǐngtyan néng   I hope you can come tomorrow.
   lái.

II. STRESSING TIME WHEN WITH THE *shr...de* CONSTRUCTION

             N (shr)   Time When   Vde
   Pattern: *Nǐ shr shémma shŕhou dàude? Wǒ shr Lǐbaiwǔ dàude.*
   When did you arrive? I arrived Friday.

1. Nèige rén   shr   něityan   dzǒude?
   Tā   shr   dzwótyan   dzǒude.

2. Nǐn Tàitai   shr   Lǐbaijǐ   dau Nyǒuywē chyùde?
   Wǒ tàitai   shr   Lǐbaisān   chyùde.

3. Jèige jwōdz   shr   něiywe   mǎide?
                 Shr   shàngywe   mǎide.

4. Jàu Syaujye   shr   jǐywe   tsúng wàigwo láide?
   Tā   shr   Shryǐywe   láide.

5. Jāng Syansheng shr něinyán   dau Jūnggwo chyùde?
   Tā shr   Yī-jyǒu-sź-lǐng-nyán chyùde.

6. Nǐde péngyou shr   jǐhau   hwéilaide?
   Tā   shr   wǔywe shrwǔ(hau)   hwéilaide.

7. Tāde háidz   shr   Èrshrjǐ(hau)   dàu jèr de (or dàude jèr)?
   Tāde háidz   shr   Èrshr-chǐ(hau)   dàude.

8. Nǐde byǎu   shr   jǐnnyán   mǎide ma?

9. Lǐ Syansheng shr   shànglǐbaisż   dzǒude bushr?

III. PROBABILITY WITH SENTENCE SUFFIX *ba*

Pattern: *Nǐmen dōu hǎu ba?* You are all well, I presume?

1. Dūngsyi dzai Měigwo syàndzài hěn gwèi ba? Bútai gwèi.

Things in America are very expensive now, I presume? Not too expensive.

2. Nǐn shr Jāng Syansheng ba? Shr̀.

You are Mr. Chang, aren't you? Yes.

3. Nǐmen búmài wàigwo chá ba? Mài. Nǐ mǎi dwōshau?

You don't sell foreign tea, do you? Yes, we do. How much do you want?

4. Sywésheng dōu hwéijyāle ba? Dwèile, dōu hwéijyāle.

I suppose the students have all returned home? You're right, they've all gone home.

5. Nǐ jīntyan buchyù ba? Buchyù.

You're not going today, I suppose? No, I'm not.

6. Nǐ tyāntyān dau tā nèr chyù ba? Wǒ yǒushŕhou chyù, yǒushŕhou búchyu.

I suppose you go to his place every day? Sometimes I go there, sometimes I don't.

FLUENCY DRILLS

Nǐn shr něinyán dau jèr láide?
  Wǒ shr Yī-jyǒu-sž-líng-nyán láide.
Nǐn shr něiywe dàude?
  Wǒ shr Èrywe dàude.
Nǐn shr Èrywe jǐhau dàude?
  Wǒ shr Èrywe báhau dàude.
Nǐn shr báhau dzǎushang dàude ma?
  Wǒ búshr dzǎushang dàude, wǒ shr wǎnshang dàude.

Nǐnde byǎu shr něinyán mǎide?
  Wǒde byǎu shr chyùnyán mǎide.
Nǐnde byǎu shr chyùnyán něiywe mǎide?
  Wǒde byǎu shr chyùnyán Chīywe mǎide.
Nǐnde byǎu shr Chīywe jǐhau mǎide?
  Wǒde byǎu shr Chīywe sānhau mǎide.
Chyùnyán Chīywe sānhau shr lǐbaijǐ?
  Chyùnyán Chīywe sānhau shr Lǐbaiwǔ.

NOTES

1. TIME WHEN AND WITHIN WHICH: In indicating the time when or within which an action occurred, or failed to occur, whether it be a
point of time or a stated period, the time element always comes
somewhere before the main verb of the sentence or clause. The
entire expression thus functions as a movable adverb, and serves
as a setting for the action:

wǒ mǐngtyan chyù.	I am going tomorrow.
Tā shr dzwótyan láide.	He came yesterday.
Wǒ jèi lyǎngtyan méi shr̀.	I have nothing to do these two days.
Jīntyan wǎnshang chǐng nǐmen dau wǒmen jyā lái chr̄ yidyǎr Jūnggwo fàn.	Please come to our home this evening for a little Chinese food.

2. STRESSING TIME WHEN: When it is desired to emphasize the time when
or within which an action did or did not take place, rather than
the action itself, the *shr...de* construction is used, as in the
case of place, purpose, etc. (see Lesson IX, Note 4, and Lesson
XII, Note 6). Contrast the following pairs of sentences:

Wǒ péngyou dzwótyan láile.	My friend came yesterday.
Tā shr dzwótyan láide.	It was yesterday that he came.
Wǒ jīntyan mǎile shū le.	I bought a book today.
Jèiběn búshr jīntyan mǎide.	This volume is not one I bought today.

3. PROBABILITY WITH SENTENCE SUFFIX *BA*: The particle *ba* suffixed to
certain statements makes them imply a probability, a conclusion
based on the best light one has, yet leaving some room for doubt.
Contrast the following pairs of sentences:

Nín hěn máng ma?	Are you very busy?
Nín hěn máng ba?	You're probably very busy, aren't you?
Tā dau Jūnggwo chyule ma?	Has he gone to China?
Tā dau Jūnggwo chyule ba?	He's gone to China, I presume?
Tā méichyù ma?	Didn't he go?
Tā méichyù ba?	I don't suppose he went, did he?

4. ORDINAL NUMBERS are formed by prefixing the ordinalizing particle

dì- to the cardinal numbers. Compare the English endings *-st, -nd, -rd,* etc.:

> *diyī* (first), *dièr* (second), etc.
>
> *diyíge* (the first), *disānběn* (the third volume), etc.

5. INQUIRING DAY OF THE WEEK, ETC.: In inquiring and giving the day of the week, etc., the verb (*shr*) is very often omitted, as in the case of asking prices (see Lesson VI, Note 6):

> *Míngtyan (shr) Lǐbaijǐ?*   What day of the week is tomorrow?
>
> *Lǐbailyòu.*   Saturday.
>
> *Jīntyan (shr) jǐhàu?*   What day of the month is today?
>
> *Jīntyan (shr) shrsānhau.*   Today is the 13th.
>
> *Jīnnyán (shr) shémma nyán?*   What year is this?
>
> *Jīnnyán (shr) Yī-jyǒu-sè-*   This year is 1947.
> *chīnyán.*

6. DATES AND ADDRESSES: When giving dates and addresses, or other detailed times and places, the larger units always precede the smaller. No *-de* is used between the different divisions:

> *Lǐbaièr wǎnshang*   Tuesday evening
>
> *disāntyan dzǎushang*   the morning of the 3rd day
>
> *Yī-jyǒu-sè-wǔnyán Báywe shrsè*   August 14th, 1945
>
> *Jūnggwo Nánjīng*   Nanking, China
>
> *Nyǒuywē Wǔshrjyǒu Jyē*   59th Street, New York City
>
> *Shrsè Jyē sānbǎihàu*   #300 14th Street

Note that the particle *dì-* is omitted in inquiring and giving the month, day of month, or number of the street.

LESSON XIV

CO-VERBS OF INTEREST, ETC. – INDEFINITES

WHO'LL GO WITH ME TO EAT?

A: Jīntyan wǎnshang wǒ syǎng dau jyēshang chyu chr̄ dyǎr Jūnggwo fàn. Shéi gēn wǒ chyù?

I'm thinking of going out for some Chinese food tonight. Who'll go with me?

B: Wǒ gēn nǐ chyù.

I'll go with you.

A: Nǐ hwèi yùng kwàidz ma?

Do you know how to use chopsticks?

B: Yidyǎr dōu buhwèi.

I don't know the first thing about it.

A: Nà buyaujǐn! Nǐ yau yùng dāudz chādz, fàngwárli dōu yǒu. Nǐ yau sywé yùng kwàidz, wǒ kéyi jyāu nǐ.

Never mind! If you want to use knife and fork, the restaurant has both. If you want to learn to use chopsticks, I can teach you.

B: Wǒmen dau něige fàngwǎr?

To which restaurant shall we go?

A: Chéng lǐtou yǒu yige syǎu fàngwǎr jyàu Syīn Hwá Lóu. Wǒ tīngshwō nèrde tsài butswò.

There is a small restaurant downtown called the New China. I hear that the food there is quite good.

B: Ou, wǒ jr̄dau nèige dìfang.

Oh, I know that place.

(AT THE RESTAURANT)

A: Nǐ dzwèi ài chr̄ shémma?

What do you like most to eat?

B: Wǒ shémma dōu ài chr̄.

I like to eat anything.

A: Nǐ syǎng chr̄ yú ma?

Would you like some fish?

B: Hěn syǎng chr̄.

I'd love to have some.

A: Hǎu, sānge tsài, yíge tāng, gòu bugòu?

Good, would three main dishes and a soup be enough?

B: Gòule!

That'll be enough!

A: Wǒmen syān hē yidyǎr jyǒu, hǎu buhǎu?

How about starting off with a little wine?

B: Syèsye, wǒ buhē jyǒu.

Thanks, I don't drink wine.

VOCABULARY

-wǎn	M:	bowl (of)	*yikwàr*	A: together (also as N)
-jyù	M:	(measure for *hwà*)	*gēn*	CV: with; and (following)
tsài	N:	vegetables; dish of Chinese food	*gěi*	CV: for; to (for benefit of)
ròu	N:	meat	*tì*	CV: for (in place of)
yú	N:	fish	*yùng*	V: use, employ
tāng	N:	soup		CV: with (using)
dāudz	N:	knife	*dwèi*	CV: to, towards (facing)
chādz	N:	fork	*yǒuyùng*	SV: be useful
shǎur	N:	spoon	*butswò*	SV: be not bad, quite good
kwàidz	N:	chopsticks		
wǎn	N:	bowl	*wár*	V: play
syìn	N:	letter, mail	*tīngshwō*	IE: hear(d) it said that
jyùdz	N:	sentence	*wèn...hǎu*	IE: inquire after another's welfare
gūngfu	N:	free or leisure time		
syān	A:	first	*gòule!*	IE: that'll be enough!

PATTERN SENTENCES

I. CO-VERBS OF INTEREST, ETC.

(a) The Co-Verb *gēn* (with; and, lit. following)

Pattern: *Wǒmen míngtyan yau gēn Lǐ Syansheng Lǐ Taitai yikwàr chī wǎnfàn.*

We are eating supper with Mr. and Mrs. Lee tomorrow.

Jāng Syansheng	gēn	Jāng Taitai dau Běijīng chyule.
Wǒ dzwèi syǐhwan	gēn	syǎu háidz wár.
Tāmen bugēn	wǒmen yikwàr chyù.
Wǒ méigēn	tā shwō shémma(hwà).
Wǒ méi gūngfu	gēn	tāmen chyù.
Nǐde Jūnggwo hwà shr	gēn	shéi sywéde?

(b) The Co-Verb *gěi* (for; to, lit. for the benefit of)

Pattern: *Lǐ Taitai yau gěi wǒmen dzwò Jūnggwo fàn.*
   Mrs. Lee is going to cook Chinese food for us.

Wǒ tàitai tyāntyān	gěi	wǒmen	dzwòfàn.
Nǐ néng bunéng syān	gěi	wǒ	mǎi yidyǎr dūngsyi?
Chǐng nǐ	gěi	wǒmen	shwō yidyǎr Yīngwén.
Wǒ méigěi	tā	dzwò shémma (shr̀).	
Wáng Syansheng	gěi	tāmen	syěle jǐge Jūnggwo dz̀ le.
Wǒ tīngshwō tā cháng(cháng)	gěi	tā fùmǔ	syěsyìn.

(c) The Co-Verb *tì* (for, lit. substituting for)

Pattern: *Lǐ Syansheng yau tì Lǐ Taitai mǎi tsài.*
   Mr. Lee is buying the meat and vegetables for Mrs. Lee.

Nǐ néng tì	wǒ	dzwò jèige(shr̀) ma?	
Chǐng nǐ tì	wǒ	gēn Chén Syansheng shwōshwo.	
Wǒ dzwótyan méitì	wǒ	mǔchin	mǎi shémma.
Chén Syansheng dzwótyan tì	Lyóu Syansheng	jyāushūle.	

(d) The Co-Verb *yùng* (with, lit. using)

Pattern: *Wǒmen yau yùng kwàidz chr̄fàn.*
   We are going to eat with chopsticks.

Jūnggwo rén	yùng	dāudz chādz	chr̄fàn ma?
Chǐng nǐ	yùng	Jūnggwo hwà shwō.	Wǒ. budǔng Yīngwén.
Shéi búyung	sháur	hē tāng?	
Wǒ	yùng	tā gěi wǒde chyán	mǎile lyǎngjang hwàr.

(e) The Co-Verb *dwèi* (to, towards, lit. facing)

Pattern: *Lǐ Syansheng Lǐ Taitai dwèi wǒmen hěn hǎu.*
   Mr. and Mrs. Lee are very nice to us.

Tā dwèi	wǒ	shwō...	
Wǒ méidwei	tāmen	shwō shémma (hwà).	
Wǒ yǐjing dwèi	wǒ tàitai	shwōle.	
Wǒ dwèi	jèige shr̀	shémma dōu bùjrdàu.	

II. QUESTION WORDS AS INDEFINITES

Pattern: *Nǐ yàu shémma? Wǒ búyau shémma.*
What do you want? I don't want anything.

1. Nǐ yǒu shémma shr̀? Wǒ méi shémma shr̀.

   What can I do for you? You can't
   do anything for me.

2. Nǐ dau nǎr chyù? Wǒ búdau nǎr·
   chyù.

   Where are you going? I'm not going
   anywhere.

3. Nǐ gēn shéi shwōhwà? Wǒ méigēn
   shéi shwōhwà.

   With whom did you speak? I didn't
   speak with anyone.

4. Nǐmen sywésyàu yǒu dwōshau
   sywésheng? Méi dwōshau.

   How many students are there in
   your school? Not many.

5. Nǐmen yǒu jǐge syīn sywésheng?
   Méi jǐge.

   How many new students do you have?
   Not many.

III. INCLUSIVENESS AND EXCLUSIVENESS (WITH INDEFINITES)

Pattern: *Nǐ yàu shémma? Wǒ shémma dōu yàu,* or
Wǒ shémma dōu (or yě) buyàu.
What do you want? Anything at all, or
Nothing at all.

1. Shéi jr̄dau jèige shr̀ching?
   Shéi dōu jr̄dau.
   Shéi dōu bùjr̄dàu.

   Who knows about this?
   Everybody knows.
   Nobody knows.

2. Nǎr yǒu fàngwǎr?
   Nǎr dōu yǒu.
   Nǎr yě méiyǒu.

   Where are there restaurants?
   Everywhere.
   Nowhere.

3. Něige chǐchē shr nǐde?
   Neige dōu búshr wǒde. Wǒde
   màile.

   Which car is yours?
   Neither (or none) of them is
   mine. Mine is sold.

4. Nǐ yau kàn něiběn shū? Něiběn
   dōu kéyi.

   Which volume do you want to look
   at (or read)? Either (or any)
   one will be all right.

5. Nǐ shwō něityan dzǒu hǎu? Něityan dōu syǐng.

   Which day do you say is the best
   to leave? Any day will do.

IV. EXCLUSIVENESS INTENSIFIED ('NOT EVEN')

Pattern: *Nǐ yàu dwōshau? Wǒ yidyǎr dōu* (or *yě*) *buyàu.*
How much do you want? Not any (lit. not even a bit).
Nǐ yàu jǐge (or *dwōshau*)? *Wǒ yǐge dōu* (or *yě*) *buyàu.*
How many do you want? Not a single one.

1. Nǐ hwèi syě dwōshau dz̀? Wǒ yǐge   How many characters can you write?
   dz̀ yě búhwei syě.   Not a single character.
2. Nǐ kànle jǐběn shū le? Wǒ yiběn   How many books have you read? I
   dōu méikàn ne.   haven't read a single volume yet.
3. Nǐn hwèi shwō Yīngwén ma? Wǒ   Can you speak English? I can't
   yidyǎr dōu búhwei shwō.   speak a bit of English.
4. Nǐ yǒu dwōshau chyán? Yimáu   How much money do you have? Not
   chyán yě meiyǒu.   even a dime.
5. Nǐ néng chr̄ jǐwǎn fàn? Bànwǎn   How many bowls of rice can you
   dōu bunéng chr̄.   eat? Not even half a bowl.
6. Wǒ shwōde hwà, nǐn dǔng dwō-   How much do you understand of what
   shau? Yíjyù wǒ dōu budǔng.   I said? Not a single sentence.
7. Nǐ yàu shémma? Wǒ yidyǎr shémma   What do you want? I don't want
   yě buyàu.   anything at all.

FLUENCY DRILL

Mǎi tsài.

Mǎi tsài chyu.

Chyù mǎi tsài chyu.

Gēn wǒ chyù mǎi tsài chyu.

Nǐ gēn wǒ chyù mǎi tsài chyu.

Nǐ gēn wǒ yikwàr chyù mǎi tsài chyu.

Nǐ gēn wǒ yikwàr dau chéngli chyù mǎi tsài chyu.

Nǐ gēn wǒ yikwàr dau chénglǐtou chyù mǎi tsài chyu.

Nǐ yǒu gūngfu gēn wǒ yikwàr dau chénglǐtou chyù mǎi tsài chyu ma?

Nǐ mǐngtyan yǒu gūngfu gēn wǒ yikwàr dau chénglǐtou chyù mǎi tsài chyu ma?

NOTES

1. CO-VERBS OF INTEREST, ETC.: In this lesson five more co-verbs are introduced: *gēn* (with), *gěi* (for or to), *tì* (for), *yùng* (with), and *dwèi* (to). The sentence pattern is the same as that introduced in Lesson X:

Nǐ gēn shéi chyù?	With whom are you going?
Tā tyāntyān gěi wǒ mǎi bàu.	He buys the paper for me every day.
Wǒ kéyi tì nǐ chyù ma?	May I go for you?
Shéi yùng dāudz hē tāng?	Who drinks soup with a knife?
Wǒ dwèi tāmen shwō wǒ bunéng chyù.	I told them I couldn't go.

2. QUESTION WORDS AS INDEFINITES: Question words like *shéi* (who?), *shémma* (what?), etc., are commonly used as indefinites like the English 'anyone', and 'anything':

Nèige wǎnli yǒu shémma? Méi shémma.	What's in that bowl? Nothing.
Chēshang yǒu dwōshau rén? Méi dwōshau rén.	How many people are there on the train. Not many.

3. INCLUSIVENESS AND EXCLUSIVENESS: To express inclusive ideas such as 'everyone' and 'everything', and exclusive ideas such as 'no one' and 'nothing', indefinites plus *dōu* (at all) are used:

Shéi syǐhwan tā? Shéi dōu syǐhwan tā.	Who likes him? Everybody likes him.
Shémma rén yàu jèige? Shémma rén dōu (or *yě*) *buyàu.*	What person wants this. Nobody wants it.

4. INTENSIFYING EXCLUSIVENESS: To express an intense degree of exclusiveness, as in the English phrase 'not even a little', *yi* and a measure, or some expression which signifies a very small number or amount, is used before *dōu* and the negative form of the verb:

Nǐ hwèi dzwòfàn ma? Wǒ yidyǎr dōu buhwèi.	Do you know how to cook? I don't know a single thing about it.
Háidz chīle jǐwǎn fàn le? Bànwǎn dōu méichī ne.	How many bowls of rice has the child eaten? Not even half a bowl yet.

Note that the adverb *yě* is often substituted for *dōu* in sentences expressing exclusiveness.

LESSON XV

SINGLE AND DOUBLE -LE - TIME SPENT

A TRIP TO ITALY

Wǒ yǒu yige péngyou, syìng Sz̄. Yǒu yityān Sz̄ Syansheng dau Yìdàlì chyule.

I have a friend named Smith. One day Mr. Smith went to Italy.

Tā búshr yǐge rén chyùde, tā shr gēn lyǎngge péngyou yikwàr chyùde.

He didn't go alone, he went with a couple of friends.

Tāmen dzwò chwán, dzwòle wǔtyān jyou dàule Fàgwo. Dàule Fàgwo, syàle chwan, tāmen jyou shàngle hwǒchē le.

They traveled by boat for five days and reached France. Upon arriving in France, they disembarked and boarded a train.

Tāmende hwǒchē shr Lǐbaisān kāide, dièrtyan dzǎushang jyou dàule Lwómǎ le.

Their train left on Wednesday, and the next morning they arrived in Rome.

Dàule Lwómǎ, tāmen jyou dzai chéng lǐtou jǎule yige lyǔgwǎn.

When they got to Rome they hunted up a hotel in town.

Tāmen dzai nèige lyǔgwánli jùle yǐgedwō lǐbài, hòulai jyou dàu yige péngyou jyā chyù jù chyule.

They lived in that hotel a week or so, and afterwards went to live at a friend's home.

Sz̄ Syansheng gēn tāde péngyou dzai nèige rénde jyāli jùle bànnyán, jyou hwéi Měigwo le.

Mr. Smith and his two friends stayed in that man's home for half a year, and then returned to America.

Míngnyán wǒ yě děi dau Yìdàlì chyu kànkan. Yǒu rén shwō búbì chyu. Hái yǒu rén shwō byé chyù. Kěshr wǒ shwō wǒmen dōu yīngdāng dau Yìdàlì chyu kànkan.

Next year I must also go to Italy to have a look around. Some say there is no need to go. Others say don't go. But I say we all ought to visit Italy.

VOCABULARY

hòulai	MA:	afterwards, and then	*shàng*	V:	ascend, go up on; go
bàntyān	(MA)N:	a long while			to
yìtyān	(MA)N:	a day; a whole day	*syà*	V:	descend, go down from
hǎují-	NU:	quite a few	*jù*	V:	live or stay in or at
hǎusyē	NU:	a good many; a good	*hwéi*	V:	return (to)
		deal of	*jǎu*	V:	look or hunt for
-kwài	M:	piece (lit. lump)	*kāi*	V:	open; start away
-kè	M:	lesson			(train, bus, ship);
-fēng	M:	(measure for letters)			operate (car)
lyǔgwǎn	N:	hotel	*shàngsywé*	VO:	go to school
jyòu	A:	then (introduces sub-	*shàngkè*	VO:	go to class
		sequent action)	*shàngchē*	VO:	board a train or car
děi	AV:	have to, must	*shàngjyē*	VO:	go to the shopping
bubì	AV:	need not			district
buyùng	AV:	no use to	*shànglóu*	VO:	come or go upstairs
yīngdāng	AV:	ought to, should	*hwéijyā*	VO:	return home
byé	AV:	don't (imperative,	*hwéigwó*	VO:	return to one's
		from *búyàu*)			native country

PATTERN SENTENCES

I. SINGLE VERB -*le* WITH SIMPLE OBJECTS (DEPENDENT CLAUSES)

Vle   O,   jyou...

Pattern: *Wǒmen chr̄le fàn, jyou shànglóule.*
When we had eaten, we went upstairs.

1. Wǒmen shàngle lóu, jyou dzwò-   When we got upstairs, we sat down.
   syale.

2. Tā mǎile táng, jyou hwéijyāle.   He returned home after he bought
                                     the candy.

3. Tāmen syàle chē, jyou shàng   After they got off the train, they
   lyǔgwǎn chyule.   went to the hotel.

4. Wǒmen dàule chējàn, hwǒchē yǐ-   When we reached the station, the
   jing kāile.   train had already left.

5. Wǒ dàule Nyǒuywe, jyou yau chyu   I am going to look up my friend as
   jǎu wǒde péngyou.   soon as I get to New York.

6. Tāmen dàule Tyānjing, jyou méi-   When they arrived at Tientsin they
   syàchwán.   didn't disembark.
7. Nín chr̄le fàn, kànle bàu, jyou   After you have eaten and read the
   chǐng nín shànglóu.   paper, please come upstairs.

II. SINGLE OR DOUBLE -*le* WITH MEASURED OBJECTS

	Vle	Meas	O	(le)

Patterns: (a) *Nèige háidz (dzwótyan) chr̄le bákwai táng.*
That child ate eight pieces of candy (yesterday).
(b) *Nèige háidz (yǐjing) chr̄le bákwai táng le.*
That child has (already) eaten eight pieces of candy.

1.(a) Wǒ shàngywe kànle sānběn shū.   I read three books last month.
  (b) Syānsheng yàu wǒmen kàn wǔ-   The teacher wants us to read five
      běn shū. Wǒ kànle sānběn le.   books. I have read three already.
2.(a) Wǒ wènle lyǎngge rén. Tāmen   I inquired of two people. They
      dōu shwō bùjrdàu.   both said they didn't know.
  (b) Wǒ wènle lyǎngge rén le. Wǒ   I have asked two people already.
      hái děi wèn jǐge rén.   I must still inquire of a few more.
3.(a) Tāmen chyùnyan dzai wàigwo   Last year while abroad they went
      yigùng dàule báge dìfang.   to eight places.
  (b) Tāmen jīnnyan yǐjing dàule   This year they have already been
      sānge dìfang le.   to three places.
4.(a) Wǒ dzwótyan wǎnshang mǎile   I bought a little candy last night.
      yidyǎr táng.
  (b) Wǒmen yǐjing chr̄le yibàn le!   We have already eaten a half of it.
5.(a) Wǒ chyùnyan dzai Jūnggwo   I learned a few sentences in Chi-
      sywéle jǐjyu Jūnggwo hwà.   nese last year.
  (b) Wǒmen nyànle shrwǔkè le.   We have studied fifteen lessons.

III. TIME SPENT (TIME ELEMENT FOLLOWS THE VERB)

Patterns: (1-4) *Chyùnyan wǒ dzai jèr jùle lyǎngge ywè.*
I lived here two months last year.
(5-7) *Wǒmen nyànle lyǎngge ywède shū le.*
We have been studying for two months already.
or *Wǒmen nyànshū, nyànle lyǎngge ywè le.*
(lit. as to our studying, we have been studying...)

1. Wǒ syānsheng dzai wàigwo jùle
   bushǎu shŕhou le.

My husband has been living abroad
for quite a while.

2. Wǒ syǎngle hěndwō shŕhou le.
   Mǐngtyan wǒ dzài syángsyang.

I have been thinking about this
for a long time. I'll give it
more thought tomorrow.

3. Tā láile yìtyān le.

He's been here an entire day.

4. Tā dzwòle bàntyān, hǒulai jyou
   dzǒule.

He sat a long while and then left.

5. Wǒ chyùnyan dzai nèige sywésyàuli nyànle jǐge ywède shū.
   or...nyànshū, nyànle jǐge ywè.

I studied in that school for a few
months last year.

6. Wǒ dzai jèr yǐjing sywéle
   lyǎnggedwō ywède Jūnggwo hwà
   le.
   or...sywé Jūnggwo hwà, sywéle
   lyǎnggedwō ywè le.

I have been here studying spoken
Chinese for more than two months.

7. Tā syěle hǎujǐnyánde dẑ le.
   or...syědẑ, syěle hǎujǐnyán le.
   Swóyi tāde dẑ dzwèi hǎu.

He has been writing characters for
a good many years, so his characters are extremely good.

IV. ACTION (WITH -le) AND ATTENDANT CIRCUMSTANCES (WITH shr...de) CONTRASTED

1. Wǒ chyùnyan dau Dégwo chyule.
   Nǐ shr gēn shéi chyùde?

Last year I went to Germany. With
whom did you go?

2. Wǒ jīnnyan sywéle yidyǎr Déwén.
   Nǐ shr gēn shéi sywéde?

This year I studied a little German. With whom did you study?

3. Wǒ shànggeywè dzai Nyǒuywe mǎile yige chìchē. Nǐ shr gěi shéi
   mǎide?

Last month I bought a car in New
York. For whom did you buy it?

4. Wǒ gěi tā syěle hǎujǐfēng syìn.
   Nèisye syìn shr gěi shéi syěde?

I wrote (or for) him a good many
letters. To (or for) whom did
you write all those letters?

5. Wǒ dzwótyan jyāule yidyǎr shū.
   Nǐn shr tì shéi jyāude?

I taught a little yesterday. For
whom were you substituting?

6. Wǒmen jīntyan dzai yige péngyou
   jyāli chŕle Jūnggwo fàn. Nǐmen
   shr yùng kwàidz chŕde ba?

We had (a meal of) Chinese food at
a friend's home today. You ate
with chopsticks, I presume?

7. Wǒ dwèi tā shwōle hǎusye hwà.   I said a good many things to him.
Nèisye hwà shr dwèi shémma rén   To whom were all those things
shwōde?   said?

FLUENCY DRILL

Nyànshū.

Nyàn Jūnggwo shū.

Wǒ nyàn Jūnggwo shū.

Wǒmen nyàn Jūnggwo shū.

Wǒmen nyàn Jūnggwo shū le.

Wǒmen nyànle Jūnggwo shū le.

Wǒmen nyànle lyǎngge ywède Jūnggwo shū le.

Wǒmen yǐjing nyànle lyǎngge ywède Jūnggwo shū le.

Wǒmen dzai jèr yǐjing nyànle lyǎngge ywède Jūnggwo shū le.

Wǒmen dzai jèige sywésyàu yǐjing nyànle lyǎngge ywède Jūnggwo shū.le.

Wǒmen dzai jèige sywésyàuli yǐjing nyànle lyǎngge ywède Jūnggwo shū le.

NOTES

1. SIMPLE OBJECTS AND VERB -*LE* ONLY: A sentence with a simple object
and verb -*le* only, is unfinished, and requires a subsequent statement to finish the sense. Such unfinished sentences function like
English dependent clauses which begin with 'when', 'after', etc.
The subsequent statement is usually introduced by the fixed adverb
jyou (then), which is not translated into English, and receives no
stress in speaking:

    Tā chr̄le fàn, jyou kàn bàu.   After he eats he reads the
                                         paper.

    Tā chr̄le fàn, jyou kàn bàu   After he ate, he went off to
     chyule.   read the paper.

    Tā chr̄le fàn, jyou syǎng kàn   After he eats, he wants to read
     bàu.   the paper.

2. MEASURED OBJECTS AND SINGLE OR DOUBLE -*LE*: A sentence in which the
object is measured as to number and quantity, may be said with verb
-*le* only, or with both verb and sentence -*le*. Both constitute
finished sentences, but there is a difference in aspect. With verb
-*le* only, simple completion at some time in the past is indicated.
With both verb and sentence -*le*, the action of the verb is brought

down to the present, and in some way related to it. Contrast the
following pairs of sentences:

Tā chŕle sānwǎn fàn.	He ate 3 bowls of rice.
Tā chŕle sānwǎn fàn le.	He has eaten 3 bowls of rice already.
Wǒ dzai Jūnggwo jùle sānnyán.	I (once) lived in China 3 years.
Wǒ dzai Jūnggwo jùle sānnyán le.	I have been living in China 3 years.

3. TIME SPENT: Expressions which indicate the period of time during
which an action went on, or has been going on up to the present,
or will go on at some future time, always follow the main verb of
the sentence. Contrast this position with time when or time within
which expressions which always precede the verb:

Wǒ chyùnyan dzai jèr jù (time when).	I lived here last year.
Wǒ jèi lyǎngge ywè dzai jèr nyànshū (time within which).	The past two months I have been studying here.
Wǒ dzai jèr jùle lyǎngge ywè le (time spent).	I have been living here for two months already.

When both verb and object are expressed, two patterns are used,
with no difference in meaning:

(a) The time spent element takes *-de*, and stands in a modifying
position before the object (as in the case of modifying
expressions of value, see Lesson VIII, Note 2):

Wǒ dzai jèr nyànle lyǎngge ywède shū le.	I have been studying here for two months (lit. studying two months' worth of books).

(b) the uninflected verb and its object are first announced, then
the verb repeated (with or without *-le* as the case may be),
followed by the time spent element:

Wǒ dzai jèr nyànshū, nyànle lyǎngge ywè le.	(lit. as to my studying here, I have studied for two months already).

Note that since time spent elements constitute measured objects,
sentences with time spent expressions behave with respect to *-le* in
the same way as those described in Note 2 above.

LESSON XVI

COMPOUND VERBS - EXPRESSING MANNER

DOWNSTAIRS AND OUT!

Yǒu yityān Jāng Syansheng jǎu wǒ láile. Wǒ tsúng lóushang syàlai, gěi tā kāi mén. Wǒ shwō: "Ou, Jāng Syansheng láile! Chǐng jìn-lai ba!"

Jāng Syansheng gēn wǒ dzwòdzai kè-tīngli tánle yihwěr hwà. Hòulai wǒde háidz dzai lóushang jyàu wǒ shwō: "Bàba, wǒmen yě yau jyànjyan Jāng Syansheng." Wǒ shwō: "Hǎu, kwài syàlai ba!" Háidz jyou syàlaile.

Háidzmen syàlóu, syàlaide hěn kwài, gēn Jāng Syansheng shwōle lyǎngjyu hwà, jyou syǎng chūchyu wár. Tāmen wèn wǒ kéyi bukeyi. Wǒ shwō kéyi, tāmen jyou pǎudau wàitou chyù wár chyule. Háidz pǎulù, pǎude jēn kwài!

Hòulai wǒ tàitai yě syàlaile, yàu chǐng Jāng Syansheng gēn wǒmen yikwàr chr wǎnfàn. Jāng Syan-sheng shwō: "Hǎu, kěshr wǒ děi syān dau sywésyàu chyù kànkan. Wǒ yihwěr jyou hwéilai."

Jāng Syansheng tsúng sywésyàu hwéilaile, wǒmen jyou dzwòsya chrfàn. Chrle fàn, Jāng Syan-sheng jyou dzǒule.

One day Mr. Chang came to look for me. I came down from upstairs to open the door for him. I said: "Oh, Mr. Chang's come! Please come in!"

Mr. Chang and I sat in the parlor and chatted awhile. Later my children upstairs called me, saying: "Papa, we want to meet Mr. Chang, too." I said: "All right, hurry up and come down." Whereupon the children came down.

The children came downstairs very rapidly, said a couple of words to Mr. Chang, and then wanted to go out to play. They asked my permission, and I gave it, and they ran outside to play. Children certainly can run fast!

Afterwards my wife came down, to invite Mr. Chang to have supper with us. Mr. Chang said: "Good, but I must first return to the school to have a look. I'll be back in a few minutes."

After Mr. Chang returned from the school we sat down to eat. When we had eaten Mr. Chang left.

VOCABULARY

yihwěr (MA)N:	(in) a moment		*jyàu*	V:	call (some one)
kètīng	N:	parlor (guest hall)		CV:	tell, order; let
mén	N:	door	*jyàn*	V:	see, meet (more
chwānghu	N:	window			formal than *kàn*)
lù	N:	road	*gwān(shang)*	V:	close(up) (opp. *kāi*)
kwài	SV:	be fast, quick	*bān*	V:	move (change resi-
	A:	quickly, soon			dence)
màn	SV:	be slow	*bānjyā*	VO:	move one's residence
jàn	V:	stand	*jìnchéng*	VO:	go into the city or
dzwò	V:	sit			downtown
jìn	V:	enter (in)	*chūmén*	VO:	go out (of the house)
chū	V:	exit (out)	*ba*	P:	(sentence suffix, in-
tán	V:	converse; chat about			dicating a request)
tánhwà	VO:	carry on conversation	*-jíle*	P:	(suffix to SVs, in-
pǎu	V:	run			dicating exaggerated
děng	V:	wait, wait for			degree)
			dwèibuchǐ	IE:	excuse me! I'm sorry!

PATTERN SENTENCES

I. VERBS OF MOTION COMPOUNDED WITH *lai* AND *chyu*

shànglai	come up (here)	*shàngchyu*	go up (there)
syàlai	come down (here)	*syàchyu*	go down (there)
jìnlai	come in (here)	*jìnchyu*	go in (there)
chūlai	come out (here)	*chūchyu*	go out (there)
hwéilai	come back (here)	*hwéichyu*	go back (there)
bānlai	move (here)	*bānchyu*	move (there)

Pattern: *Wǒ yau chūchyu, yihwěr jyou hwéilai.*

I'm going out, and will be back in a moment.

1. Tā jyàu nǐ shàngchyu, nǐ wèi-   He asked you to go up, why don't
   shémma bushàngchyu?   you go up?
2. Chǐng jìnlai dzwò yihwěr!   Please come in and sit awhile!
3. Nèige wūdz wǒmen bunéng jìnchyu.   We can't go into that room.
4. Jīntyande bàu hái méichūlai ne.   Today's paper hasn't come out yet.
5. Nín fùchin hwéilaile meiyou?   Has your father returned yet?

6. Dwèibuchǐ, wǒ děi syān hwéichyu.   Pardon me, but I must be getting back.

7. Nǐmen shr něityan bānlaide?   Which day was it that you moved (here)?

8. Nǐmen shémma shŕhou bānchyu?   When do you move (there)?

II. dzai AS A SUFFIX TO VERBS OF LOCATION

<i>jàndzai...</i>	stand at...
<i>dzwòdzai...</i>	sit at...
<i>jùdzai...</i>	live or stay at...

Pattern: <i>Chǐng nǐ jùdzai wǒmen jèr.</i> Please stay here with us.

1. Chǐng nǐ jàndzai jwōdz chyántou.   Please stand in front of the table.
2. Nǐ ywànyi dzwòdzai nǎr?   Where do you wish to sit?
3. Byé dzwòdzai nèige yǐdzshang!   Don't sit in that chair!
4. Jintyan wǎnshang nǐ jùdzai nǎr?   Where are you stopping tonight?

III. dau AS A SUFFIX TO VERBS OF MOTION

<i>jìndau...(lái</i> or <i>chyù)</i>	enter into ...(here or there)
<i>hwéidau..(lái</i> or <i>chyù)</i>	return to...(here or there)
<i>bāndau...(lái</i> or <i>chyù)</i>	move to...(here or there)
<i>dzǒudau..(lái</i> or <i>chyù)</i>	walk or travel to...(here or there)
<i>pǎudau...(lái</i> or <i>chyù)</i>	run or hurry to...(here or there)
<i>nyàndau...</i>	read or study to...

Pattern: <i>Tāmen dōu bāndau Běipíng chyùle.</i>
They have all moved to Peiping.

1. Chǐng nǐ jìndau jèige wūdz lái kànkan.   Come into this room and have a look.

2. Nǐ shémma shŕhou hwéi(dau) Měigwo chyù?   When are you returning to America?

3. Wǒmen yau dzǒudau fēijī chyántou jyou hwéilai.   We are going to the front of the plane and then come back.

4. Háidz dōu pǎudau chéng wàitou chyù wár chyule.   The children have all run outside the city to play.

5. Nǐmen yǐjing nyàndau nǎr le?   Where have you read to?

IV. DESCRIBING THE MANNER OF AN ACTION

(chr̄fàn)	chr̄de tài kwài	eats too fast
(shwōhwà)	shwōde hěn màn	speaks very slowly
	shwōde yǒuyìsz	talks interestingly
(syědz̀)	syěde hǎujǐle	writes extremely well
(chànggēr)	chàngde jēn hǎu	really sings well
(dzwòshr)	dzwòde hěn hǎu	works quite well
(dzǒulù)	dzǒude bumàn	walks quite fast
(kāichē)	kāide butswò	drives quite well

Patterns:
$$\text{Vde} \qquad \text{SV}$$
Tā sywé Jūnggwo hwà, sywéde hěn kwài.

He learns Chinese very quickly (lit. as to his
learning Chinese, he learns...)

or Tāde Jūnggwo hwà, sywéde hěn kwài.

(lit. as to his Chinese, he learns...)

1. Nèige háidz chr̄fàn, chr̄de tài kwài.

That child eats too fast.

2. Tāde Yīngwén shwōde hěn hǎu.

He speaks English very well.

3. Lyóu Syansheng syědz̀, syěde dzwèi hǎu.

Mr. Liu writes the best (characters).

4. Jèige shr̀ching nǐ dzwòde butswò.

You did this quite well.

5. Lǐ Syaujye dzwò Jūnggwo fàn, dzwòde jēn hǎuchr̄!

Miss Lee certainly cooks delicious Chinese food!

6. Lǎu tàitaimen dzǒulù, dzǒude hěn màn.

Elderly ladies walk very slowly.

7. Wǒ kāichē, kāide butài hǎu. Wǒ jyějye kāide hǎujǐle!

I don't drive too well. My elder sister drives extremely well!

V. EXPRESSING MANNER IN COMMANDS AND REQUESTS

Patterns: Kwài shàngchē ba! Chē yihwěr jyou kāi!

All aboard! The train is about to leave!

Kwài yidyǎr pǎu, or Pǎu kwài yidyǎr!

Run a little faster!

1. Kwài chyù gēn Lǐ Syansheng shwōyishwo!

Hurry up and go speak to Mr. Lee about it!

2. Chǐng nǐ kwài kāikai (or gwān-shang) nèige mén (or chwānghu)! — Please open (or close) that door (or window) immediately!

3. Tā mǔchin jyàu tā kwài dzwòsya, kěshr tā dzwòsyade hěn màn. — His mother told him to sit down at once, but he sat down very slowly.

4. Pyányi yidyǎr ba! — A little cheaper, please!

5. Chǐng nín màn yidyǎr shwō! — Please say it a little slower!

6. Wǒmen děi dzǒu kwài yidyǎr. — We must walk a bit faster.

7. Nǐ dzǒude tài kwài. Nǐ néng màn yidyǎr dzǒu ma? — You walk too fast. Can you walk a little slower?

8. Wǒ syīwang nín kwài yidyǎr hwéilai. — I hope you'll come back soon.

VI. SOME OTHER COMMON COMPOUND VERBS

1. Tāmen dōu hwéijyāle. Jèr yíge rén dōu méiyǒu. — They've all gone home. There isn't a single person here.

2. Mǎ Syansheng hwéigwóle. — Mr. Ma has returned to his native country.

3. Wǒ tàitai jìnchéng mǎi dūngsyi chyule. Tā yihwěr jyou hwéilai. — My wife has gone downtown to shop. She'll be back in a few moments.

4. Wǒ syānsheng chūménle. Tā shwō tā syàywe hwéilai. — My husband has gone away on a trip. He says he's coming back next month.

5. Jāng Taitai shàngjyēle. — Mrs. Chang has gone shopping.

6. Tāmen yǐjing bānjyāle, bāndau chéng wàitou chyùle. — They have already moved. They moved outside the city.

FLUENCY DRILL

Háidz wár chyule.

Háidz chyù wár chyule.

Háidz dou chyù wár chyule.

Háidz dōu dau wàitou chyù wár chyule.

Háidz dōu dau chéng wàitou chyù wár chyule.

Háidz dōu pǎudau chéng wàitou chyù wár chyule.

Wǒmen háidz dōu pǎudau chéng wàitou chyù wár chyule.

Wǒmen syǎu háidz dōu pǎudau chéng wàitou chyù wár chyule.

Wǒmende syǎu háidz dōu pǎudau chéng wàitou chyù wár chyule.

NOTES

1. VERBS COMPOUNDED WITH *LAI* AND *CHYU*: The verbs *lái* (come) and *chyù* (go) may be affixed to certain verbs of motion to form compound verbs, *lái* indicating direction toward the speaker, and *chyù* direction away from the speaker, and toward some definite object. These compounds do NOT take objects, since 'here' or 'there' is inherent in them:

> *Wǒ bunéng syàchyu. Chǐng nǐ*   I can't come down. Please come
> *shànglai ba!*   up!

Note that *lái* and *chyù* as suffixes never receive stress in speaking.

2. *DZAI* AS A VERB SUFFIX: *Dzài* has already been presented as a main verb and as a co-verb (see Lesson X). *Dzài* is also used as a suffix to certain verbs of location, such as *jàn* (stand), *dzwò* (sit), *jù* (live), etc. Used in this way, *dzài* becomes part of the action itself. (Compare English prepositions which are related to verbs, such as stand on, sit in, live at, etc.). In all three uses, *dzài* requires a positional noun as object:

> *Chǐng nǐ jàndzai jèr.*   Please stand here.
> *Wǒ yau dzwòdzai jèige yǐdz-*   I want to sit on this chair.
> *shang.*
> *Wǒ busyǐhwan jùdzai lyúgwǎnli.*   I don't like to live in hotels.

3. *DAU* AS A VERB SUFFIX: The word *dàu* (to) was first introduced as a co-verb of motion and direction (Lesson XI). It is also used as a suffix to certain verbs of motion, such as *hwéi* (return), *bān* (move), etc. The resulting compounds require positional nouns as objects. *Lái* and *chyù* often follow these positional nouns as directional particles:

> *Wǒmen míngnyan yau bāndau Nán-*   We are moving to Nanking next
> *jīng chyù.*   year.
> *Háidz dōu p̌ǎudau chéng lǐtou*   The children have all run into
> *chyù wár chyule.*   the city to have fun.

Note that in this last sentence denoting purpose, the final *chyù* functions as a directional suffix (see Note 5, Lesson XI).

4. DESCRIBING MANNER: In describing the manner in which the action of a verb is carried out, a modifying clause (with *-de*) which contains this verb is used. This stands before the main stative verb which

denotes the intensity of degree of that manner:

Tā syĕde (style) *hĕn hău.*	She writes very well.
Tā tău̯de (speed) *bumàn.*	She runs quite fast.
Tā chàngde (manner) *hău̯jĭle!*	She sings wonderfully!

Note how this pattern resembles the basic pattern for modifying clauses (with nouns modified understood) which were first introduced in Lesson VIII:

Tā chr̄de (food) *hĕn dwō.*	She eats a lot.
Tā chàngde (song) *shr Dégwo gēr.*	She is singing a German song.

When the object is expressed, it may be transposed to the front of the sentence; or the uninflected verb and its object may first be given out, then the verb repeated with *-de* affixed, followed by the stative verb:

Tāde dè syĕde hău.	The characters she writes are
Tā syĕdè, syĕde hău.	well-written.

Note the similarity between this pattern (VOVde) and one of the time spent patterns (VOVle) introduced in the last lesson (see Note 3 b).

5. EXPRESSING MANNER IN COMMANDS: In indicating the manner in which an action is expected to be performed, the unqualified adverb of manner stands immediately before the verb:

kwài syàlai!	Hurry and come down!
Kwài lái chr̄fàn!	Come quickly and eat!

Yidyăr or just *dyăr* (a little) is often added to the adverb to express a greater or less degree. These qualified expressions of manner may stand just before or just after the verb:

Chĭng nĭ màn yidyăr shwō.	Please say it a little slower.
Chĭng nĭ shwō màn yidyăr.	(same)
Kwài dyăr dzŏu!	Go a little faster!
Dzŏu kwài dyăr!	(same)

6. SENTENCE SUFFIX *BA*, added to a command, changes its aspect to that of a mild command, request, or suggestion:

Gĕi wŏ ba!	Give it to me, or Better give it to me!
Wŏmen dzŏu ba!	Let's be going!
Wŏmen syān chr̄fàn ba!	Let's eat first!

LESSON XVII

THE *BA* CONSTRUCTION – CONTINUANCE WITH -*JE*

WEʻRE GOING TO MOVE!

A: Wǒmen yau bānjyā, nín tīngshwō-le meiyou?

We're going to move, had you heard?

B: Tīngshwōle, swóyi wǒ yau lái kàn nǐmen. Dūngsyi dōu bāndau syīn fángdz chyule ma?

Yes, I had, so that's why I wanted to come to see you. Has everything been moved to the new house?

A: Dà dūngsyi dōu bānchyule. Hái yǒu sye syǎu dūngsyi wǒmen jèngdzai bān ne.

The large things have all been moved. There is still some small stuff which we are just in the midst of moving.

B: Wǒ kéyi bāng nǐmen bǎ jǐjyan syǎu dūngsyi bānchyu, hǎu bu-hǎu?

How about letting me help you move a few of the little things?

A: Nín yǒu chìchē ma?

Do you have a car?

B: Yǒu.

Yes, I do.

A: Nín méi gūngfu ba?

You don't have time, do you?

B: Wǒ jīntyan yidyǎr shr̀ dōu mei-yǒu.

I haven't a thing to do today.

A: Wǒmen jyālide shū bushǎu. Bùjr-dàu nín néng buneng bǎ jèisye shū gěi wǒmen bānchyu.

We have quite a few books in our home. I don't know whether or not you could move these books for us?

B: Dōu fàngdzai shūfángli ma?

Are they all to be put in the study?

A: Dōu dzai shūfángli fàngje bu-syíng. Méi dìfang. Wǒmen syǎng ba chwānghu dǐsya neisye shū fàngdzai kètīngli.

It won't do to have them all in the study. No room. We think we will put the books which are under the window in the living room.

B: Hái yǒu shémma?

Anything else?

A: Hái yǒu jèi lyǎngge syǎu jwōdz.   There are still these two little
                                       tables.

B: Hǎu, wǒ syān bǎ jèijǐjyàn sùng-   Good, I'll take these few pieces
   chyu, hwéilai dzài ná byéde.   first, and when I get back I'll
                                         take some other things.

A: Láujyà, láujyà!   I'm putting you to a lot of trouble!

B: Méi shémma!   That's nothing at all!

VOCABULARY

−jyàn	M:	article, piece, item	fàng	V:	let go of; put, place
fàntīng	N:	dining room (eating hall)	bān	V:	move (heavier articles)
shūfáng	N:	study, den (book room)	dài	V:	take or bring along
dì(sya)	N:	ground, floor	sùng	V:	send, deliver (things); send, escort, see off
shǒu	N:	hand			
tóu	N:	head	sùng(gěi)	V:	present as a gift
kǒudar	N:	pocket	bāng(ju)	V:	help (some one)
jèng(dzai)	A:	just in the midst of	bāngmáng	VO:	render assistance
dzài	A:	again (in future)	nǎchilai	V:	pick up
yòu	A:	again (in past)	fàngsya(lai)	V:	put down
bǎ	CV:	(brings object to front of main verb)	−je	P:	(verb suffix, indicating continuance)
ná	V:	take hold of; take, carry (smaller articles	−r	P:	(diminutive suffix to nouns)
			láujyà!	IE:	may I trouble you? much obliged!

PATTERN SENTENCES

I. THE *ba* CONSTRUCTION

              S   CV − N   V   (O)

Pattern: *Wǒ bǎ shū fàngdzai jwōdzshang le.*

        I have put the books on the table.

1. Nǐmen míngtyan kéyi	bǎ	nǐmende shū	dōu nálai.
2. Nǐ kéyi	bǎ	nǐde háidz	jyàulai.
3. Nǐmen jīntyan	bǎ	bǐ	dàilaile meiyou?

4.	Wǒ dzwótyan méibǎ	wǒ háidz	dàichyu. Tā buywànyi chyù.
5.	Nǐmen yǐjing bǎ	dūngsyi	dōu bānchyule ma?
6.	Nǐ bǎ	wǒ syěde nèifeng syīn	sùngchyule meiyou?
7.	Kwài yidyǎr bǎ	jèige ròu	nádzǒu!
8.	Shéi bǎ	wǒde bǐ	nádzǒule?
9.	Byé bǎ	mén (or chwānghu)	kāikai!
10.	Láujyà, chǐng nǐn bǎ	mén (or chwānghu)	gwānshang dyǎr!
11.	Nǐmen búyau bǎ	màudz	dàishang.
12.	Chǐng nǐ bǎ	shàngtoude nèiběn shū	násyalai, gěi wǒ.
13.	Nǐmen kéyi bǎ	nǐmende yìsz	syěsyalai.
14.	Bǎ	nèi lyǎngge yǐdz	bānjinlai ba.
15.	Wǒ jyàu háidz bǎ	kǒudarlide dūngsyi	dōu náchulai.
16.	Nǐ kéyi dzài bǎ	nǐde yìsz	shwōchulai.
17.	Tā yòu bǎ	tāde yìsz	shwōchulaile.
18.	Láujyà, chǐng nǐn bǎ	wǒde màudz	náshangchyu.
19.	Nǐ wèishémma bùbǎ	jèige dà jwōdz	bānchuchyu?
20.	Chǐng nǐ bǎ	jèige	fàngdzai lóushang.
21.	Bǎ	nǐde shǒu	fàngdzai nǐde kǒudarli.
22.	Nǐ yīngdāng bǎ	jèisye shū	gēn nèisye fàngdzai yikwàr.
23.	Bǎ	nèijang hwàr	nádau wǒ jèr lái.
24.	Chǐng nǐ bāng wǒ bǎ	jèi jǐge yǐdz	bāndau lóushang chyu.
25.	Byé bǎ	nǐde péngyou	dàidau lóusyà chyu.
26.	Nǐ kéyi bǎ	nǐde chìchē	kāidau fángdz hòutou chyu.
27.	Kwài bǎ	jèifeng syìn	sùngdau wǒ jyāli chyu!
28.	Wǒ yǐjing bǎ	wǒ neige chìchē	màigěi nèige rén le.
29.	Wǒ buywànyi bǎ	jèijang hwàr	sūnggěi byéren.
30.	Tā cháng bǎ	nèige gùshr	shwōgěi rén tīng.
31.	Tāmen yǐjing bǎ	syǎu hár	dàihwéi jyā chyule.
32.	Wǒmen búbi bǎ	nèisye dūngsyi	dōu bānjin jèige wūdz lai.
33.	Wǒ yǐjing bǎ	wǒde chìchē	màile.
34.	Nǐmen dōu bǎ	shū	kànle ma?
35.	Chǐng nǐ bǎ	nǐde bǐ	gěi wǒ. Wǒ yau kànyikan.
36.	Tā hái méibǎ	chyán	dōu gěi wǒ ne.
37.	Nǐ búyau bǎ	jèijan shr̀	gàusung rén!
38.	Wǒ bunéng bǎ	tāde shr̀ching	dōu gàusung nǐ.
39.	Nǐ yidìng děi bǎ	jèige shr̀ching	gēn ta shwōyishwo.
40.	Tā bǎ	hwà	shwōle jyou dzǒule.

II. CONTINUANCE WITH VERB -*je*

jànje	standing	*dzǒuje*	walking
dzɐòje	sitting	*děngje*	waiting, waiting for
jùje	living, staying	*dàije*	taking or carrying along
nǎje	taking, carrying	*kāije*	being open
fàngje	lying (of things)	*gwānje*	being shut

Patterns: (1-5) *Chǐng nǐ dzai jèr děngje wǒ. Wǒ yihwěr jyou hwéilai.*
Please wait here for me. I'll be back in a moment.
(6-10) *Nǐ dàije háidz chyù ma?*
Are you taking the children along?
(lit. taking-children go).

1. Nǐ wèishémma jànje? Dzwòsya ba! › Why are you standing? Sit down!
2. Tā shwō cháng dzai yìge dìfang jùje méiyìsz. — He says that always living in one place is dull.
3. Nǐde bǐ dzai jwōdzshang fàngje. — Your pen is lying on the table.
4. Nǐ shǒuli nǎje shémma? — What are you holding in your hand?
5. Gwānje chwānghu buhǎu. Kāije yidyǎr hǎu. — It's not good to keep the window closed. It's better to keep it open a little.
6. Rénrén dōu syǐhwan dzwòje chr̄fàn. — Everybody likes to eat sitting down.
7. Tāmen dzai wàitou jànje tánle bushǎude hwà. — They stood outside chatting for quite a while.
8. Nǐmen méidàije syǎu dìdi chyù ma? Méiyou. — Didn't you take 'little brother' along? No, we didn't.
9. Wǒmen dzǒuje shwō ba. — Let's talk about this as we walk.
10. Yǒude rén kànje shū chr̄fàn. — Some people read while eating.

III. REVIEW OF CONTINUANCE WITH SENTENCE *ne*

Pattern: *Lǐ Syansheng dzai nǎr ne. Tā dzai jyā ne.*
Where is Mr. Lee? He's at home.

1. Tā dzai jyā dzwo shémma ne? Chr̄fàn ne. — What's he doing at home? Eating.
2. Lǐ Taitai dzai nǎr ne? Tā dzai chúfángli dzwòfàn ne. — Where's Mrs. Lee? She's in the kitchen cooking.

3. Nǐ syěle nèifeng syìn le mei-   Have you written that letter? I'm
   you? Wo jèng syě ne.   just writing it.
4. Byé nádzǒu, wǒ hái yàu ne.   Don't take it away, I still want
                                       some.

5. Wǒmen jèr hái yǒu ne. Nǐ hái   We still have some here. Do you
   yàu ma?   still want some?

IV. CONTINUANCE WITH BOTH VERB -*je* AND SENTENCE *ne*

Pattern: *Nǐde byǎu hái dzai jwǒdzshang fàngje ne.*
Your watch is still lying on the table.

1. Tāmen hái dzai nèr jànje shwō-   They are still standing there
   hwà ne.   talking.
2. Tā mǔchin dzai Nánjīng jùje ne.   His mother is living in Nanking.
3. Nǐ shóuli náje shémma ne?   What are you holding in your hand?
4. Nǐ tàitai dzai sywésyàu děngje   Your wife is at the school waiting
   nǐ ne.   for you.
5. Mén kāije ne, kěshr tāmen bǎ   The door is open, but they have
   chwānghu dōu gwānshangle.   closed all the windows.

CLASSROOM ACTIVITY

Bǎ bǐ náchilai.   Pick up the pen.
Bǎ bǐ fàngsya.   Put the pen down.
  Dzài náchilai.   Take it up again.
  Dzài fàngsya.   Put it down again.
Bǎ bǐ gěi wǒ.   Give the pen to me.
  Náhweichyu.   Take it back.
  Dzài gěi wǒ.   Give it to me again.
  Nádzǒu.   Take it away.
Bǎ bǐ nádau wàitou chyu.   Take the pen outside.
  Nájinlai.   Bring it in.
  Dzài náchuchyu.   Take it out again.
  Náhweilai.   Bring it back.
Bǎ bǐ fàngdzai nǐde tóushang.   Place the pen on your head.
  Násyalai.   Take it off.
Bǎ bǐ fàngdzai nǐde kǒudarli.   Put the pen in your pocket.
  Náchulai.   Take it out.

Dzài fàngjinchyu.	Put it in again.
Bǎ bǐ fàngdzai dìsya.	Put the pen on the floor.
Náchilai.	Pick it up.
Bǎ bǐ gēn shū fàngdzai yikwàr.	Put the pen and the book together.
Bǎ bǐ nádau wǒ jer lái.	Bring the pen to me here.
Fàngdzai wǒde shǒushang.	Place it on my hand.
Nádzǒu.	Take it away.

FLUENCY DRILL

Dàije háidz.

Dàije syǎuháidz.

Dàije nǐ syǎuháidz.

Dàije nǐmen syǎuháidz.

Dàije nǐmende syǎuháidz.

Dàije nǐmende syǎuháidz chyù

Dàije nǐmende syǎuháidz chyù ma?

Nǐmen dàije nǐmende syǎuháidz chyù ma?

Nǐmen mǐngnyán dàije nǐmende syǎuháidz chyù ma?

Nǐmen mǐngnyán chyù, dàije nǐmende syǎuháidz chyù ma?

Nǐmen mǐngnyán dau Jūnggwo chyù, dàije nǐmende syǎuháidz chyù ma?

NOTES

1. THE *BA* CONSTRUCTION: The co-verb *bǎ* serves to draw the object of the sentence up to just in front of the main verb, from which position it receives the action of that verb. One of the commonest uses of the *bǎ* construction is in sentences with compound verbs ending in *lái* and *chyù:*

    Chǐng nǐ bǎ nǐde shū nádau wǒ   Please bring your book here to
    jer lái.   me.
    Bǎ yǐdz bānchuchyu.   Move the chairs out.
    Wǒ yǐjing bǎ chìchē màile.   I have already sold the car.

    Note that no attempt is made to give an English equivalent for *bǎ*, or to translate literally sentences using the *bǎ* construction.

2. COMPOUND VERBS AS SUFFIXES: Verbs compounded with *lái* or *chyù* serve not only as main verbs (as shown in the last lesson), but they in turn may be suffixed to certain other verbs, such as, *ná* (take), *dài* (take along), *bān* (move), *dzǒu* (walk), *pǎu* (run), etc.:

Wǒmen shr dzǒushangchyude.	We walked up.
Bǎ jwōdz bānjinlai.	Move the table in.
Tāmen bǎ háidz dōu dàihwei-chyule.	They have taken all the children back with them.

When a specific place is indicated, these combinations split up, and an appropriate place noun inserted just before the final *-lái* or *-chyù:*

Bǎ yǐdz bānjin fàntīngli lai.	Bring the chairs into the dining room.
Tā pǎuhwei jyā chyule.	He has run back home.
Bǎ jèibǎn shū náhwei sywésyàu chyu.	Take this book back to the school.

3. CONTINUANCE WITH VERB *-JE*: The addition of the particle *-je* to a limited number of verbs prolongs the action of these verbs:

Wǒ jyòu dzai jèr jànje ba.	I'll just be standing here.
Dzǒuje hǎu.	It would be better to walk (lit. walking is better).

Verbs with *-je* also serve adverbially to describe the **manner** in which the action of the main verbs which immediately follow **is** carried out:

Wǒmen kéyi dzwòje tánhwà.	We may sit down to chat (lit. sitting chat).
Wǒmen shr dzǒuje chyùde.	We walked there (lit. walking went).

A sentence may have both verb *-je* and sentence *ne*, as for example:

Chwānghu gwānje ne.	The window is shut.
Tāmen jèngdzai chrje fàn ne.	They are just in the midst of eating.

4. DIMINUTIVE SUFFIX *-R*: The suffix *-r* is commonly added to a large number of nouns. It is not pronounced as a separate syllable, and usually modifies the primary form of the word to which it is attached. It is derived from *ér* (child, smallness), but its effect on a word is not limited to this elemental meaning. Compare the words with the suffix *-r* already learned:

> *hwàr, gēr, jèr, nèr, nǎr?, shǎur, syǎuhár,*
> *fàngwǎr, kǒudàr, yidyǎr, yihwěr, yikwàr.*

Note that many other nouns already learned may take this suffix.

LESSON XVIII

CHANGED STATUS AND IMMINENT ACTION WITH -LE

"COMING, MOTHER!"

Wǒ yǒu yige Měigwo péngyou. Tā yǒu yige syǎu nyǔhár jyàu - ài, wǒ wàngle! Nà búyaujǐn, wǒmen kéyi jyàu ta Syǎu Māur!

Syǎu Māur jīnnyan báswèile. Yǒu yityān tā dzai lóushang gēn ta dìdi wár. Ta mǔchin dzai chúfángli dzwōfàn.

Nèityan ta mǔchin hěn máng, swóyi ta syǎng jǎu Syǎu Māur bāngmáng. "Syǎu Māur, nǐ lái bāng wǒ yidyǎr máng!" "Láile! láile!" - kěshr Syǎu Māur méichyù.

Ta mǔchin yòu jyàu ta: "Syǎu Māur, kwài syàlai!" "Láile! láile!" - kěshr tā háishr méichyù.

Mǔchin disāntsz jyàu tade nyǔer: "Syǎu Māur, nǐ dzěmma bulái? Syàndzài nǐ búbi láile. Wǒ búyung nǐ bāngmáng le."

Syǎu Māur tīngjyan jèige hwà jyou syàchyule. Ta mǔchin hěn shēngchì. "Wǒ jyàu nǐ, nǐ wèishémma bulìkè lái?"

Syǎu Māur kūje dwèi ta mǔchin shwō "Mā, wǒ jēn dwèibuchǐ nín. Nín syàtsz dzài jyàu wǒ, wǒ yidìng

I have an American friend. He has a little girl named - oh, I've forgotten! Never mind, we can call her Kitty.

Kitty is eight years old this year. One day sne was upstairs playing with her little brother. Her mother was in the kitchen cooking.

Her mother was very busy that day, so she wanted to get Kitty to help. "Kitty, come and help me!" "Coming, coming!" - but she didn't go.

Her mother called her again: "Kitty, hurry and come down!" "Coming, ·coming!" - but still she didn't go.

The mother called her daughter for the third time: "Kitty, why don't you come? Now you don't need to come. I don't need your help any longer."

When Kitty heard this she went down. Her mother was very angry. "Why don't you come immediately when I call?"

Kitty, crying, said to her mother: "Mama, I am really sorry. When you call me again the next

lìkè jyou lái."	time, I'll come right away."
Ta mǔchin tīngjyan jèige hwà jyou bùshengchìle.	When her mother heard this, she was no longer angry.

VOCABULARY

tsúngchyán	MA:	formerly	hwài	SV:	be bad
měi-	NU:	each	buhwài	SV:	be not bad, pretty good
-hwéi	M:	a time; occurrence			
-tsz̀	M:	a time; occasion	shēngchì	SV:	get angry, be angry
-swèi	M:	year(s) old	yǒubìng	SV:	be sick
bìng	N:	sickness	kū	V:	cry, cry about
dyǎnsyin	N:	light refreshments	wàng	V:	forget
chúfáng	N:	kitchen	míngbai	V:	understand (clearly)
búdà	A:	not very	kànjyan	V:	see
jyòu	A:	at once	tīngjyan	V:	hear
lìkè(jyou)	A:	immediately	bìngle	V:	become sick
dzěmma	A:	why?how is it that?	hǎule	V:	be well again; it's ready, done
chīngchu	SV:	be clear (in meaning)			
gāusying	SV:	be happy, in high spirits	hwàile	V:	become spoiled, get out of order
shūfu	SV:	be comfortable	tóu-	P:	first (see Note 5)
bushūfu	SV:	be uncomfortable; indisposed, not feel well	dzěm(ma)leIE:		what's happened? what's the matter?

PATTERN SENTENCES

I. CHANGED STATUS WITH -le

SVle

Patterns: (1-4) Háidz dōu dàle (or busyǎule).

The children are all grown now (or quite big).

negVle

(5-8) Chǐng nín dzài chī yidyǎr. Buchīle, syèsye.

Have a little more. No more, thank you.

AV - V　　　　(o)　　le

(9-12) Wǒ syàndzài hwèi shwō Jūnggwo hwà le!

Now I can speak Chinese!

1. Syàndzài dūngsyi dōu gwèile.   Everything has become expensive now.

2. Wǒ dzwótyan mǎide ròu yǐjing hwàile.   The meat I bought yesterday has already gone bad.

3. Tā fùchin lǎule, bunéng dzwò shr̀le.   His father has aged, and can't work any more.

4. Tā dzwótyan hěn hǎu, kěshr jīntyan tā yòu buhǎule.   He was fine yesterday, but today he is bad again.

5. Dzwótyan tā shwō tā yǐding lái. Jīntyan tā shwō buláile.   Yesterday he said he would surely come. Today he says he's not coming after all.

6. Nín míngtyan hái chyù buchyu? Buchyùle.   Are you still going tomorrow? No, I'm not going after all.

7. Nín hái yàu shémma? Búyau shémma le.   What else do you want? Nothing now.

8. Nǐmen hái yǒu táng meiyou? Méi-yǒule.   Do you have any more sugar? No, we don't have any more.

9. Wǒ tsúngchyán hwèi shwō Fǎwén. Syàndzài búhwei shwōle.   Once I could speak French. Now I can't speak it any longer.

10. Tsúngchyán wǒ búai chr̄ Jūnggwo fàn. Syàndzài wǒ hěn ài chr̄ le.   Formerly I didn't like Chinese food. Now I have come to love it.

11. Tā chyùnyan méichyán, kěshr tā jīnnyan yǒuchyánle.   He was poor last year, but now this year he has become rich.

12. Wǒ syǎude shr̀hou syǐhwan chàng-gēr. Syàndzài wǒ búda syǐhwan le.   When I was small I liked to sing. Now I don't care much for it.

II. IMMINENT ACTION WITH -*le*

A   Vle

Patterns: (1-3) *Jāng Syansheng kwài láile.*

Mr. Chang will be coming soon.

AV   V (O) le

(4-7) *Wǒmen yau chr̄fàn le.*

We're about to eat now.

1. Chr̄fànde shr̀hou kwài dàule.   It's almost time to eat.
2. Kwài kāichēle! Chǐng shàngchē!   Train is about to leave! All aboard!
3. Wǒmen yihwěr jyou shàngkèle.   We will be going to class shortly.

4. Lǐ Syansheng jyòu yau dzǒule.   Mr. Lee will be leaving presently.
5. Dwèibuchǐ, wǒ děi hwéichyule.   I'm sorry but I must be getting
                                         back.
6. Shŕhou dàule, wǒmen děi dzǒule.   Time's up, we must be going.
7. Wǒ syǎng tā mǐngtyan jyou hǎu-   I think he will be all right by
   le.   tomorrow.

III. USE OF MEASURES -*tsz* AND -*hwei*

(a) following Time When pattern (precedes verb)

Pattern: *Wǒ shàngtsz chyù méikànjyan nǐ.*
         The last time I went I didn't see you.

1. Syàhwei wǒ yidìng gēn nǐ chyù.   I'll certainly go with you the
                                         next time.
2. Wǒ tóulyǎngtsz chyù, tāmen gēn   The first two times I went they
   wǒ hěn hǎu. Wǒ jèilyǎngtsz chyù,   were lovely to me. The last two
   tāmen gēn wǒ shēngchìle. Bùjr-   times they were angry with me.
   dàu wèishémma.   Don't know why.
3. Jèi shr wǒ dièrhwei chŕ Jūnggwo   This is the second time I have
   fàn. Tóuyihwéi shr dzài Lǐ Syan-   eaten Chinese food. The first
   sheng jyā chŕde.   time was at Mr. Lee's home.
4. Wǒ měitsz dau ta jyā chyu, tā   Each time I go to his house, he
   dōu gěi wǒ chá hē, gěi wǒ dyǎn-   gives me tea and cakes.
   syin chŕ.

(b) following Time Spent pattern (follows verb)

Pattern: *Wǒ jyòu kànjyan tā yihwéi.*
         I only saw him once.

1. Tā chyùnyan dau Fàgwo chyule   He went to France twice last year.
   lyǎngtsž.
2. Nǐ dau Nyǒuywe chyule dwōshau   How many times have you been to
   hwéi le?   New York?
3. Wǒ dau tā jyā chyule hǎujǐtsž   I have been to his home a good
   le.   many times.
4. Tā shwōle sżwǔhwéi, wǒ háishr   He said it four or five times, but

bumíngbai tāde yìsz.   I didn't get his meaning.

5. Chǐng nǐn dzài shwō yihwéi.   Please say it again.

IV. REVIEW OF VERBS REDUPLICATED

1. Wǒ mǎile yige syīn byǎu. Chǐng   I have bought a new watch. Have a
   nǐ kànyikan.   look at it.

2. Mǎ Syansheng kwài láile. Chǐng   Mr. Ma will be here soon. Please
   nǐ dzai jèr děngyiděng (or děng-   wait here.
   yihwěr.

3. Ta chǐng wǒ jìnchyu dzwòyidzwo,   He asked me in to sit awhile. I
   wǒ jyou jìnchyu dzwòle yidzwo.   went in and sat awhile, and then
   Hòulai wǒ jyou dzǒule.   left.

4. Wǒmen dzai wàitou dzǒule yidzǒu.   We took a stroll outside.

5. Wǒde bǐ meiyǒule. Chǐng nǐ bāng   My pen is gone. Please help me hunt
   wǒ jáujau.   for it.

6. Wǒ buhwèi yùng kwàidz. Wǒ děi   I don't know how to use chopsticks.
   sywéyisywé.   I must learn.

7. Tā yau chàng jǐge gēr. Wǒmen   He's going to sing a few songs.
   chyù tīngting, hǎu buhǎu?   Let's go and listen in.

8. Wǒ mǐngtyan bulái. Chǐng nǐ tì   I'm not coming tomorrow. Please
   wǒ gēn syānsheng shwōyishwo.   say a word to the teacher about
       it for me.

9. Wǒ yòu syǎngle yisyǎng, háishr   I thought it over again, and still
   méichyù.   didn't go.

FLUENCY DRILL

Shwō sāntsɀ.

Shwōle sāntsɀ.

Tā shwōle sāntsɀ.

Tā gěi wǒ shwōle sāntsɀ.

Tā bǎ shr̀ gěi wǒ shwōle sāntsɀ.

Tā bǎ shr̀ching gěi wǒ shwōle sāntsɀ.

Tā bǎ nèijyan shr̀ching gěi wǒ shwōle sāntsɀ.

Tā jyou bǎ nèijyan shr̀ching gěi wǒ shwōle sāntsɀ.

Wǒ chyù, tā jyou bǎ nèijyan shr̀ching gěi wǒ shwōle sāntsɀ.

Wǒ chyù kàn tā, tā jyou bǎ nèijyan shr̀ching gěi wǒ shwōle sāntsɀ.

Wǒ tóuyihwéi chyù kàn tā, tā jyou bǎ nèijyan shr̀ching gěi wǒ shwōle sāntsɀ.

NOTES

1. CHANGED STATUS WITH *-LE*: It has been seen that the particle *-le*, whether as verb suffix or sentence final, basically indicates completion of action, without respect to tense. However, in actual use it most often points to completion of action at some time in the past. One aspect of completed action in the past with *-le* needs to be pointed out, chiefly because certain additional English words are usually needed to convey the sense, namely, that of changed status. Three common patterns are found:

   (a) The addition of *-le* to stative verbs in their positive or negative forms (with *bu-*), leads to a changed condition or state of affairs:

Tā yǐjing hǎule.	He is already well again.
Gòu bugou? Gòule.	Is that enough? Yes, that will be enough.
Syàndzài bundnle.	It's not difficult any more.
Tā méisyīwangle.	There's no hope for him now.

   Note that the verb-object *méisyīwang* may be regarded as a stative verb (compare *yǒuchyán, méiyìsz,* etc.).

   (b) The addition of *-le* to the negative form (with *bu-*) of sentences containing other than stative verbs also implies a change in condition or intention:

Tā buyàule.	He doesn't want (it) any more.
Wǒ buchyùle.	I'm not going after all.
Wǒmen búdzai jèr jùle.	We're not living here any more.

   (c) The addition of *-le* to some statements using auxiliary verbs also denotes a change of status:

Wǒmen dōu hwèi shwō yidyǎr Jūnggwo hwà le.	Now we can all speak a little Chinese.
Wǒ busyǎng chyùle.	I don't care to go any longer.
Nǐ búbi láile.	You don't need to come after this.
Wǒ búai chr̄ táng le.	I don't like to eat candy any more.

2. IMMINENT ACTION WITH *-LE*: The addition of *-le* to verbs modified by appropriate adverbs (such as *kwài,* soon), or to verbs or sentences

using certain auxiliary verbs (such as **yau,** going to), indicates
that the action has already been decided upon, and that it is
expected to be completed at some time in the not too distant future:

Lǐ Syansheng kwài láile.	Mr. Lee will be here soon.
Háidz kwài hǎule.	The child is almost well.
Wǒmen yau chr̄fànle.	We're about to eat.
Tāmen jyòu yau dàule.	They're just about to arrive.
Wǒ děi dzǒule. Dzàijyàn ba!	I must be going. See you again!

3. THE MEASURES *-TSZ* and *-HWEI*: Specified occasions with the measures
-tsž or *-hwéi* follow the time when pattern, and precede the verb:

Wǒ diyǐtsz chyù, tā búdzaijyā.	The first time I went, he wasn't home.
Tā jèijǐhwéi lái méidàije màudz.	The last few times he came he didn't wear a hat.

Frequency of occurrences with *-tsž* or *-hwéi* follow the time spent
pattern, and come after the verb:

Wǒ chyùle hǎujǐhwéi le.	I have been there a good many times already.
Wǒ chyù kànle lyǎngtsž jyou budzài chyùle.	I went to see it a couple of times, and then didn't go any more.

When an object is expressed, the frequency expression stands
after the verb and before this object:

Wǒ chr̄le lyǎngtsz Egwo fàn le.	I have eaten Russian food twice.

EXCEPTION: When this object is a person or a place, the frequency
expression stands after the object:

Wǒ chyùnyan kànjyan tā shr̄jǐhwéi.	I saw him ten or fifteen times.
Wǒ shàng Nyǒuywe bùshǎutsž le.	I've been to New York quite a few times up till now.
Wǒ gàusung(le) tā hǎujǐhwéi le.	I've told him a good many times.

4. REDUPLICATED VERBS AND COMPLETED ACTION: It was noted in Lesson IX,
Note 5, that certain active verbs are sometimes doubled, and that
this often gives a casualness to the sense. When completed action
is indicated, the particle *-le* is attached to the first verb only:

Wǒmen dzai wàitou dzǒule yidzǒu.	We took a stroll outside.
Wǒ syǎngle yisyǎng jyou chyùle.	I thought it over and went.

5. ORDINALIZING PREFIXES *DI-* AND *TOU-* CONTRASTED: The ordinalizing
   prefix *dì-* is equivalent to the English endings -st, -nd, -rd,
   etc., and signifies any single unit of a series (as *diyī*, number
   one, *dièrge*, the second one, etc.).

   The ordinalizing prefix *tóu-*, on the other hand, denotes the
   first one or more persons or things (as *tóuyíge*, the first one,
   tóulyǎngge rén, the first two persons, *tóushŕtyān*, the first ten
   days, etc.).

6. *JYOUSHR*, ETC.: The addition of *shŕ* to certain adverbs such as *jyòu*
   (just), *hái* (still), etc., serves to make them more emphatic:

Wǒ jyòushr busyĭhwan dzwòfàn.	I just simply don't like to cook.
Tā háishr méilái.	He still hasn't come.
Háishr jèige hǎu.	After all this is better.
Nèige háidz jēnshr tsūngming.	That child is really bright.

LESSON XIX

READING THE CLOCK – SUPPOSITION

WHAT DO YOU DO ALL DAY?

A: Nǐ měityan dzǎushang shémma shŕ-hou chǐlai?

What time do you get up each morning?

B: Wǒ měityan chàbudwō lyǒudyǎn jūng chǐlai.

I get up at about six o'clock each day.

A: Nǐ jǐdyǎn jūng chŕ dzǎufàn?

What time do you eat breakfast?

B: Lyǒudyǎn-sānkè.

At quarter to seven.

A: Nǐ shémma shŕhou jìnchéng?

When do you go into the city?

B: Wǒ chǐdyǎn-yíkè shàng chǐchē-jàn. Chē chǐdyǎn-szshrwǔ kāi.

I go to the bus station at 7:15. The bus leaves at 7:45.

A: Nǐ měityan dzwòshŕ dzwò jǐge jūngtóu?

How many hours do you work each day?

B: Chǐge jūngtóu. Shàngwǔ, tsúng bādyǎnbàn dzwòdau shrèrdyǎn; syàwu, tsúng yìdyǎn-yíkè dzwòdau sżdyǎn-sānkè. Yàushr shŕ-ching máng, wǒ jyou dzwòdau wǔdyǎndwō jūng.

Seven hours. I work forenoons from 8:30 until 12:00; afternoons from 1:15 until 4:45. If work is **pressing, then I work until after five o'clock.**

A: Wǎnshang nǐ búdzwoshŕ ba?

You don't work evenings, do you?

B: Wǎnshang wǒ búdzwoshŕ. Tsúng-chyán wǒ wǎnshang chángcháng dzwò lyǎngge jūngtoude shŕ, kě-shr syàndzài wǒ lǎule, wǎnshang bunéng dzwòshŕle!

No, I don't work evenings. I used to work two hours every evening, but now I'm old and can no longer work evenings!

A: Nǐ méi shŕ de shŕhou dzwò shémma?

What do you do when you are not working?

B: Yǒude shŕhou wǒ dzai shūfángli kànkan shū, yǒude shŕhou wǒ dzai lóushang gēn háidzmen wár.

Sometimes I read in the study, sometimes I play upstairs with the children.

A: Hǎu, tyān budzǎule, wǒ děi dzǒu-le. Dzàijyàn ba!

Well, it's getting late, and I must be going. I'll be seeing you!

B: Dzàijyàn!

Goodbye!

VOCABULARY

shàngwǔ	(MA)N:	forenoon	*dzǎu*	SV:	be early
jūngwǔ	(MA)N:	noon	*wǎn*	SV:	be late
syàwǔ	(MA)N:	afternoon	*hēi*	SV:	be black; dark
báityan	(MA)N:	daytime, during the day	*bái*	SV:	be white; fair
			lyàng	SV:	be light or bright
yèli	(MA)N:	nighttime, during the night			(opp. dark)
			gāng(gāng)	A:	just this minute
yǐyè	(MA)N:	a night; the whole night	*chà*	A:	differ by; lack, be short
gāngtsái	MA:	just a moment ago	*kě*	A:	indeed, **certainly**, however
yàushr	MA:	if, in case			
-dyǎn	M:	hour	*gwò*	V:	pass, exceed; cross over
-kè	M:	quarter-hour			
-fēn	M:	minute	*chǐlai*	V:	rise, get up
-yè	M:	night	*gàusung*	V:	tell, inform
r̀dz	N:	day; a special day	*shwèijyàu*	VO:	sleep, retire
jūngtóu	N:	an hour	*chàbudwō*	IE:	almost, about
wǔfàn	N:	noon meal	*dzěmma bàn?*	IE:	what can be done about it?

POINTS IN TIME, BY THE CLOCK

Question: *Shémma shŕhou(le)?* What time is it?

  Jǐdyǎn jūng(le)? (same)

yìdyǎn jūng	1:00 o'clock
yìdyǎn shŕfēn	1:10
yìdyǎn-shŕwǔfēn	1:15
(or *yìdyǎn-yíkè*	or quarter past one)
yìdyǎn-èrshrfēn	1:20
yìdyǎn-sānshrfēn	1:30
(or *yìdyǎnbàn*	or half past one)
yìdyǎn-sèshrfēn	1:40
yìdyǎn-sèshr-wǔfēn	1:45
(or *yìdyǎn-sānkè*	or quarter to two)
yìdyǎn-wǔshrfēn	1:50
lyǎngdyǎn jūng	2:00 o'clock
lyǎngdyǎndwō jūng	after 2 o'clock

AMOUNTS OF TIME, BY THE CLOCK

Question: *Nǐ kànshū, kànle dwōshau shŕhou le?*

...kànle jǐge jūngtóu le?

How long have you been reading?

yìfen jūng	one minute	*yìdyǎndwō jūng*	**over an hour**
lyǎngfen jūng	two minutes	*yìdyǎn(lǐng)shŕfen*	1 hr. 10 mins.
sì-wǔfen jūng	4 or 5 mins.	*yìdyǎn-sānkè jūng*	1¾ hrs.
shŕjìfen jūng	'10 or 15' mins.		
shŕwǔfen jūng	15 mins.	*bànge jungtóu*	a half-hour
(or *yíkè jūng*	¼ hour)	*yíge jūngtóu*	an hour
sānshrfen jūng	30 mins.	*yígedwō jūngtóu*	over an hour
(or *bàndyǎn jūng*	½ hour)	*yígebàn jūngtóu*	1½ hrs.
sìshr-wǔfen jūng	45 mins.	*lyǎngge jūngtóu*	two hrs.
(or *sānkè jūng*	¾ hour)	*sì-wǔge jūngtóu*	4 or 5 hrs.
yìdyǎn jūng	an hour	*shŕjǐge jūngtóu*	'10 or 15' hrs.

PATTERN SENTENCES

I. TIME WHEN, BY THE CLOCK

Patterns: *Chē shémma shŕhou kāi? Chē lyǎngdyǎn jūng kāi.*

When does the train leave? It leaves at two o'clock.

Nǐ měityan jǐdyǎn jūng chr wǔfàn? Shrèrdyǎnbàn.

When do you eat lunch each day. At twelve-thirty.

1. Chē shémma shŕhou dàu? Syàwǔ sāndyǎn-wǔshrfēn dàu.

   When does the train arrive? At 3:50 P.M.

2. Wǒmen míngtyan jǐdyǎn jūng chyù? Dzǎushang jyǒudyǎn jūng, hǎu bu-hau?

   What time tomorrow shall we go? How about 9:00 o'clock in the morning?

3. Nǐ Syàlǐbaisān jǐdyǎn jūng dàu wǒ jèr lái? Wǒ shŕdyǎn-sānkè lái.

   At what hour are you coming here next Wednesday? I'm coming at a quarter to eleven.

4. Wáng Syansheng shr shémma shŕhou dzǒude? Tā shr jīntyan shàngwǔ shryīdyǎn-shŕfēn dzǒude.

   When did Mr. Wang leave? He left this forenoon at ten past eleven o'clock.

5. Lǐ Taitai shr jǐdyǎn jūng dau chéng lǐtou chyùde? Syàwǔ sān-dyǎn bàn.

   When did Mrs. Lee go downtown? At half past three.

6. Chē shr jǐdyǎn jūng dau jèr de? (or dàude jèr?) Sìdyǎn-yikè.

     When did the train arrive here? Quarter past four.

7. Nǐmen dzwótyan shr shémma shŕhou shwèijyàude? (or shwèide jyàu?) Chàbudwō yèli yìdyǎn jūng le!

     What time did you get to bed last night? It was almost one o'clock!

8. Chǐng nǐ mǐngtyan dzǎu yidyǎr lái. Wǒ chīdyǎn-sìshrfen lái, syǐng busyǐng?

     Please come a little earlier tomorrow morning. Would twenty to eight be all right?

II. TIME SPENT, BY THE CLOCK

Patterns: *Wǒmen měityan shàng sège jūngtóude kè.*
                 Wǒmen měityan shàngkè, shàng sège jūngtóu.
We attend classes four hours a day.

1. Wǒ jīntyan yǐjing nyànle báge jūngtóude shū le. Nà kě jēn bushǎu!

     I have already studied eight hours today. That's really quite a lot!

2. Tā gēn wǒ tánle yǐgedwō jūngtóude hwà jyou hwéichyule.

     He chatted with me an hour and more, and then returned.

3. Tā gēn wǒmen háidz wárle chàbudwō sānge jūngtóu le.

     He played with our children for about three hours.

4. Wǒ děng ta sānke jūng le[1]. Wǒ dzài děng bàndyǎn jūng, yàushr tā bulái, wǒ jyou děi dzǒu.

     I have been waiting for him three quarters of an hour. I'll wait another half hour, and if he doesn't come, I must leave.

5. Nǐ tyāntyan shwèijyàu, shwèi jǐge jūngtóu? Wǒ shwèi chǐge jūngtóu jyou chǐlai.

     How many hours do you sleep each night? I sleep seven hours and then I get up.

6. Aiyou, dzěmma ban a? Wǒde háidz kūle lyǎngdyǎndwō jūng le!

     My, what'll I do? My child has been crying for more than two hours!

---

[1]See Lesson XVIII, Note 3 Exception

III. USE OF *cha* (LACK) AND *gwo* (EXCEED)

1. Dàu(le) shàngkède shŕhou le ma? Is it time for class?
   Hái méidàu ne. Not yet.
   Hái dzǎu ne. It's early yet.
   Hái chà bàndyǎn jūng ne. There's half an hour yet.
   Dàule. Yes, it is.
   Yǐjing dàule. It's already time.
   Dzǎu dàule. It was time long ago.
   Gānggang dàu shŕhou. It's just time.
   Gwòle. It's past time.
   Dzǎu gwò shŕhou le. It's long past time.

2. Dàu(le) lyǎngdyǎn jūng le meiyou? Is it two o'clock yet?
   Méidàu ne. Not yet.
   Hái méidàu lyǎngdyǎn ne. It isn't two yet.
   Hái chà dwōshau? (or jǐfen?) How long before it'll be two?
     Hái chà shŕfen jūng. It lacks ten minutes.
   Yǐjing gwòle. It's already past two.
   Dzǎu gwòle. It's long past two.
   Gwò dwōshau le? How much past?
     Gwò(le) yǐke jūng le. It's quarter past two.

3. Hái chà dwōshau chyán? How much do I still owe you?
   Hái chà sānmau chyán ne. You owe me thirty cents yet.

4. Wǒ chà yidyǎr méikànjyan nǐ. I almost didn't see you.

5. Gwòle nèityau lù jyou dàu sywé- The school is just past that road.
   syàu le.

6. Dzài gwò bàndyǎn jūng wǒmen jyòu We must be going after another
   děi dzǒule. half hour.

7. Gwò yihwěr dzài tán ba! Let's chat about this after a lit-
     tle while!

8. Gwò lyǎngtyan dzài jyàn ba! I'll be seeing you in a couple of
     days!

IV. 'JUST AS SOON AS' (EMPHATIC)

Patterns: (1-4) *Tyān yilyàng(le), wŏmen jyou chĭlaile.*
             Just as soon as it was light, we got up.
        (5-6) *Wŏ yikànjyan syŏuhár jyou syĭhwan.*
             Whenever I see children I am happy.
        (7-8) *Tā yidàu(le), wŏmen jyou yau chr̄fàn.*
             We will eat just as soon as he arrives.

1. Wŏ yitīngshwō wŏ mŭchin bìngle, wŏ lìkè jyou hwéijyā le. — As soon as I heard that my mother was ill, I returned home.

2. Tā yishwō syíng, wŏ jyou bă chyán dōu gěi ta le. — As soon as he said all right, I gave him all the money.

3. Wŏ bă chyán yigěi ta, tā jyou dzŏule. — He left as soon as I gave him the money.

4. Wŏ yikànjyan nĭ jyou jr̄dau nĭ yidìng shr̄ ge tsūngming rén. — As soon as I saw you, I knew that you definitely were an intelligent man.

5. Háidz yibunyànshū, fùmŭ jyou bùgausyìng. — Whenever children don't study, parents are unhappy.

6. Rén yihējyŏu, jyou hĕn rúngyi bă shr̄ching wàngle. — Whenever people drink, they very easily forget things.

7. Wŏmen yidàule Nyŏuywe, wŏ jyou yau syān chyu kàn yige péngyou. — Just as soon as we get to New York, I want to go to see a friend.

8. Wŏ yihwèi shwō yidyăr Jūnggwo hwà, jyou yàu dau Jūnggwo chyu. — As soon as I can speak a little Chinese, I expect to go to China.

V. SUPPOSITION (WITH OR WITHOUT *yaushr*)

Pattern: (*Yàushr*) *wŏmen dzŏu yidyăr chyù, wŏmen jyou
         kéyi dzŏu yidyăr hwéilai.*
        If we go a little earlier, we can get back
        a little earlier.

1. (Yàushr) nĭmen bumíngbai wŏde yìsz, wŏ jyou kéyi dzài shwō yihwéi. — If you don't get what I mean, I can say it once again.

2. Lău Sān yàushr dzài jèr, chĭng nĭ bă jèijyan syău dūngsyi gěi ta. — If Lau San is here, please give him this little thing.

3. (Yàushr) wǒ shwōde tài kwài,   If I speak too fast, please tell
   chǐng nǐ gàusung wǒ, wǒ jyou   me and I can speak more slowly.
   kéyi shwō màn yidyǎr.

4. Nǐ yàushr méi shr̀, nǐ néng bu-   If you don't have anything to do,
   neng bāng wǒ yidyǎr máng?   could you help me a little?

5. (Yàushr) nǐ jēn kànjyan ta le,   If you have really seen him, please
   chǐng gàusung wǒ shwō tā hǎu   tell me if he is well.
   buhau.

6. Tā (yàushr) yǐjing dzǒule, wǒ-   We needn't wait any longer for him
   men jyou búbi děng ta le.   if he has already left.

7. (Yàushr) wǒ wàngle dzěmma bàn? What if I forget? (or have for-
                                   gotten?)

8. (Yàushr) nǐ dzwótyan méichyu   If you didn't go to see him yes-
   kàn ta, nǐ dzěmma jr̄dau ta   terday, how do you know he's
   bìngle?   sick?

9. Tā yàushr hái shwèijyàu ne, nǐ   If he is still sleeping, don't
   jyou byé jyàu ta.   call him.

10. (Yàushr) nǐ chyù jyou hǎule.   If you go, all is well. If you
    (Yàushr) nǐ buchyù, wǒ yě jyou don't go, then I won't be going
    buchyùle.   either.

FLUENCY DRILL

Buchyùle.

Wǒ buchyùle.

Wǒmen buchyùle.

Wǒmen syàwǔ buchyùle.

Nǐ bulái, wǒmen syàwǔ jyou buchyùle.

Yàushr nǐ bulái, wǒmen syàwǔ jyou buchyùle.

Yàushr nǐ bulái, wǒmen syàwǔ jyou bunéng chyùle.

Yàushr nǐ shàngwǔ bulái, wǒmen syàwǔ jyou bunéng chyùle.

Yàushr nǐ shàngwǔ bunéng lái, wǒmen syàwǔ jyou bunéng chyùle.

Yàushr nǐ mǐngtyan shàngwǔ bunéng lái, wǒmen syàwǔ jyou bunéng chyùle.

NOTES

1. TELLING TIME BY THE CLOCK: The three commonest units of measurement
   of time by the clock are the measures *-dyǎn* (hour), *-kè* (quarter
   hour), and *-fēn* (minute). These measures are preceded by appropri-

ate number words, and followed by the noun *jūng* (clock). See
Vocabulary for examples.

Note that for even hours the full expression with *jūng* is usually
used, whereas in fractional expressions *jūng* is usually dropped,
as for example:

yìdyǎn jūng	one o'clock
yìdyǎn-sānkè	one forty-five

2. AMOUNTS OF TIME BY THE CLOCK: See the Vocabulary for list of whole
   and fractional units used in reckoning amounts of time by the
   clock. Since *-dyǎn jūng* denotes quantity as well as a point in
   time, the noun *jūngtóu* (hour) is often used when sixty minutes of
   time is meant. The following three sentences express the same
   meaning:

   > *Wǒ shwèile bàndyǎn jūngde jyàu jyou chǐlaile.*
   > *Wǒ shwèile bànge jūngtóude jyàu jyou chǐlaile.*
   > *Wǒ shwèile bàndyǎn jūngde gūngfu jyou chǐlaile.*

   I slept for half an hour and then got up.

3. LARGER UNITS OF TIME: Larger units of time, such as weeks, days, and
   divisions of the day, always precede the time by the clock:

jīntyan syàwǔ sèdyǎn jūng	four o'clock this afternoon
Shànglǐbaityān dzǎushang bā-	eight-thirty last Sunday morn-
dyǎnbàn	ing

4. INQUIRING THE TIME OF DAY: In asking and giving the time of day,
   as in asking prices (see Lesson VI, Note 6), no verb is necessary,
   although *shr̀* or *yǒu* is sometimes used. The particle of completion
   -le is sometimes attached to both question and reply:

Shémma shŕhou (le)? Wǔdyǎnbàn	What time is it? 5:30.;
(le).	
Syàndzài jǐdyǎn jūng (le)? Sān-	What time is it now? Quarter
dyǎn-yikè (le).	past three.

5. SUPPOSITION: Supposition, as in English, is expressed by condi-
   tioning clauses, which (unlike English) always precede the main
   statements which they condition. Whereas 'if' is essential to the
   English clause, *yàushr* is not necessary to the Chinese. And vice
   versa, whereas 'then' is seldom used in English to introduce the
   subsequent statement, *jyòu* in Chinese is often used (compare
   dependent clauses in Lesson XV):

(*Yàushr*) *tā buldi, wǒmen jyou buchyùle.*	If he doesn't come, we won't go.
Nǐ (*yàushr*) *bunéng chr róu, jyou kéyi chr yú. Swéibyàn.*	You can eat fish if you can't eat meat. Do as you wish.

6. 'JUST AS SOON AS': The Chinese equivalent of the more explicit expression 'just as soon as' is formed by affixing the numeral *yī* (one, once, used adverbially) to the verb of the dependent clause. The subsequent statement is usually introduced by the adverb *jyòu* (then). (Compare dependent clauses in Lesson XV.):

Wǒ yigēn tā shwōhwà, tā jyou shēngchìle.	Just as soon as I talked with him, he got angry.
Wǒ yichr yú jyou bushūfu.	Whenever I eat fish I don't feel well.
Nǐ gēge yihwéilai, wǒ jyou yau jyàn ta.	We want to see your elder brother as soon as he returns.

LESSON XX

EXPERIENTIAL SUFFIX -GWO - RELATIVE TIME

MY INDIAN FRIEND VISITS CHINA

Wǒ yǒu yige Yìndu péngyou. Wǒ rèn-shr ta hǎujǐnyán le. Yǒu yinyán tā dǎswan dau Jūnggwo chyù. Tā syésyìn gàusung wǒ tā yǐchyán méidau Jūnggwo chyùgwo.

I have an Indian friend. I have known him for a good many years. One year he planned on going to China. He wrote me that he had never been to China before.

Wǒde péngyou dzai chwánshangde shŕhou sywéle jǐjyu Jūnggwo rén cháng yùngde hwà. Syàchwán yǐ-chyán tā yǐjing hwèi shwō: Nǐn hǎu a, Syèsye, Dzàijyàn. Syàle chwán yǐhòu tā yòu sywéle hǎusyē.

While my Indian friend was aboard the ship he learned a few common expressions in Chinese. Before he disembarked he could say: How are you, Thanks, Goodbye. After getting off he learned a lot more.

Tā syān dzai Shànghǎi jùle sye r̀dz, hòulai jyou dzwò tèbyé-kwàichē dau Nánjīng chyùle. Nánjīng shr Jūnggwode Hwáshengdwèn. Dǎjàng yǐchyán, chénglǐtoude rén hěn dwō. Dǎjàngde shŕhou rén jyou shǎule. Syàndzài bùdǎjàngle, rén dōu hwéilaile.

He first stayed several days in Shanghai, after which he went by Limited Express to Nanking. Nanking is the Washington of China. Before the war the city was well-populated. During the war the people became fewer. Now that the war is over, the people have all returned.

Wǒ péngyou hěn syǎng jyànjyan jǐ-wèi yǒumíngde Jūnggwo rén. Yīn-wei tā burènshr tāmen, buhǎu dz̀-jǐ chyu jyàn tāmen, swóyi tā jǎu-le yige péngyou gěi ta jyèshau.

My friend was anxious to meet a few of China's well-known people. Since he did not know them, and could not easily go himself to see them, he found a friend to introduce him.

Tā jyànle tāmen yǐhòu jyou hwéi Yìndu chyùle. Tā dzǒude shŕhou

After he had visited them he returned to India. As he left he

jywéde hěn gāusying. Yǒu jǐge
péngyou sùng ta shàngchwán, kāi-
chwánde shŕhou dwèi ta shwō:
Dzàijyàn! Yílù-pǐngān!

felt very happy. There were a few
friends to see him off, who as
the ship started said: Goodbye,
and a pleasant trip!

VOCABULARY

yǐchyán	MA:	previously; formerly	rènde,	V:	know, recognize, be
...yǐchyán	MA:	before..., ...ago	rènshr		acquainted with
yǐhòu	MA:	(t)hereafter	jywéde	V:	feel that, consider
...yǐhòu	MA:	after...	kàn	V:	see, think, consider
běnldi	MA:	originally	dǎswan	V:	plan to
chyántyan	(MA)N:	day before yesterday	jyèshau	V:	introduce
hòutyan	(MA)N:	day after tomorrow	syàu	V:	laugh or smile
chyán-	N:	front; former	syàu(hwa)	V:	laugh at
dzjǐ	N:	self, oneself	dǎjàng	VO:	fight, make war
syàuhwa	N:	a joke	-gwò	P:	(experiential
lǎu	A:	always, keep on			suffix to verbs)
pǐngchǎng	SV:	be ordinary, common	a	P:	(sentence suffix,
tèbyé	SV:	be special, dis-			see Note 4)
		tinctive	bùgǎndāng!	IE:	you flatter me!
yǒumíng,	SV:	be prominent,	yílù-	IE:	a pleasant journey!
		well-known	pǐngān!		

PATTERN SENTENCES

I. VERB SUFFIX -gwo

Patterns: (1-6) Nǐ chŕgwo Rběn fàn meiyou? Chŕgwo.
Have you ever eaten Japanese food? Yes, I have.
(7-8) Nǐ chŕgwo fàn le ma? Chŕgwole, syèsye.
Have you eaten? Yes, thankyou.

1. Nǐ dàugwo Jūnggwo meiyou? Méi-
dàugwo. Wǒ dǎswan jīnnyan chyù.

Have you ever been to China? No, I
haven't. I plan to go this year.

2. Tā dzai Jūnggwo jùgwo ma? Jùgwo.

Has he ever lived in China? Yes,
he has.

3. Nǐ méikàngwo jèiběn shū ma?
Kàngwo. Wǒ jywéde jèiben shū
tài méiyìsz!

Haven't you ever read this book?
Yes, I have, and I think it's
too dull for anything!

4. Tā jyāli méichyán, swóyi nèige háidz méinyàngwo shū.

That child has never been to school since his family doesn't have the money.

5. Nǐ jyàngwo Lǐ Syansheng ma? Méijyàngwo, chǐng nǐ gěi jyè-shau jyeshau.

Have you met Mr. Lee before? No, I haven't, please introduce me.

6. Měigwo gēn Jūnggwo dǎgwo jàng meiyou? Méiyou.

Have America and China ever fought? No, they haven't.

7. Nǐ yùnggwo kwàidz meiyou? Wǒ yùnggwo jǐhwéi(le), kěshr háishr búda hwèi yùng.

Have you ever used chopsticks? Yes, a few times, but I still don't know much about it.

8. Nǐ chyù kàn tāmen le meiyou? Chyùgwole, kěshr jyāli méi rén.

Have you been to see them? Yes, but there was nobody home.

.II. GENERAL RELATIVE TIME

Pattern: *Nǐ yǐchyán dzai nǎr nyànshū?*
Where have you studied previously?

1. Nèige rén yǐchyán hěn ywànyi dzwòshr̀. Tā hòulai yǒuchyán le, jyou buywànyi dzwòshr̀le.

That man previously was very willing to work. He later came into money and became unwilling.

2. Yǐchyán wǒmen jùdzai Nyǒuywē. Hòulai wǒmen bāndau jèr láile.

Before this we've been living in New York. Later we moved here.

3. Nǐ tsúngchyán cháng shwō Jūnggwo hwà. Nǐ dzěmma syàndzài bu-shwōle?

You formerly spoke Chinese a lot. Why don't you speak it now any more?

4. Tsúngchyán wǒ burènde ta. Syàn-dzài wǒmen shr hǎu péngyou.

Formerly I didn't know him. Now we are good friends.

5. Wǒ běnlai yě dǎswan chyù. Hòu-lai shr̀ching mángle, wǒ jyou bunéng chyùle.

I had originally planned on going. Later because things piled up, I gave up going.

6. Chyánjǐtyān wǒ tèbyé máng. Jèi-lyǎngtyan hǎu yidyǎr le.

I was specially busy a few days ago. It is a little better the past couple of days.

7. Gwò lyǎngtyan dzài kàn ba.

Let's consider this again after a few days.

III. SPECIFIC RELATIVE TIME

(a) ...*yǐchyán* (before; ago)

Pattern: *Wǒ chīfàn yǐchyán cháng kàn bàu.*
I often read the paper before I eat.

1. Shwèijyàu yǐchyán, wǒ yǒu shŕ-
   hou kàn yidyǎr shū.

   I sometimes read a little before I
   go to sleep.

2. Dau wàigwo chyù yǐchyán, wǒmen
   děi mǎi bushǎu dūngsyi.

   Before we go abroad, we must buy
   quite a few things.

3. Nǐ shàngchwán yǐchyán, byé wàng-
   le syěsyìn gàusung wǒ něityan
   dzǒu.

   Don't forget to write me before
   you embark what day you are leav-
   ing.

4. Tāmen bānjyā yǐchyán jùdzai
   Tyānjing.

   They lived in Tientsin before they
   moved.

5. Wǒmen sānge ywè yǐchyán, yǐ-
   jyù Jūnggwo hwà yě búhwei shwō.
   Syàndzài nǐ kàn, wǒmen dǔng
   dwōshau le!

   Three months ago we couldn't speak
   a word of Chinese. Now see how
   much we can understand!

6. Tā shr bàndyǎn jūng yǐchyán
   hwéilaide.

   He returned a half hour ago.

(b) ...-*de shŕhou* (while; when)

Pattern: *Wǒ chīfànde shŕhou cháng gēn jyāli rén tánhwà.*
I often chat with the family while eating.

1. Jūnggwo rén chīfànde shŕhou bú-
   da ài shwōhwà.

   Chinese don't much like to talk
   while eating.

2. Byéren chànggērde shŕhou, búyau
   shwōhwà.

   We shouldn't talk while others are
   singing.

3. Wǒ bādyǎn jūng shàngkède shŕhou,
   hái jywéde lèi.

   I still feel tired when I go to
   class at eight o'clock.

4. Nín chyántyan lái kàn wǒ de shŕ-
   hou, wǒ shàng Běijīng chyule.

   When you came to see me day be-
   fore yesterday, I had gone to
   Peking.

5. Wǒ shwō Jūnggwo hwà de shŕhou,
   chǐng nǐ byé syàu(hwa) wǒ.

   Please don't laugh at me when I
   speak Chinese.

(c) ...*yǐhòu* (after)

Pattern: *Wǒ chīfàn yǐhòu jyou chyù dzwòshr̀.*
After I have eaten I go to work.

1. Měityan chr̄ wǔfàn yǐhòu, wǒ děi
   shwèi yihwěr. Bushwèi busyíng!

   I have to have a little nap each
   day after lunch. It won't do if
   I don't!

2. Wǒmen bānjyā yǐhòu, chǐng nǐ
   dau wǒmen jyā lái chr̄fàn.

   After we have moved, please come
   to our home for a meal.

3. Wǒ dżjǐ míngbaile yǐhòu, jyou
   rúngyi jyāu rén le.

   After I understand it myself, then
   I can easily teach others.

4. Tā dzǒule yǐhòu, wǒmen jyou
   chr̄fànle.

   We ate after he left.

5. Dūngsyi màile yǐhòu, wǒmen jyou
   dau chējàn chyule.

   After the things had been bought,
   we went to the station.

6. Wǒ bàndyǎn jūng yǐhòu jyou hwéilai.

   I'll be back in half an hour.

7. Bànnyán yǐhòu wǒmen jyou yàu
   dau Jūnggwo chyule.

   We'll be going to China in six
   months.

8. Dżài gwò sānge ywè (yǐhòu), wǒmende Jūnggwo hwà yidìng jyou
   butswòle!

   After another three months, our
   Chinese will certainly be quite
   good!

FLUENCY DRILL

Nyànshū.

Nyàn Jūnggwo shū.

Nyàn yidyǎr Jūnggwo shū.

Děi nyàn yidyǎr Jūnggwo shū.

Wǒ děi nyàn yidyǎr Jūnggwo shū.

Wǒmen děi nyàn yidyǎr Jūnggwo shū.

Wǒmen děi syān nyàn yidyǎr Jūnggwo shū.

Wǒmen chyù yǐchyán, děi syān nyàn yidyǎr Jūnggwo shū.

Wǒmen dau Jūnggwo chyù yǐchyán, děi syān nyàn yidyǎr Jūnggwo shū.

Wǒmen míngnyan dau Jūnggwo chyù yǐchyán, děi syān nyàn yidyǎr Jūnggwo shū.

Wǒmen míngnyan méidau Jūnggwo chyù yǐchyán, děi syān nyàn yidyǎr Jūnggwo shū.

NOTES

1. EXPERIENTIAL VERB SUFFIX *-GWO*: When it is desired to indicate that an action has or has not ever been experienced, the verb suffix *-gwo* is used with both positive and negative forms of the verb:

   Nǐn dzwògwo fēijī meiyou? Méi-   Have you ever been in a plane?
   dzwògwo. Wǒ cháng syǎng dzwò.   No, I never have. I often wish
                                         I might.

   Nǐn kàngwo jèibǐn shū ma? Kàn-   Have you read this book? Yes,
   gwo, yǒuyìszjìle!   and it's most interesting!

   The verb suffix *-gwo* often indicates little more than what is indicated by *-le*. In this use it can be considered as an integral part of the verb, and the resulting compound behaves with respect to *-le* like any other verb:

   Nǐ dau ta jyā chyule ma? Chyù-   Did you go to his house? Yes, I
   gwole.   did.

   Jīntyande bàu nǐ kànle ma?   Have you read today's paper?
   Kàngwole. Méi shémma yàujǐn-   There's nothing of importance.
   de shr̀.

2. GENERAL RELATIVE TIME: Taking the immediate present, or some point of reference as a pivot, general relative time is expressed by time words such as the following:

tsúngchyán	formerly
hòulai	afterwards, later on
yǐchyán	(t)heretofore, previously
syàndzài	at present, now
yǐhòu	(t)hereafter, afterwards

   These words are movable adverbs, and the sentences follow the time when pattern:

   Yǐchyán wǒ méichr̄gwo Jūnggwo   I have never eaten Chinese food
   fàn. Yǐhòu wǒ yau cháng chr̄.   before. I expect to eat it
                                         often after this.

3. SPECIFIC RELATIVE TIME: To be specific in time relationships, the time element, or a descriptive sentence, stands just before the time words *yǐchyán* or *yǐhòu,* and a descriptive sentence before *-de shŕhou.* The resulting expressions behave like movable adverbs:

Nǐn shàngchwán yǐchyán kéyi   Before you embark let me know,
gěi wǒ yige syìn, wǒ syǎng   as I want to see you off.
sùngsung nín.

Shàngkède shŕhou byé shwō Yīng-   Don't talk English while class
wén!   is in session!

Sānnyán yǐchyán wǒ búdzai jèr.   I wasn't here three years ago.

Bànnyán yǐhou tā jyou yau láili-   He'll be coming in six months.
le.

Wǒ dàule Jūnggwo yǐhòu jyou   I'll be happy when I get to
gāusyingle.   China.

Note that the sentence: *Wǒ chŕfàn yǐchyán kàn bàu* is often said: *Wǒ méichŕfàn yǐchyán kàn bàu.* The same holds true for sentences 1-4 under Pattern III(a) above, where a descriptive sentence precedes *yǐchyán.*

4. SENTENCE SUFFIX *a*: The particle *a* adds nothing in content to the word or sentence to which it is affixed, but it changes the mood of the speaker. One of the commonest uses of *a* is in direct address as in: *Nǐ hǎu a!* (How are you!), *Lǎu Jàu a!* (Oh, Chao!)

LESSON XXI

RESULTATIVE COMPOUND VERBS

A QUEER LAD

Wǒ yǐchyán dzai Měigwo kànjyanle yige shŕjǐswèide nánháidz. Nèige háidz jēn chígwài!

Previously in America I saw a teen-age boy. That child is really very queer!

Yǒu yityān dzǎushang tā mǔchin jyàu ta chǐlai, kěshr tā bùkěn chǐlai. Tā dwèi mǔchin shwō: "Mā, wǒ hái děi shwèi yihwěr, dzwótyan wǎnshang méishwèihǎu."

One morning his mother called him to get up, but he wouldn't get up. He said to his mother: "Moth-er, I've got to sleep a little longer, I didn't get enough sleep last night."

Tā chǐlaile yǐhòu, tā fùchin jyàu ta syǐlyǎn chrfàn. Háidz jyou shwō: "Wǒ yidyǎr yě buè, shémma yě busyǎng chr."

After he got up, his father told him to wash up and eat. The child said: "I'm not a bit hungry, I don't want to eat anything."

Gwò yíge jūngtou, tā fùchin jyàu ta shàngsywé. Háidz shwō: "Bàba, yǐhòu wǒ búshangsywéle. Wǒ sywébulyǎu shémma, wǒ tài bèn!"

After an hour, his father told him to go to school. The boy said: "Daddy, I'm not going to school any more. I can't learn anything, I'm too dumb!"

Yàushr nǐ jyàu ta shàngjyē, gěi nǐ mǎi yidyǎr dūngsyi, tā lǎushr shwō nèige dūngsyi dzai jèr mǎibujáu, swóyi búyung chyùle.

If you ask him to go upstreet to buy something for you, he always says that that can't be bought here, and so there's no use to go.

Yàushr nǐ jyàu ta tǐ nǐ bàn yijyàn shŕching, dièrtyan wèn ta bànle meiyou, tā jyou shwō nèijyan shŕching hái méibanwán ne, yìtyān bànbuwán.

If you tell him to do something for you, and the next day ask him if he has done it, he will say that the job is not yet finished, and that it can't be finished in a day.

Nèige háidz chígwàide dìfang tài
dwō le, shwō yìtyān yě shwōbuwán. Kěshr nà búyaujǐn, děng ta
dàle tā jyou hǎule!

The queer points of that boy are
too numerous to mention. You
couldn't exhaust them in a day's
time! But never mind, wait till
he grows up and he'll be all
right!

VOCABULARY

shān	N:	hill, mountain	*syǐ*	V:	wash
yīshang	N:	clothes	*yùbei*	V:	prepare
lyǎn	N:	face (lit. or fig.)	*bàn*	V:	manage; carry out
fǎdz	N:	way, method	*chwān*	V:	wear; put on (clothes)
lóutī	N:	stairs	*twō*	V:	take off (clothes)
è	SV:	be hungry	*jāi*	V:	take off (hat)
kě	SV:	be thirsty	*dyōu*	V:	lose, misplace
bǎu	SV:	be satisfied (after	*pà*	V:	be afraid of; fear
		eating)			that
bèn	SV:	be stupid; clumsy	*kǔngpà*	V:	be afraid that; per-
chígwài	SV:	be strange; queer			haps, probably
dzāng	SV:	be dirty	*dyōulyǎn*	IE:	lose face (publicly)
gānjing	SV:	be clean	*méi(you)*	IE:	there's no way out!
kěn	AV:	be willing to	*fǎdz*		it can't be helped!

A FEW OF THE COMMONER ENDINGS TO RESULTATIVE COMPOUND VERBS

-*jyàn*   indicates perception of what is seen, heard, or smelled
-*dǔng*   indicates understanding of what is seen, heard, or read
-*dàu*   indicates arrival at the goal of the action
-*jáu*   indicates success in attaining object of the action
-*hǎu*   indicates satisfactory completion of the action
-*wán*   indicates end or completion of the action
-*lyǎu*   indicates capacity for doing something, or for carrying
           it through to completion
-*lái*   indicates arrival here
-*chyù*   indicates arrival there

EXAMPLES OF RESULTATIVE COMPOUNDS OF BOTH TYPES

(Actual)	*Nǐ kànjyanle ma?*	*Kànjyanle.*	*Méikanjyàn.*
	Did you see it?	Yes, I did.	No, I didn't.
(Potential)	*Nǐ kàndejyàn ma?*[1]	*Kàndejyàn.*[2]	*Kànbujyàn.*[2]
	Can you see it?	Yes, I can.	No, I can't

THE POTENTIAL TYPE

	(Positive)	(Negative)	(Other Verbs taking These Endings)
1.	tīngdejyàn	tīngbujyàn	(kàn)
2.	kàndedŭng	kànbudŭng	(tīng)
3.	sùngdedàu	sùngbudàu	(dzwò, bàn, dzǒu, chǐng, syǎng)
4.	mǎidejáu	mǎibujáu	(jǎu, jyàn, wèn, yùng, shwèi)
5.	bàndehǎu	bànbuhǎu	(dzwò, bàn, syě, sywé, yùbei)
6.	shwōdewán	shwōbuwán	(tán, syě, sywé, nyàn, jyāu, chr̄, hē, dzwò, bàn, mǎi, yùng, ná, bān, chàng)
7.	nádelyǎu[8]	nábulyǎu	(same as those under *-wán* above)
8.	hwéidelái	hwéibulái	(shàng, syà, jìn, chū, chǐ, gwò)
9.	shàngdechyù	shàngbuchyù	(syà, hwéi, jìn, chū, gwò)
10.	bāndeshanglái	bānbushanglái	(ná, dzǒu)
11.	dzǒudeshangchyù	dzǒubushangchyù	(ná, bān)
12.	nádesyalái	nábusyalái	(bān, dzǒu, twō, jāi)
13.	chr̄desyachyù	chr̄busyachyù	(hē, ná, bān, dzǒu, fàng, dzwò)
14.	bāndejinlái	bānbujinlái	(ná, dzǒu)
15.	fàngdejinchyù	fàngbujinchyù	(ná, bān, dzǒu)
16.	syǎngdechulái	syǎngbuchulái	(ná, bān, dzǒu, shwō)
17.	dzǒudechuchyù	dzǒubuchuchyù	(ná, bān)
18.	syǎngdechǐlái	syǎngbuchǐlái	(ná, bān, jàn, dzwò)
19.	mǎidechǐ[8]	mǎibuchǐ	(chr̄, hē, chwān, dài, jù, dzwò)
20.	kāidekāi	kāibukāi	
21.	gwāndeshàng	gwānbushàng	(chwān, dài)
22.	chr̄debǎu	chr̄bubǎu	
23.	syǐdegānjing	syǐbugānjing	
24.	kàndechǐ[8]	kànbuchǐ	

[1]Potential questions use both the simple type (*kàndejyàn ma?*), and the choice type (*kàndejyàn kànbujyàn?*)

²The main stress in both forms of the potential type falls on the last syllable (with the exception of *syĭdegānjing*).

³The endings *-lyău* and *-chĭ* appear only in the potential type.

PATTERN SENTENCES

I. USE OF RESULTATIVE COMPOUNDS

Pattern: *Nèige shānshang yŏu lyăngge rén, nĭ kàndejyàn ma? Wŏ kànbujyàn.*
There are two people on that hill, can you see them? No, I can't make them out.

1. Wàitou yŏu rén shwōhwà, nĭ tīng-dejyàn ma? Tīngdejyàn. — There are some people talking outside. Can you hear them? Yes, I can.

2. Jèisye jyùdz nĭ kàndedŭng ma? Yŏude kàndedŭng, yŏude kànbudŭng. — Can you understand these sentences that you are reading? Some I can, some I can't.

3. Tài wănle, jīntyan kŭngpà sùng-budàu. Mĭngtyan gěi nĭ sùngchyu, hău buhău? — It's too late, I'm afraid we can't get it there today. How about sending it there tomorrow?

4. Jūnggwo bĭ dzai Měigwo măidejáu măibujáu? Măidejáu. Wŏ dzai Nyŏuywe gāng măile jĭge. — Can you buy Chinese pens in America? Yes, you can. I just bought a few in New York.

5. Nèige shĭching bànhăule ma? Wŏ bànbuhău. Chĭng nĭ jău byéren tì nĭ bàn ba. — Has that been put through? I can't do it. Better find some one else to do it for you.

6. Wŏ yŏu hăusye hwà yau dwèi nĭ shwō, kŭngpà shwō yityān yě shwōbuwán! — I have a great deal to say to you, We could talk a whole day and not finish talking!

7. Nĭ nádelyău jèisye dūngsyi ma? Nábulyău. Nín néng buneng tì wŏ ná yidyăr? — Can you carry all these things? No, I can't. Could you take a few of them for me?

8. Wŏmen mĭngtyan hwéidelái hwéi-bulái? Mĭngtyan yidĭng néng hwéilai. — Can we get back tomorrow? We certainly can.

9. Jèige shān hěn gāu, wŏ pà nĭ — This is a high mountain, I fear

shàngbuchyù. Nǐ shàngchyule yǐhòu, wǒ pà nǐ syàbulái. — you won't make it. After you have climbed it, I fear you can't get down.

10. Nèige jwōdz lyǎngge rén bānbushanglái ba? Bāndeshanglái. — Two people can't move that table up here, can they? Yes, they can.

11. Jèige lóutī bùhaudzǒu, kǔngpà nǐ dzǒubushangchyù. — These stairs are not easy to climb. I fear you can't climb them.

12. Nèijang hwàr nábusyaláile. — You can't get that picture down.

13. Wǒ jīntyan bushūfu, dūngsyi chrbusyachyù. — I don't feel well today, so can't eat anything (lit. get anything down).

14. Mén tài syǎu, jwōdz bānbujinlái. — The door is too small so we can't move the table inside.

15. Dūngsyi tài dà, dìfang tài syǎu, fàngbujinchyù. — The thing is too large and the place too small, so we can't place it in.

16. Nǐ yǒu fádz meiyou? Wǒ syǎngbuchu fádz lai. — Have you a way? I can't think of a way.

17. Jèige mén dzǒubuchuchyù. Chǐng nǐmen dzǒu nèige mén. — You can't go out this door. Please go by that door.

18. Wǒ wàngle tā syìng shémma, wǒ dzěmma yě syǎngbuchilái! Ou, wǒ syǎngchǐláile, tā syìng Chén! — I've forgotten his name, try as I may, I can't recollect it! -- oh, I have it, his name is Chen!

19. Jèige jūng tài gwèi, wǒ mǎibuchǐ. — This clock is too expensive, I can't afford to buy it.

20. Nèige mén kāidekāi kāibukāi? Mén yǐjing kāikaile. — Can that door be opened? It has already been opened.

21. Jèige chwānghu wǒ gwānbushàng. Chǐng nǐ bāng wǒ gwānshang. — I can't close this window. Please help me close it.

22. Wàigwo fàn nín chrdebǎu ma? Chrdebǎu. — Can you feel satisfied when you eat foreign food? Yes, I can.

23. Wèishémma jèijyan yīshang wǒ lǎu syǐbugānjing? — Why is it that I can never wash this garment clean?

24. Wǒ kànbuchǐ nèige rén! Ai, byé kànbuchǐ rén! — I despise that man! Goodness, you mustn't look down on people!

FLUENCY DRILL

Syĭbugānjing.

Yīshang syĭbugānjing.

Jèijyan yīshang syĭbugānjing.

Wŏ jèijyan yīshang syĭbugānjing.

Wŏ jèijĭjyan yīshang syĭbugānjing.

Wŏmen jèijĭjyan yīshang syĭbugānjing.

Wŏmen jèijĭjyan yīshang dzāng, syĭbugānjing.

Wŏmen jèijĭjyan yīshang dzāngde lìhai, syĭbugānjing.

Wŏmen jèijĭjyan yīshang dzāngde lìhai, kŭngpa syĭbugānjing.

Wŏmen jèijĭjyan yīshang dzāngde lìhai, kŭngpa bàntyan syĭbugānjing.

Wŏmen jèijĭjyan yīshang dzāngde lìhai, kŭngpa bàntyan yě syĭbugānjing.

NOTES

1. RESULTATIVE COMPOUND VERBS: Resultative verbs are compounds of two members, in which the first or root verb indicates the kind of action involved, while the second shows the result or extent of the action expressed by the first.

   There are two types of resultative compounds: (a) ACTUAL, in which the result or goal has been actually attained, and (b) POTENTIAL, in which the result or extent of the action is conceived of as being possible or impossible of attainment. The potential type is formed by inserting between the first and second members -de- for the positive, and -bu- for the negative:

   (a) Actual Type:

Nĭ kànjyan tā le ba?	You saw him, I presume?
Kànjyan tā le.	Yes, I did.
Nĭmen chr̄wánle meiyou?	Have you finished eating?
Hái méichrwǎn ne.	Not yet.
Fàn yùbeihǎule ma?	Is the food ready?
Yùbeihǎule.	It's all ready.

   (b) Potential Type:

Tā shwōde hwà nĭ tīngdedŭng ma? Wŏ yijyù yě tīngbudŭng.	Do you understand what you hear him say? I don't understand a word of it.

Wǒmen mǐngtyan dzǒudelyǎu ma? Can we get away from here to-
  Yàushr shr̃ching bànwánle jyou   morrow? If we get through with
  dzǒudelyǎu.   everything we can.
Nǐ shàngdechyù nèige shān ma? Can you climb that mountain? No,
  Busyǐng, shàngbuchyù.   I can't do it.

Note that a resultative compound verb does not necessarily have both actual and potential 'types. Compare, for example, those with the endings *-lyǎu* and *-chǐ* which have only the potential types (*dzǒudelyǎu,* able to leave; *chr̃dechǐ,* can afford to eat).

Note also that objects follow a resultative verb, or stand in the transposed position:

Nǐ chr̃delyǎu jèisye fàn ma?   Can you eat all this rice?
Jèisye fàn nǐ chr̃delyǎu ma?   (same)

Note again that not all compound verbs are resultative. For example, *tīngshwō, jyèshàu, rènshr, yùbei, mǐngbai,* are not. The test for resultatives is whether the compound can be converted into the potential type or not.

LESSON XXII

SIMILARITY AND COMPARISON

CHINA AND AMERICA

Jūnggwo bǐ Měigwo dà, Jūnggwo rén yě bǐ Měigwo rén dwō.

China is bigger than America, and there are more Chinese than Americans, too.

Měigwode shān hěn gāu, kěshr Jūnggwode gèng gāu.

The mountains of America are high, but those of China are higher.

Jūnggwode hé méiyou Měigwode nemma cháng.

China's rivers are not as long as America's.

Jūnggwode tyānchi gēn Měigwode chàbudwō yiyàng.

The climate of China is about like that of America.

Jūnggwo yǒu bushǎu dà chéng, kěshr méiyou Měigwo nemma dwō.

There are quite a few big cities in China, but not so many as in America.

Shànghaide lóu buǎi, kěshr méiyou Nyǒuywede nemma gāu. Shr jyèshang dzwèi gāude lóu dzai Nyǒuywe.

Shanghai's buildings are quite high, but they're not as high as New York's. The world's highest building is in New York.

Jūnggwo rén gēn Měigwo rén chřde dūngsyi bùyiyàng. Chřfànde fádz yě bùyiyàng, kěshr chřfànde shrhou chàbudwō.

Chinese and Americans don't eat the same things. They don't eat the same way either, but the times they eat don't differ much.

Jūnggwo rén gēn Měigwo rén hēde dūngsyi yě bùyiyàng. Jūnggwo rén pǐngcháng hē chá. Měigwo rén dzwèi ài hē 'kāfēi'.

What Chinese and Americans drink is different, too. Chinese ordinarily drink tea. Americans love most to drink coffee.

Jūnggwo hwà fēicháng rúngyi shwō, bǐ byéde hwà dōu rúngyi shwō, kěshr Jūnggwo dž tèbyé nánsyě.

Chinese is extraordinarily easy to speak, easier than all other languages. But Chinese characters are specially difficult to write.

Jūnggwode gwógē jēn hǎutīng, gēn
Měigwode yíyang hǎutīng. Kěshr
Měigwode gwógē bǐ Jūnggwode nán-
chàng.

The national anthem of China is
really pretty, just as pretty as
America's. But the American national anthem is harder to sing.

VOCABULARY

tyānchi	N:	weather, climate	fāngbyan	SV:	be convenient
hé	N:	river	cháng	SV:	be long
shrjyè(shang)	N:	the world	dwǎn	SV:	be short(opp. cháng)
yàngdz	N:	style, appearance; sample	lěng	SV:	be cold
			rè	SV:	be hot
swǒyǒude	N:	all	pàng	SV:	be fat (of persons)
-yàng	M:	kind, sort, way	shòu	SV:	be thin (opp. pàng)
-tyáu	M:	(measure for rivers, roads, fish, etc.)	ǎi	SV:	be short (opp. gāu)
			lìhai	SV:	be fierce, strong, severe
jèm(ma), dzèm(ma)	A:	in this way, to this degree, so	yíyàng	SV:	be the same, alike, similar
nèm(ma)	A:	in that way, to that degree, so	bǐ	CV:	compared with; than
gèng	A:	still more, even	yǒu	CV:	be as much as; be as
	SV:	-er		SV:	as
yiyàng	A:	equally, similarly	dzěmmayàng	IE:	how about...?; how's everything?
fēicháng	A:	unusually			

PATTERN SENTENCES

I. DESCRIPTION (ONE LONG TABLE)

Pattern: *Jèige jwōdz hěn cháng.* This is a very long table.

Jèige jwōdz cháng buchang? Cháng.	Is this table long? Yes, it is.
Jèige jwōdz hěn cháng.	This table is quite long.
Jèige jwōdz chángde hěn.	This table is very long.
Jèige jwōdz fēicháng cháng.	This table is unusually long.
Jèige jwōdz tèbyé cháng.	This table is specially long.
Jèige jwōdz jēn cháng!	This table certainly is long!
Jèige jwōdz chángde lìhai!	This table is terribly long!
Jèige jwōdz chángjíle!	This table is extremely long!
Jèige jwōdz tài cháng!	This table is too long!

II. SIMILARITY (TWO TABLES OF EQUAL LENGTH)

Patterns: *Jèige jwōdz gēn nèige yǐyang chǎng.*
This table is the same length as that one.
Jèige jwōdz yǒu nèige nemma chǎng.
This table is as long as that one.

Jèige jwōdz gēn nèige yǐyang chǎng
ma? Yǐyang chǎng. Jèilyǎngge jwōdz dōu yǐyang chǎng.

Jèige jwōdz yǒu nèige jwōdz nemma
chǎng ma? Yǒu. Yǒu wǒ jyāli neige jwōdz nemma chǎng ma? Yǒu.

Is this table the same length as
that one? Yes, it is. These two
tables are both the same length.

Is this table as long as that one?
Yes. Is it as long as the one in
my home? Yes.

III. DISSIMILARITY AND COMPARISON

(TWO TABLES, ONE LONG AND ONE SHORT)

Patterns: *Jèige jwōdz gēn nèige bùyiyàng chǎng.*
This table is not the same length as that one.
Jèige jwōdz bǐ nèige chǎng.
This table is longer than that one.
Nèige jwōdz méi(you) jèige jwōdz (dzemma jemma,
or *nemma) chǎng.*
That table is not as long as this table.

Jèige jwōdz gēn nèige bùyiyàng
chǎng ba? Bùyiyàng chǎng. Jèilyǎngge jwōdz bùyiyàng chǎng.

Jèilyǎngge jwōdz, něige chǎng?
Jèige chǎng. Jèige jwōdz bǐ nèige chǎng.

Nèige jwōdz yǒu jèige jemma chǎng
ma? Méiyou. Nèige jwōdz méiyou
jèige jemma chǎng?

This table is not the same length
as that one, is it? No, it isn't.
These two tables are not of equal
length.

Which is the longer of these two
tables? This is the longer. It's
longer than that one.

Is that table as long as this one?
No, it isn't. That table is not
as long as this one.

IV. DEGREES OF COMPARISON WITH ADVERBS *geng* AND *dzwei*

(THREE TABLES OF DIFFERENT LENGTHS)

Patterns:　*Tóuyǐge jwōdz hěn chǎng.*
　　　　　The first table is quite long.
　　　　　Dièrge jwōdz (bǐ tóuyǐge) gèng (or hái) chǎng.
　　　　　The second table is even longer (than the first).
　　　　　Disānge jwōdz dzwèi chǎng, bǐ nèi lyǎngge dōu chǎng.
　　　　　The third table is the longest, longer than the
　　　　　　other two.

Jèi sānge jwōdz dōu yǐyang chǎng ma? Budōu yiyàng chǎng.

Are these three tables all the same length? No, they're not.

Něige dzwèi chǎng? Disānge jwōdz dzwèi chǎng.

Which is the longest? The third table is the longest.

Něige dzwèi dwǎn? Diyǐge jwōdz dzwèi dwǎn.

Which is the shortest? The first table is the shortest.

Dièrge jwōdz dzěmmayàng? Dièrge jwōdz hěn chǎng, kěshr méiyou disānge nemma chǎng. Disānge jwōdz chǎngjǐle, bǐ nèi lyǎngge dōu chǎng. Wǒ syǎng shrjyèshang swǒyǒude jwōdz dōu méiyou disānge jwōdz nemma chǎng. Nǐ shwō dzěmmayàng?

What about the second table? It is very long, but it isn't as long as the third. The third table is extremely long, longer than the other two. I think that none of the tables in the world are as long as the third table. What do you say?

FOUR MEN DESCRIBED AND COMPARED

Wǒ rèndede rén lǐtou yǒu sžge rén: yíge syìng Jāng, yíge syìng Wáng, yíge syìng Lǐ, yíge syìng Jàu.

Among the people I know there are four men: one is named Chang, one Wang, one Lee, and one Chao.

Lǎu Jāng gēn Lǎu Wáng yǐyang gāu, yǐyang pàng.

The two persons Chang and Wang are the same height and build.

Lǎu Lǐ dzwèi ǎi, bǐ tāmen dōu ǎi. Tā yě dzwèi páng, bǐ tāmen dōu pàng.

Lee is the shortest, shorter than all of them. He is the stoutest too, stouter than the others.

Lǎu Jàu dzwèi gāu, bǐ tāmen sānge rén dōu gāu. Tā yě dzwèi shòu,

Chao is the tallest, taller than the other three. He is the thin-

bǐ tāmen dōu shòu.

Lǎu Lǐ pàngjǐle! Tāmen dōu méiyou tā nemma pàng. Tā syǎude shŕhou yě hěn pàng. Wǒ syǎng tā nèmma pàng, dzǒulù yidìng hěn bufāngbyan!

Lǎu Jàu gāude lìhai! Wǒ jywéde tā tāi gāu. Tā yě tài shòu. Kěshr kàn rén buyīngdāng kàn tāmen gāu bugau, pàng bupang, yīngdāng kàn tāmen bāngju byéren bubāngju byéren, shr hǎu rén búshr hǎu rén.

nest too, thinner than the rest.

Lee is extremely fat! None of them are as fat as he. He was fat when he was small. I think walking must surely be difficult when one is so fat!

Chao is terribly tall! I think he is too tall. He is too thin, too. But in judging people one shouldn't look to see if they are tall or not, stout or not. One should consider if they are out to help people or not, if they are good people or not.

MORE SENTENCES ILLUSTRATING SIMILARITY AND COMPARISON

1. Lyóu Syansheng gēn tā tàitai yíyang gāu ma? Yíyang gāu.

Are Mr. and Mrs. Liu the same height? Yes, they are.

2. Nánháidz bùgen nyǔháidz yíyang tsūngming ba? Chàbudwō.

Boys and girls are not equally intelligent, are they? Just about.

3. Wǒde yìsz gēn nǐde yiyàng.

My idea is the same as yours.

4. Jèige gēr méi nèige hǎuchàng. Nèige gēr hǎuchàngde hěn.

This song is not as easy to sing as that one which is very easy to sing.

5. Tā méi nǐ dzwòfàn dzwòde hǎu. Nǐ dzwòde fàn jēn hǎuchŕ!

He doesn't cook as well as you do. The food you cook is delicious!

6. Dau Nyǒuywe chyu, dzwò hwǒchēde méiyou dzwò chìchēde dwō. Dzwò chìchēde jēn bushǎu!

In going to New York, not as many people go by train as by car. Really quite a few go by car!

7. Hwǒchē yǒu fēijī nemma kwài ma? Méiyou. Fēijī bǐ shémma dōu kwài.

Are trains as fast as airplanes? No, planes are faster than anything else.

8. Tā sywé Jūnggwo hwà bǐ ta tàitai sywéde kwài. Ta tàitai sywéde fēicháng màn.

He is learning Chinese faster than his wife. His wife is learning it unusually slowly.

9. Jèiyangde bǐ bǐ nèiyangde pyányi.

This kind of pen is cheaper than that kind.

10. Dau Yīnggwo chyu, dzwò fēijī   In going to England, it is more
    bǐ dzwò chwán shūfu.   comfortable to go by plane than
                                       by boat.

11. Nèiyangde byǎu hěn gwèi, kěshr   That kind of watch is quite expen-
    jèiyangde gèng (or hái) gwèi.   sive, but this kind is even more
                                       expensive.

12. Nǐmen jǐge rén, něige dzwòfàn   Which one of you cooks the best
    dzwòde dzwèi hǎu?   food?

13. Jīntyan bǐ dzwótyan rè.   Today is hotter than yesterday.

14. Chyùnyán méiyou jīnnyán lěng.   It wasn't as cold last year as it
                                       is this.

FLUENCY DRILL

Yiyàng, kěshr pyányi.

Gen nǐde yiyàng, kěshr pyányi.

Wǒde gen nǐde yiyàng, kěshr pyányi.

Wǒde byǎu gen nǐde yiyàng, kěshr pyányi.

Wǒ mǎide byǎu gen nǐde yiyàng, kěshr pyányi.

Wǒ mǎide byǎu gēn nǐ mǎide yiyàng, kěshr pyányi.

Wǒ mǎide jeige byǎu gēn nǐ mǎide yiyàng, kěshr pyányi.

Wǒ mǎide jeige byǎu gēn nǐ mǎide neige yiyàng, kěshr pyányi.

Wǒ mǎide jeige byǎu gēn nǐ mǎide neige yiyàng, kěshr bǐ nǐde pyányi.

Wǒ mǎide jeige byǎu gēn nǐ mǎide neige yiyàng, kěshr bǐ nǐ mǎide pyányi.

NOTES

1. SIMILARITY AND DISSIMILARITY: To indicate similarity and dissimilarity between two or more persons or things, the co-verb pattern
   with *gēn* (with; and), and the stative verb *yiyàng* (be similar,
   alike) in its positive or negative form, are used:

   Jèige gēn nèige yiyàng.   This is the same as that.

   Jūng gēn byǎu bùyiyàng.   Clocks and watches are different.

   In refuting a statement expressing similarity, the negative
   particle *bù-* is prefixed to the entire expression:

   Jèige bùgen nèige yiyàng.   This is not the same as that.

   To indicate in what particular respect the two are similar or
   different, an appropriate SV follows *yiyàng,* which latter then
   functions adverbially:

Jèige gēn nèige yíyang dà. This is the same size as that.

Jèige bùgen nèige yíyang cháng. This is not the same length as this.

Jūng gēn byǎu bùyiyàng gwèi. Clocks and watches are not the same price.

Another way to approach similarity and dissimilarity is with the verb *yǒu* (be as much as) and *jèmma* or *nèmma* (so):

Jèige yǒu nèige (nemma) dà. This is as big as that.

Jèige méiyou nèige (nemma) dà. This is not as big as that.

Note that the adverb *jèmma* (or *dzèmma*) and *nèmma* are often omitted.

2. COMPARISON WITH CO-VERB *BI*: To express comparison between persons or things, or groups of the same, the co-verb pattern with *bǐ* (in comparison with), and an appropriate SV, are used:

Jèige bǐ nèige dà. This is bigger than that.

Jèige bùbǐ nèige hǎutīng. This is not prettier than that.

Note that in comparisons with *bǐ*, the positive form of stative verbs is usually used. For example, one says: *Jèige chìchē bǐ nèige gwèi*, not *Jèige chìchē bǐ nèige bugwèi.*

Note also that *bǐ* is used when both of the objects to be compared are expressed. When that with which something is being compared is clear from the context, the simpler form of comparison introduced in Lesson IV is sufficient:

Jèi lyǎngge shān, něige gāu? Which of these two hills is
Jèige shān gāu (for *Jèige* higher? This one is higher
shān bǐ nèige gāu). (than that one).

3. DEGREES OF COMPARISON WITH ADVERBS *GENG* AND *DZWEI*: When it is desired to state that a person or thing is larger, for instance, than one which is already regarded as large, the adverb *gèng* (even more), or *hái* (still) is used:

Jèrde tyānchi hěn rè, kěshr The weather here is hot, but
nèrde (bǐ jèrde) gèng (or there it is even hotter (than
hái) rè. here).

The adverb *dzwèi* (the most, -est) before SVs indicates the superlative degree:

Tāmen sānwei syānsheng, něiwei- Of the three teachers, whose
de Yīngwén dzwèi hǎu? Jāng. English is the best? Mr. Chang's
Syanshengde dzwèi hǎu. is the best.

LESSON XXIII

SEPARATION AND DISTANCE – DEGREES OF COMPARISON

THREE ROUTES TO CHINA

A: Wǒ syǎng syàywè dau Jūnggwo, Jūnggwo lí Měigwo yǒu dwó ywǎn?

I'm thinking of going to China next month. How far is China from America?

B: Kàn nǐ dzǒu něityau lù.

It depends on which route you take.

A: Dzwèi jìnde lù shr něityau lù?

Which is the shortest route?

B: Dzwèi jìnde lù shr jīnggwo Běi-jí.

The nearest route is via the North Pole.

A: Nèityau lù dzěmma dzǒu?

How do you travel by that route?

B: Tsúng Nyǒuywe dzwò fēijī, yijŕ wàng běi fēi, jīnggwo Jyānadà dau Běijí. Tsúng Běijí dzài wàng nán fēi, jīnggwo Ègwode dūngbù jyou dàu Jūnggwo le.

From New York you fly by plane straight north, across Canada to the North Pole. From the North Pole you fly south, cross the eastern part of Russia and you reach China.

A: Jèityau lù yǒu dwōshau yīnglǐ?

What is the length of this route?

B: Yǒu chīchyāndwo-yīnglǐ.

More than seven thousand miles.

A: Dau Jūnggwo méiyou bǐ jèityau gèng jìnde lù ma?

Isn't there a shorter route to China than this one?

B: Méiyou. Jīnggwo Oūjōu yǒu yì-tyau lù, kěshr nèityau bǐ jèi-tyau ywǎn yidyǎr.

No. There is a way through Europe, but that route is a little long-er than this one.

A: Nèityau lù dzěmma dzǒu?

How do you go by that route?

B: Yau wàng dūng chyu, dzwò chwán dau Dégwo. Dzài dzwo hwǒchē, jīnggwo Mwòszkē, búdau lyǎngge lǐbài jyou kéyi dau Nánjīng.

You must go east by boat, crossing the Atlantic (Great West Ocean) to Germany. Then you go by train, through Moscow, and in less than two weeks you can reach Nanking.

A: Jèityau lù bǐ nèityau ywǎn dwō-shau?

How much longer is this route?

B: Ywǎn lyǎngchyāndwo-yīnglǐ.

It's 2,000 some miles longer.

A: Wǎng syī chyu dàubulyǎu Jūnggwo   Can't you reach China by going
   ma?   west?

B: Dàudelyǎu, kěshr lù gèng ywǎnle.   You can, but it is still longer. If
   Yàushr dzǒu jèityau lù, děi syān   you travel this route, you must
   dzwo hwǒchē dau Jyǒujinshān,   first go by train to San Fran-
   dzài dzwo chwán, gwò Tàiping-   cisco, then by boat across the
   yáng dau Shànghǎi. Jèityau lù   Pacific to Shanghai. This is the
   dzwèi cháng dzǒu.   most commonly travelled route.

A: Fèisyīn, fèisyīn!   I'm sorry to have troubled you!

B: Méi shémma!   It wasn't any trouble!

VOCABULARY

-byar	M: -side, border; part	
-bù	M: section, part	
-lǐ(lù)	M: a Chinese li ($\frac{1}{3}$ mile)	
-yīnglǐ(lù)	M: an English mile	
-chǐ	M: a Chinese foot (N: ruler)	
hǎi	N: sea	
dūng	N: east	
nán	N: south	
syī	N: west	
běi	N: north	
dzwǒ	N: left	
yòu	N: right	
swèishu	N: age (year count)	
pángbyār	N: the side of, flank	
lù	N: route	
dwó(ma)	A: how SV? to what degree; oh, how SV!	

tsái	A: just; merely
yijrí	A: straight on, direct
ywǎn	SV: be far
jìn	SV: be near
dī	SV: be low
lí	CV: from (be separated or distant from)
wàng	CV: towards (in direction of)
jīnggwo	V: pass through or by, via
dzǒu	V: go by way of; go (of cars, watches, etc.)
líkai	V: leave (a place)
fēi	V: fly
kàn	V: it depends on
fèisyīn	IE: I have put you to much trouble!

PATTERN SENTENCES

I. DESCRIPTION OF A PARTICULAR DISTANCE

Pattern: *Nǐ jyā lí sywésyàu ywǎn buywǎn? Buywǎn.*
         Is your home far from the school? No, it isn't.

Wǒ jyā lǐ sywésyàu hěn jìn.	My home is quite near to the school.
lǐ sywésyàu jìnde hěn.	very near to the school.
lǐ sywésyàu buywǎn.	not far from the school.
lǐ sywésyàu bùhěn ywǎn.	not so far from the school.
lǐ sywésyàu bútai ywǎn.	not too far from school.
Tā jyā lǐ sywésyàu ywǎn buywǎn? Ywǎn.	Is his home far from school? Yes.
lǐ sywésyàu hěn ywǎn.	It is quite far from school.
lǐ sywésyàu ywǎnde hěn.	very far from school.
lǐ sywésyàu fēicháng ywǎn.	unusually far from school.
lǐ sywésyàu tèbyé ywǎn.	specially far from school.
lǐ sywésyàu jēn ywǎn!	really far from school!
lǐ sywésyàu ywǎnde lìhai!	terribly far from school!
lǐ sywésyàu ywǎnjǐle!	extremely far from school!
lǐ sywésyàu tài ywǎn!	too far from school!

II. COMPARISON OF DISTANCES AND DEGREES OF COMPARISON

Patterns: *Wǒ jyā (lǐ sywésyàu) bǐ nǐ jyā lǐ sywésyàu jìn.*
My home is nearer to the school than yours.
Jìn dwōshau? Jìndwōle! Jìn hǎujǐlǐ lù.
How much nearer? Very much nearer. Quite a few 'li' nearer.

Nǐ jyā (lǐ sywésyàu) gēn wǒ jyā lǐ sywésyàu bùyiyàng ywǎn ba? Bù- yiyàng ywǎn. Shéi jyā lǐ sywé- syàu ywǎn? Nǐ jyā ywǎn.	Your home and mine are not the same distance from the school, are they? No, they're not. Whose home is farther from the school? Yours.
Nǐ jyā (lǐ sywésyàu) bǐ wǒ jyā	Your home is a little farther from
lǐ sywésyàu ywǎn yidyǎr.	the school than my home.
lǐ sywésyàu ywǎn hǎusyē.	a good deal farther.
lǐ sywésyàu ywǎnde dwō.	much farther
lǐ sywésyàu ywǎndwōle!	very much farther
lǐ sywésyàu ywǎnde dwōle.	(same)
Wǒ jyā (lǐ sywésyàu) méiyou nǐ jyā lǐ sywésyàu nemma ywǎn. Wǒ jywé- de nǐ jyā lǐ sywésyàu tài ywǎn! Nǐ jywéde dzěmmayàng?	My home is not as far from the school as your home is. I feel that your home is too far from the school. What do you think?
Chējàn lǐ sywésyàu ywǎn buywǎn? Nà	Is the station far from the school?

kě gèng ywǎnle! Bǐ wǒmen lyǎng-
jyā lǐ sywésyàu ywǎnde dwō! Swóyi wǒ bucháng dzwò hwǒchē!

That's even farther! It's farther from school than our two
homes! So I seldom go by train!

III. MEASURING DISTANCE

Pattern: *Nǐ jyā lǐ sywésyàu yǒu dwóma ywǎn. Yǒu bànlǐ lù.*
How far is your home from the school? Half a li.

Wǒ jyā lǐ sywésyàu yǒu bànlǐ lù.
Nǐ jyā lǐ sywésyàu yǒu dwó ywǎn?
Yǒu sānlǐ lù. Nà bǐ wǒ jyā lǐ
sywésyàu ywǎn èrlǐ lù, dwèi bu-
dwei?
Chējàn lǐ sywésyàu yǒu jǐlǐ lù?
Yǒu lyòuyīnglǐ méiyou? Chàbu-
dwō.

My home is half a li from school.
How far is your home from school?
Three li. That's two li farther
from the school than my home. Is
that right?
How far is the station from the
school? Is it six miles? Just
about.

IV. MEASURING DISTANCE, LENGTH, AGE, ETC.

1. Jyòujinshān lǐ Nyǒuywe yǒu dwōshau yīnglǐ? Yǒu sānchyāndwo
   yīnglǐ.
2. Shànghǎi lǐ Jyòujinshān dwóma
   ywǎn? Bǐ Jyòujinshān lǐ Nyǒuywe
   ywǎn èrchyān yīnglǐ.
3. Jèige jwōdz jǐchǐ cháng? Sān-
   chǐbàn. Bǐ nèibyar neige jwōdz
   cháng dwōshau? Cháng yichǐ.
4. Měigwo dzwèi chángde hé yǒu dwó
   cháng? Yǒu yìchyān yīnglǐ cháng
   ma? Wǒ bùjrdàu, nǐ kéyi wèn tā ba!
5. Nǐ neige chìchē yíge jūngtóu
   néng dzǒu dwōshau yīnglǐ? Néng
   dzǒu bāshr yīnglǐ.
6. Nǐ kàn nèige rén dwóma gāu a!
   Tā yǒu bāchǐ gāu ba?

How many miles is it from San Francisco to New York? It is 3,000
and more miles.
How far is it from Shanghai to San
Francisco? It is 2,000 miles farther than from Frisco to New
York.
How long is this table? Three and
a half feet. How much longer than
that one? One foot.
How long is America's longest river? Is it 1,000 miles long? I
don't know, ask him!
How many miles an hour can your
car go? It can go eighty miles
an hour.
See how tall that man is! He is
eight feet tall, isn't he?

7. Nǐ jǐswèi le? Nǐ gēge jǐswèi le? Nǐ fùchin dwó dà swèishu-le? Tā yǒu sèshrswèi meiyou?

How old are you? How old is your elder brother? How old is your father? Is he forty years old yet?

8. Nǐn yǒu dwó dà swèishu? Wǒ wǔ-shrdwō le!

How old are you? I'm more than fifty already!

9. Jèityau lù bǐ nèityau ywǎn dwōshau? Ywǎn hǎujǐshrlǐ lù. Nèityau lù jìndwōle!

How much farther is this road than that one? Many, many 'li'. That road is much nearer!

10. Nèige shān yǒu dwó gāu? Yǒu yiwànchǐ gāu ma? Dwō! Hái yǒu gèng gāude shān ma? Yǒu. Shì-jyèshang dzwèi gāude shān dzai Yìndude běibyar, yǒu sānwànchǐ gāu.

How high is that mountain? Is it 10,000 feet high? It's more. Are there even higher mountains? Yes, there are. The world's highest mountain is north of India, it's 30,000 feet high.

V. MEASURES *-byar* AND *-bu* COMPARED

1. Nyǒuywe dzai Měigwode dūngbù (or dūngbyar). Jyǒujinshān dzai syībù (or syībyar).

New York is in the eastern part of America. San Francisco is in the western part.

2. Běijīng dzai Jūnggwode běibù (or běibyar), Nánjing dzai dūng-bù (or dūngbyar), Hànkǒu dzai Jūnggwode jūngbù.

Peking is in the north of China, Nanking is in the east, and Han-kow is in the middle of China.

3. Dūngsanshěng dzai Jūnggwode dūngběibù (or dūngběibyār).

Manchuria (East Three Provinces) is in northeast China.

4. Wǒ shr tsái tsúng Jyānadà jūng-bù láide, kěshr wǒ búshr Jyā-nadà jūngbùde rén.

I just came from the central part of Canada, but I am not a Cen-tral Canadian.

5. Měigwo dūngbyar gēn syībyar dōu yǒu hǎi: dūngbyarde hǎi jyàu Dàsyiyáng, syībyarde hǎi Tàipingyáng.

There is water both east and west of America: on the east it is called the Atlantic Ocean (Great West), on the west it is the Pa-cific.

6. Wǒmen neibyar yǒu yige hěndàde lyǔgwǎn. Bùjrdàu nǐmen jeibyar yǒu dà lyǔgwǎn meiyou?

We have a big hotel over where we are. I wonder if you have big hotels over in your section?

7. Chyánbyar neige pùdz shr wǒmen   The store up in front is ours. The
   kāide. Pángbyār neige búshr.   one to the side of it isn't ours.
8. Chǐng lǐbyar dzwòdzwo!   Come in and sit down!
9. Chǐng nǐ jàndzai dzwǒbyar, nǐ   Will you please stand on the left,
   tàitai jàndzai yòubyar, nǐmen   your wife on the right, and your
   lyǎngge háidz kéyi jàndzai   two children on the two sides.
   lyǎngbyār.
10. Háidz dzwèi syǐhwan dzai hǎi-   Children love most to play on the
    byārshang wár.   seashore.

FLUENCY DRILL

Ywǎn.

Lǐ chējàn ywǎn.

Wǒ lǐ chējàn ywǎn.

Wǒ jyā lǐ chējàn ywǎn.

Wǒmen jyā lǐ chējàn ywǎn.

Wǒmen jyā lǐ chējàn, bǐ nǐmen ywǎn.

Wǒmen jyā lǐ chējàn, bǐ nǐmen jyā ywǎn.

Wǒmen jyā lǐ chējàn, bǐ nǐmen jyā lǐ chējàn ywǎn.

Wǒmen jyā lǐ chējàn, bǐ nǐmen jyā lǐ chējàn ywǎndwōle!

Nǐmen jyā lǐ chējàn, bǐ wǒmen jyā lǐ chējàn ywǎn dwōshau?

Wǒmen jyā lǐ chējàn, bǐ nǐmen jyā lǐ chējàn ywǎn sān yīnglǐ!

NOTES

1. DISTANCE WITH CO-VERB *LI*: To indicate the distance between two
points, the co-verb pattern with *lǐ* (be distant from) is used,
together with the stative verb *ywǎn* (be far) or *jin* (be near), as
the case may be:

Měigwo lǐ Jūnggwo hěn ywǎn.   America is quite far from China.

Wǒ jyā lǐ chējàn jìnde hěn.   My home is very near the station.

The extent of separation is indicated by appropriate adverbs
standing just before the stative verb, or by endings attached to
the stative verbs such as *-de hěn*, *-de lìhai*, and *-jǐle*. (See
Pattern Sentences I above for list).

3. COMPARING DISTANCES: In describing the relation between distances,
whether they are similar or dissimilar, the co-verb pattern holds,
but phrases replace the simple nouns. Compare the following pairs

of sentences:

(a) *Wǒ gēn tā yǐyang gāu. Wǒ jyā*   I am the same height as he is.
    (lǐ sywésyàu) gēn tā jyā lǐ   My home is the same distance
    sywésyàu yǐyang ywǎn.   from school as his home.

(b) *Wǒ yǒu tā nemma gāu. Wǒ jyā*   I am as tall as he. My home
    (lǐ sywésyàu) yǒu tā jyā nem-   is as far from the school
    ma ywǎn.   as his.

(c) *Nǐ bǐ wǒ gāu. Nǐ jyā (lǐ sywé-* You are taller than I am. Your
    syàu) bǐ wǒ jyā lǐ sywésyàu   home is farther from school
    ywǎn. Wǒ jyā jìn.   than my home is. My home is
                                       nearer.

(d) *Wǒ méiyou nǐ nemma gāu. Wǒ*   I'm not as tall as you. My home
    jyā (lǐ sywésyàu) méiyou nǐ   is not as far from school
    jyā lǐ sywésyàu nemma ywǎn.   as your home is. Your home
    Nǐ jyā ywǎn.   is farther.

Note the phrase in the parentheses above. This first CV-N phrase
is often omitted when distances between two points and a common
third point are compared. In the case of comparisons of distances
between two points and two different points, the full form with
both CV-N phrases is necessarily used. Compare the following
sentences:

(a) *Rběn lǐ Jūnggwo, gēn Yīnggwo*   Japan is about as far from
    lǐ Fàgwo chàbudwo yǐyang ywǎn.   China as England is from
                                       France.

(b) *Tyānjing lǐ Běipǐng, méiyou*   It isn't as far from Tientsin
    Shànghǎi lǐ Nánjīng nemma   to Peiping, as it is from
    ywǎn.   Shanghai to Nanking.

(c) *Chējàn lǐ wǒ jyā, bǐ wǒ jyā*   It is farther from the sta-
    lǐ nǐ jyā ywǎn.   tion to my home, than it is
                                      from my home to your home.

3. USE OF *YOU* IN MEASUREMENT: It was seen in the last Lesson (see Note
   1) that *(méi)yǒu* and *jèmma* or *dzèmma*, together with appropriate
   stative verbs, are used in measuring relative distances. For measuring particular distances, heights, ages, etc., *(yǒu)* and *dwó(ma)*
   (or *dwō(ma)*, how? to what degree or extent?) are used with stative
   verbs in making inquiries, and *(yǒu)* and appropriate number-measure
   phrases are used with stative verbs in making replies:

Ní yǒu dwóma gāu? Wǒ yǒu lyòu-   How tall are you? I am six feet
   chř gāu.   tall.

Syáuhár dwó dà le? Gānggāng   How old is the child? Just a
   yǐswèi le.   year old.

Tsúng jèr dau Nyǒuywe yǒu dwó   How far is it from here to New
   ywǎn? Yǒu dwōshau yīnglǐ?   York? How many miles?

Nín dwó dà swèishu le? Wǒ sz̀-   How old are you? (to adult) I
   shrdwō le!   am over forty!

Jwōdz yǒu dwóma chǎng? Yǒu jǐ-   How long is the table? How many
   chř chǎng?   feet long?

4. DEGREES OF COMPARISON: In Lesson XXII degrees of comparison between three or more persons or things with *gèng* and *dzwèi* was
presented (see Note 3). In this Lesson degrees of comparison of
particular distances, etc. are shown to be indicated by elements
such as *yidyǎr* (a little), *-de dwō* (much), etc., affixed to the
stative verb (see Pattern Sentences II for list).

5. MEASURES -BYAR and *-BU* COMPARED: The measures *-byar* and *-bù* are
alike in that they both indicate a part or a section:

   Shànghǎi dzai Jūnggwo dūngbyar   Shanghai is in the eastern part
     (or *dūngbù*).   of China.

These two measures differ in that *-bù* can only indicate part or
section, whereas *-byar* may also refer to the regions beyond the
border:

   Tàipingyáng dzai Jūnggwode dūng-   The Pacific is east of China.
     byar (NOT *dūngbù*).

Note that *-byar* with the positional words *shàng, syà, lǐ, wài, chyán,*
and *hòu* is used interchangeably with *-tou* (introduced in Lesson X).

LESSON XXIV

SELECTION AND INCLUSION – CO-VERBS OF AGENT

I DON'T REMEMBER WHO INVITED ME!

A: Lǎuèr, nǐ dzěmmale? Nǐ wèishémma dzèmma jāujǐ a ?

What's the matter, Lauer? Why are you so worried?

B: Yǒu rén chǐng wǒ chrfàn, kěshr wǒ bujìde shr shéi chǐng wǒ le.

Some one has invited me to dine, but I don't remember who it was.

A: Yěsyǔ shr Lyóujya, yàuburán jyòushr Chénjya. Nǐ dzài syáng-syang ba!

Perhaps it was the Lius; if it wasn't, then it was the Ch'ens. Think it over again!

B: Ou, wǒ syángchilaile - jyòushr Chénjya. Kěshr wǒ wàngle shr něityān le.

Oh, I recollect it now! It was the Ch'en. But I have forgotten which day it was.

A: Tāmen shr syěsyìn chǐngde nǐ, háishr gēn nǐ shwōde ne?

Did they invite you by letter, or did they speak to you about it?

B: Tāmen gěi wǒ syěle yifeng syìn, kěshr nèifeng syìn ràng wǒ syǎu dìdi gěi rēngle.

They wrote me a letter, but that letter has been thrown away by my little brother.

A: Hài, nǐ wèishémma dzèmma busyǎusyin ne? Tāmen chǐngle byéren meiyou?

My, why are you so careless? Did they invite anyone else?

B: Tāmen budàn chǐngle wǒ, yě chǐngle jǐwei Jūnggwo syānsheng. Ai, dzěmma bàn ne? Wǒ yòu bujìde rdz, yòu bujìde dìfang.

They not only invited me, they also asked a few Chinese gentlemen. Oh, what'll I do? I don't recall the day nor the place.

A: Hòutyan wǎnshang yǒu yiwei Chén Déhwèi Syansheng chǐng wǒ chrfàn. Shr bushr tā?

There is a Mr. Ch'en Te-hui who has invited me for dinner day after tomorrow. Is that the one?

B: Dwèile, jyòushr tā!

You're right, that's just who it is!

A: Nèmma, nǐ kéyi fàngsyīnle. Wǒ yǒu chìchē. Wǒmen kéyi yikwàr chyù.

So you can 'rest your heart'. I have a car, and we can go together.

B: Hǎujǐle! Wǒ bùjrdàu dzěmma syèsye nín tsái hǎu.

Wonderful! I don't know how best to thank you.

A: Byé kèchile!

Stop being so polite!

VOCABULARY

yěsyǔ	MA:	perhaps, maybe
dàgài	MA:	probably
dāngrán	MA:	of course, naturally
hwòshr	MA:	either, or; whether
budàn	MA:	not only
yàuburán	MA:	if not, then; otherwise, or else
yàubúshr	MA:	(yàushr búshr)
kèren	N:	guest
tsái	A:	then and only then, not until
húng	SV:	be red
hwáng	SV:	be yellow
lán	SV:	be blue
lyù	SV:	be green

syǎusyin	SV:	be careful
	V:	look out for
jāují	SV:	be worried, get excited
fàngsyīn	SV:	rest assured
bùfàngsyīn	SV:	be uneasy (about)
jìde	V:	remember, recollect
rēng	V:	throw (away)
jyàu or *ràng*	CV:	(indicates agent) by
lyán	CV:	even including, even
ne	P:	(suffix to questions, see Note 2)
swéibyàn	IE:	as one pleases (lit. follow convenience)

PATTERN SENTENCES

I. ALTERNATIVE ANSWERS (EITHER...OR)

Patterns: (1-5) *Jèi lyǎngge chìchē, shr jèige kwài, shr nèige kwài? Jèige kwài.*

Which is faster of these two cars, this one or that one? This one.

(6-12) *Wǒmen dzwò chē chyù, háishr dzǒuje chyù? Dzwò chē chyù ba!*

Shall we go by car or walk? Let's go by car!

1. Nǐmen lyǎngge háidz, něige dà, nǐ dà, háishr tā dà? Tā dà. Tā bǐ wǒ dà lyǎngswèi.

Which of you two children is older, you or he? He is older, two years older.

2. Něige hǎuchr̄, yú hǎuchr̄ shr ròu hǎuchr̄? Wǒ shwō ròu hǎuchr̄. Nǐ ne?

Which is better eating, fish or meat? I say meat is tastier. What about you?

3. Nín gāng mǎide shr yú háishr ròu? Wǒ lyǎngyàng dōu mǎile yidyǎr.

Did you just buy fish or meat? I bought a little of both.

4. Jèige bǐ shr shéide, shr nǐde

Whose pen is this, yours or his?

háishr tāde? Búshr wǒde. Yěsyǔ shr tāde, yěsyǔ shr tā jyějyede.

It isn't mine. Maybe it's his, or maybe it's his elder sister's.

5. Nǐ mǎide neijang hwàr jǐkwai chyán, sānkwai chyán lyǎngkwai chyán? Sānkwai chyán.

How much was the painting you bought, three dollars or two dollars? It was three dollars.

6. Nǐ yàu jèisye, háishr yàu nèisye? Wǒ dāngran yàu jèisye.

Do you want these or those? of course I want these.

7. Nǐ gēn wǒ, shr shéi chyù, shr nǐ chyù shr wǒ chyù? Hwòshr nǐ chyù, hwòshr wǒ chyù, dōu kéyi.

Who's going, you or I? Whether you go or I go, it's all right with me.

8. Tāmen chǐng nǐ chyù, shr nǐ dz̀jǐ yàu chyù? Dāngrán shr tāmen chǐng wǒ, yàuburán wǒ yidìng buchyù.

Did they invite you, or are you going of your own accord? Of course they invited me, otherwise I definitely wouldn't go.

9. Jèige táng shr shéi mǎide, shr nǐ, shr nǐ tàitai? Dàgài shr wǒ tàitai mǎide, yàuburán jyòushr tā dzwòde.

Who bought this candy, you or your wife? My wife probably bought it, otherwise she made it.

10. Jèige táng shr mǎide, háishr jyāli dzwòde? Shr jyāli dzwòde, kěshr dzwòde buhǎu.

Did you buy this candy, or is it home-made? It was made at home, but it's no good.

11. Nǐ háishr gēn wǒ chyù, háishr gēn tā chyù? Hwòshr gēn nǐ chyù, hwòshr gēn tā chyù, dōu syǐng.

Are you going with me or with him? It doesn't matter whether I go with you or with him.

12. Nǐ dàule Jūnggwo yǐhòu yàu jyāushū, shr yàu dzwò mǎimai? Yěsyǔ jyāushū, yěsyǔ dzwò mǎimai, yěsyǔ dzwò byéde shr̀. Syàndzài hái bùyidìng.

When you get to China, are you going to teach or go into business? Perhaps I'll teach, perhaps I'll carry on business, or perhaps I'll do something else. It is still uncertain.

II. INCLUSIVE AND EXCLUSIVE ANSWERS (BOTH...AND; NEITHER...NOR)

Patterns: (1-3) *Tāmen neige jūng yòu pyányi yòu hǎukàn.*

That clock of theirs is both inexpensive and pretty.

(4-6) *Nèige syǎuhár budàn hwèi kànshū, yě hwèi syědz̀.*

That child can not only read, but also write.

(7-9) *Lyán Jūnggwo dž tā dōu (or yě) hwèi syě!*
He can even write Chinese characters!

1. Jāng Syansheng yòu gāu yòu pàng. — Mr. Chang is both tall and stout.

2. Nǐ kàn Jāng Taitai, tā yě bugāu yě bupàng. — Look at Mrs. Chang, she is neither tall nor stout.

3. Wǒ dàide jeige màudz yòu gwèi yòu nánkàn. — This hat which I am wearing is both expensive and ugly.

4. Tā budàn hwèi shwō, tā yě hwèi dzwò. — He not only knows how to talk, but also knows how to act.

5. Wǒ budàn buywànye chyu, wǒ yě chyùbulyǎu. — I not only don't wish to go, I can't go.

6. Nèige rén budàn yǒu lyǎngge chì-chē, tā hái yǒu yige syǎu fēijī. — That man not only has two cars, he has a small airplane, too.

7. Tāmen dōu dǎswan lái ma? Dōu dǎswan lái. Lyán Měishēng yě lái! — Are they all planning to come? Yes, even Měishēng is coming, too!

8. Tā budàn dàugwo Běijǐ, lyán Nán-jǐ tā dōu dàugwo! — He's not only been to the North Pole. He's even been to the South Pole!

9. Nín dàije chyán meiyou? Wǒ lyán yìmáu chyán dōu méidài. — Do you have any money with you? No, I didn't even bring along a dime.

III. CO-VERBS OF AGENT (*jyau* OR *rang*)

	S	CV – N	(gěi)	V(le)	
Pattern:	Táng	jyau háidz	(gěi)	chŕle.	The candy was eaten by the children.
	Táng	jyau háidz dōu	(gěi)	chŕle.	...was all eaten by the children.
	Táng dōu jyau háidz		(gěi)	chŕle.	(same)

1. Ròu jyau byéren mǎiwánle. — The meat was all bought up by others.

2. Chá dōu rang kèren gěi hēwánle. — The tea has been all consumed by the guests.

3. Wǒ tàitai neige shǒubyǎu jyau tā gēge nádzǒule. — My wife's wrist watch was taken away by her elder brother.

4. Wǒ syǎng shwōde hwà rang tā dōu gěi shwōwánle. — He has said everything I intended to say.

5. Kwàidz byé jyau syǎu mèimei gěi rēngdzai dìsya. — Don't let little sister throw the chopsticks onto the floor.

FLUENCY DRILL

Jyāushū, dzwò mǎimai?

Yau jyāushū, yau dzwò mǎimai?

Yau jyāushū, shr yau dzwò mǎimai?

Shr yau jyāushū, shr yau dzwò mǎimai?

Shr yau jyāushū, háishr yau dzwò mǎimai?

Háishr yau jyāushū, háishr yau dzwò mǎimai?

Háishr yau jyāushū ne, háishr yau dzwò mǎimai?

Háishr yau jyāushū ne, háishr yau dzwò mǎimai ne?

Nǐ háishr yau jyāushū ne, háishr yau dzwò mǎimai ne?

Nǐ dàu Jūnggwo, háishr yau jyāushū ne, háishr yau dzwò mǎimai ne?

Nǐ dàu Jūnggwo yǐhòu, háishr yau jyāushū ne, háishr yau dzwò mǎimai ne?

Nǐ dàule Jūnggwo yǐhòu, háishr yau jyāushū ne, háishr yau dzwò mǎimai ne?

NOTES

1. CHOICE-TYPE QUESTIONS ACCENTUATED: The alternatives presented in choice-type questions, whether the questions involve a choice between positive or negative, or between various other possible alternatives, are accentuated when one of the following patterns is used:

Nǐ chyù, shr bùchyu?	Are you going or not?
Nǐ chyù, háishr bùchyu?	(same)
Nǐ shr chyù, shr bùchyu?	(same)
Nǐ shr chyù, háishr bùchyu?	(same)
Nǐ háishr chyù, háishr bùchyu?	(same)
Nǐ shwō chīdyǎn jūng chyù hǎu, háishr bādyǎn jūng chyù hǎu?	Did you say it was better to go at seven or at eight?
Nǐ shr yau hwángde, shr yau lánde?	Do you want yellow or do you want blue?
Nǐ shr gēn Lǐ Syansheng sywéde, háishr gēn ta tàitai sywéde?	Did you study with Mr. Lee or with his wife?
Nǐ háishr ài chī yú, háishr ài chī ròu?	Do you like fish or do you like meat?

Note that the first part never overbalances the second.

2. SENTENCE SUFFIX *NE* WITH QUESTIONS: The sentence suffix *ne* is often added to certain questions as follows:

(a) *Ne* may be attached to either one or both of the alternatives presented in the accentuated choice-type question pattern:

> *Nǐ gēn péngyou chyù ne, shr*   Are you going with friends
> *dějǐ yíge rén chyù?*   or alone?
>
> *Nǐ shr dau Jūnggwo chyù,*   Are you going to China or to
> *shr dau Rběn chyù?*   Japan?
>
> *Nǐ shr yau jyāushū chyu ne,*   Are you going to teach or to
> *hǎishr yau dzwò mǎimai*   carry on business?
> *chyù ne?*

(b) *Ne* is sometimes attached to sentences containing question words:

> *Wǒmen míngtyan dōu yau dau*   Tomorrow we're all going to
> *hǎibyār chyù wár chyu. Nǐ*   the beach to have fun. Why
> *wèishémma buchyù ne? Yàu-*   aren't you going? If you
> *shr nǐ buchyù, wǒmen dzěm-*   don't go, how can we go?
> *ma néng chyù ne?*

(c) *Ne* may take the place of several words in the statement immediately preceding it:

> *Wǒmen dōu shwō ròu bǐ yú*   We all say that meat is tast-
> *hǎuchr̄. Nǐ ne?*   ier than fish. And you?

3. CO-VERBS OF AGENT (*JYAU* AND *RANG*): When it is desired to point out the agent of an action, the co-verbs *jyàu* or *ràng,* with agent-nouns, are used:

> *Táng jyàu* (or *ràng*) *háidz* (*gěi*)   The candy has been eaten by the
> *chr̄le.*   children.

Note that *gěi* (give) sometimes stands immediately before the main verb, without change in meaning.

When the adverb *dōu* is required, it may stand either before the co-verb, or before the main verb, with no difference in meaning:

> *Táng dōu jyàu háidz gěi chr̄le.*   All of the candy has been eaten
>   by the children.
>
> *Táng jyàu háidz dōu gěi chr̄le.*   (same)

Note that sentences using these co-verbs of agent translate into the English passive, although there is no indication of this in the Chinese verbs.

VOCABULARY

a	P: (sentence suffix, see note 4)	20
ǎi	SV: be short (opp. *gāu*)	22
ài	V: love	7
	AV: like or love to	
bā	NU: eight	3
bǎ	CV: (brings object to front of main verb)	17
-ba	P: (sentence suffix implying probability)	13
	P: (sentence suffix indicating a request)	16
bái	SV: be white; fair	19
báityan (MA)N: daytime, during the day		19
-bǎi	NU: hundred	6
bān	V: move (change residence)	16
	V: move (heavier articles)	17
bānjyā	VO: move one's residence	16
bàn-,-bàn	NU: half	6
bàn	V: manage; carry out	21
bàntyān (MA)N: a long while		15
bāng(ju)	V: help (someone)	17
bāngmáng	VO: render assistance	17

bǎu	SV: be satisfied (after eating)	21
bàu	N: newspaper	2
běi	N: north	23
-běn	M: volume (books)	4
běnlái	MA: originally	20
bèn	SV: be stupid; clumsy	21
bǐ	N: pen, pencil; any writing instrument	2
bǐ	CV: compared with; than	22
bìng	N: sickness	18
	SV: be sick	18
bìngle	V: become sick	18
bú-, bù-	P: (negative prefix to verbs and adverbs)	1
-bù	M: section, part	23
búbì	AV: need not	15
búdà	A: not very	18
búdàn	MA: not only	24
búfangsyīn SV: be uneasy (about)		24
búhwài	SV: be not bad, pretty good	18
bútswò	SV: be not bad, quite good	14
búyaujǐn	IE: that's nothing! never mind!	13
búyùng	AV: no use to	15
bùgǎndāng! IE: you flatter me!		20

bùshūfu	SV:	be uncomfort-able; indisposed, not feel well	18
bùyidìng	A:	not necessarily; uncertain	11
-byār	M:	-side, border; part	23
byǎu	N:	watch	3
byé	AV:	don't (impera-tive, from búyàu)	15
byéde	N:	(an)other (person or thing)	12
byéren	N:	other people	12
chādz	N:	fork	14
chá	N:	tea	9
chà	V:	differ by; lack, be short	19
chàbudwō	IE:	almost, about	19
cháng	SV:	be long	22
cháng(cháng)	A:	often, usually, always	9
chàng	V:	sing	7
chē	N:	any wheeled vehicle	11
chējàn	N:	station	13
chéng	N:	city	10
chī	NU:	seven	3
chígwài	SV:	be strange; queer	21
chǐlai	V:	rise, get up	19
chichē	N:	automobile, car	11
chichejàn	N:	bus station or stop	13
chīngchu	SV:	be clear (in meaning)	18
chǐng	V:	invite, request; please	3

chǐng dzwò!	IE:	please sit down!	11
chr̄	V:	eat	7
-chř	M:	a Chinese foot	23
chū	V:	exit (out)	16
chūmén	VO:	go out (of the house)	16
chúfáng	N:	kitchen	18
chwān	V:	wear; put on (clothes)	21
chwán	N:	boat, ship	11
chwānghu	N:	window	16
chyān	NU:	thousand	6
chyán	N:	money	3
chyán-	N:	front; former	20
chyántou	N:	front	10
chyántyan (MA)	N:	day before yesterday	20
chyù	V:	go (there)	11
-chyù	PV:	indicates arrival there	21
chyùnyán (MA)	N:	last year	13
dǎjàng	VO:	fight, make war	20
dǎswan	V:	plan to	20
dà	SV:	be big, large	4
dàgài	MA:	probably	24
dàrén	N:	adult, grownup	7
dài	V:	wear, put on (hat, watch, etc.)	8
dài	V:	take or bring along	17
dāngrán	MA:	of course, naturally	24
dāudz	N:	knife	14
dàu	CV:	to (towards)	11
	V:	arrive at, reach	13
-dàu	PV:	indicates arrival at the	21

		goal of the action			ment)
-de	P:	(N and V suffix indicating modification)	8	dwō	SV: be much, many	8
				dwōshau	NU: how much? how many?	6
Dégwo	N:	Germany (Deutschland)	5	dwó(ma)	A: how? to what degree?	23
děi	AV:	have to, must	15	-dyăn	M: hour	19
děng	V:	wait, wait for	16	dyănsyin	N: light refreshments	18
dī	SV:	be low	23	dyōu	V: lose, misplace	21
dĭsya	N:	underneath	10	dyōulyăn	IE: lose face (publicly)	21
dì-	P:	(ordinalizing prefix to numbers)	13	dž	N: word (written character)	7
dìdi	N:	younger brother	8	džjĭ	N: self, oneself	20
dìfang	N:	place	10	dzài	V: be at, in, or on	10
dìjĭ	SP:	which? (of series)	13		CV: at, in, or on
dōu	A:	all, both; in all cases	2	dzài	A: again (in future)	17
dūng	N:	east	23	dzàijyàn	IE: goodbye! (lit. see you again)	6
dūngsyi	N:	thing	5	dzāng	SV: be dirty	21
dŭng	V:	understand	4	dzău	SV: be early	19
-dŭng	PV:	indicates understanding of what is seen, heard, or read	21	dzăufàn	N: breakfast (early meal)	12
				dzăushang(MA)	N: morning	12
dwăn	SV:	be short (opp. cháng)	22	dzěm(ma)	A: How? in what way?	11
dwèi	SV:	be right, correct	4		A: why? how is it that?	18
dwèi	CV:	to, towards (facing)	14	dzěmma bàn?	IE: what can be done about it?	19
dwèibuchĭ	IE:	excuse me! I'm sorry!	16	dzěma(ma)le	IE: what's happened? what's the matter?	18
dwèile!	IE:	that's right! (Indicates agree-	13	dzěmmayàng?	IE: how about...? how's everything?	22

dʐèm(ma)	A:	in this way, to this degree, so	22
dʐŏu	V:	walk; go, leave	12
	V:	go by way of; go (of watches, cars, etc.)	23
dʐwèi	A:	the most, -est	9
dʐwótyan(MA)	N:	yesterday	12
dʐwŏ	N:	left	23
dʐwò	V:	do, make; act part of	7
dʐwò	V:	ride on (sit on)	11
	CV:	go by	
	V:	sit	16
dʐwòsya	V:	sit down	11
érdz	N:	son	9
è	SV:	be hungry	21
Ègwo	N:	Russia	5
èr	NU:	two	3
èrshŕ	NU:	twenty	3
èrshŕyī	NU:	twenty-one	3
fádz	N:	way, method	21
Fàgwo	N:	France	5
fàn	N:	food (cooked rice)	7
fàngwăr	N:	restaurant food-eating-place)	10
fàntīng	N:	dining room (eating hall)	17
fāngbyan	SV:	be convenient	22
fángdz	N:	house, building	10
fàng	V:	let go of; put, place	17
fàngsya(lai)	V:	put down	17
fàngsyīn	SV:	rest assured	24
fēi	V:	fly	23

fēicháng	A:	unusually	22
fēijī	N:	airplane (flying machine)	11
fèisyīn	IE:	I have put you to much trouble!	23
-fēn	M:	cent	6
	M:	minute	19
-fēng	M:	(measure for letters)	15
fùchin	N:	father	8
fùmŭ	N:	parents	8
gānjing	SV:	be clean	21
gāng(gāng)	A:	just this minute	19
gāngtsái	MA:	just a moment ago	19
gāu	SV:	be tall, high	1
gāusyìng	SV:	be happy, in high spirits	18
	AV:	be glad to	
gàusung	V:	tell, inform	19
gēge	N:	elder brother	8
gē(r)	N:	song	7
-ge	M:	single person or thing	4
gĕi	V:	give	3
	CV:	for; to (for benefit of)	14
gēn	CV:	with; and (following)	14
gèng	A:	still more, even	22
	SV:	-er	
gòu	SV:	be sufficient, enough	6
gòule!	IE:	that'll be enough!	14
gùshr	N:	story	12
gūngfu	N:	free or leisure	14

time

gwān(shang)	V:	close (up) (opp. kāi)	16
gwèi	SV:	be expensive	2
gwèisying	IE:	what is your (sur)name?	5
gwó	N:	country, nation	5
gwò	V:	pass, exceed; cross over	19
-gwò	P:	(experiential suffix to verbs)	20
hái	A:.	still, yet, again	12
háidz	N:	child	5
hǎi	N:	sea	23
hǎu	SV:	be good, well	1
-hǎu	PV:	indicates satisfactory completion of the action	21
hǎu buhǎu	IE:	how about (it)?	6
hǎujǐ	NU:	quite a few	15
hǎukàn	SV:	be goodlooking	2
.hǎule	V:	be well again; it's ready, done	18
hǎusyē	NU:	a good many; a good deal of	15
hǎutīng	SV:	be good to listen to, pretty	9
-hàu	M:	day (of month); number (of house, room, etc.)	13
hē	V:	drink	9
hé	N:	river	22
hēi	SV:	be black; dark	19
hěn	A:	very; quite	1

hòulai	MA:	afterwards, and then	15
hòutou	N:	back	10
hòutyan (MA)	N:	day after tomorrow	20
húng	SV:	be red	24
hwà	N:	speech (spoken words); language	7
hwà	V:	draw or paint	9
hwài	SV:	be bad	18
hwàile	V:	become spoiled, get out of order	18
hwàr	N:	picture(drawing or painting)	6
hwáng	SV:	be yellow	24
-hwéi	M:	a time; occurrence	18
hwéi	V:	return (to)	15
hwéigwó	VO:	return to one's native country	15
hwéijyā	VO:	return home	15
hwéilai	V:	come back, return here	12
hwèi	AV:	can, know how to	7
hwǒchē	N:	train	11
hwǒchejàn	N:	railroad station	13
hwòshr	MA:	either, or; whether	24
jāi	V:	take off (hat)	21
jàn	V:	stand	16
jànchilai	V:	stand up	11
-jāng	M:	(measure for paper, pictures, tables, etc.)	6
jāují	SV:	be worried, get excited	24
-jáu	PV:	indicates	21

	success in	
	attaining object	*Jūnggwo* N: China 2
	of the action	*jūngtóu* N: an hour 19
jǎu	V: look or hunt for 15	*jūngwǔ* (MA)N: noon 19
-je	P: (verb suffix, 17	*jwōdz* N: table 4
	indicating	*jyā* N: home; family 10
	continuance)	*jyàn* V: see, meet (more 16
jèi-	SP: this (here) 4		formal than *kàn*)
jèm(ma)	A: in this way, to 22	*-jyàn* M: article, piece, 17
	this degree, so		item
jēn	A: truly, really 7	*-jyàn* PV: indicates per- 21
jèng(dzai)	A: just in the 17		ception of what
	midst of		is seen, heard,
jèr	N: here 10		or smelled
-jíle	P: (suffix to SVs, 16	*jyāu* V: teach 9
	indicating ex-	*jyāushū* VO: teach 9
	aggerated degree)	*jyàu* EV: is called, named 5
jǐ-	NU: how many? (answer 4		V: call (some one) 16
	usually implies		CV: tell, order; let 16
	only a few)		CV: (indicates 24
jìde	V: remember, 24		agent) by
	recollect	*jyē* N: street 11
jīnnyán (MA)N: this year 13	*jyějye* N: elder sister 8
jīntyan (MA)N: today 12	*jyèshau* V: introduce 20
jìn	V: enter (in) 16	*jyǒu* NU: nine 3
jìn	SV: be near 23	*jyǒu* N: wine or liquor 9
jìnchéng	VO: go into the city 16	*jyòu* SV: be old (not new) 8
	or downtown	*jyòu* A: only, just 6
jīnggwo	V: pass through or 23		A: at once 18
	by, via		A: then (indroduces 15
jīdau	V: know, know of or 5		subsequent
	about		action)
jǐ	N: paper 6	*-jyù* M: (measure for 14
jù	V: live or stay in 15		*hwà*)
	or at	*jyùdz* N: sentence 14
jūng	N: clock 3	*jywéde* V: feel that, 20
jūngfàn	N: lunch (middle 12		consider
		meal)

kāi	V:	open; start away (train, bus, ship); operate (car)	15			arrival here
				lán	SV:	be blue	24
				láujyà	IE:	may I trouble you? much obliged!	17
kàn	V:	look; look at; read	2			
	V:	see, visit	11	*lău*	SV:	be old (in years)	8
	V:	see, think, consider	20		A:	always, keep on	20
	V:	it depends upon	23	*-le*	P:	(verb and sentence suffix, indicating completion of action)	12
kànjyan	V:	see	18			
kéyi	AV:	may, can, be permitted to	7			
kě	SV:	be thirsty	21	*lèi*	SV:	be tired	1
kě	A:	indeed, certainly, however	19	*lěng*	SV:	be cold	22
				lí	CV:	from (be separated or distant from)	23
kěshr	MA:	but, however	4			
-kè	M:	lesson	15	*ʿkái*	V:	leave (a place)	23
-kè	M:	quarter-hour	19	*lǐ(lù)*	M:	a Chinese li (1/3 mile)	23
kèchi	SV:	be polite, stand on ceremony	7			
				lǐbài	N:	week	13
kèren	N:	guest	24	*lǐtou*	N:	inside	10
kètīng	N:	parlor (guest hall)	16	*lìhai*	SV:	be fierce, strong, severe	22
kěn	AV:	be willing to	21	*lìkè (jyou)*	A:	immediately	18
kǒudar	N:	pocket	17	*líng*	NU:	zero	6
kū	V:	cry, cry about	18	*lóu*	N:	storied building	10
kǔngpà	V:	be afraid that; perhaps, probably	21	*lóushang*	N:	upstairs	10
				lóutī	N:	stairs	21
				lù	N:	road, route	16
kwài	SV:	be fast, quick	16	*lyán*	CV:	even including, even	24
	A:	quickly, soon				
-kwài	M:	dollar	6	*lyǎn*	N:	face (lit. or fig.)	21
	M:	piece(lit. lump)	15			
kwàidz	N:	chopsticks	14	*lyǎng-*	NU:	two or couple of	4
lái	V:	come (here)	11	*lyàng*	SV:	be light or bright (opp.	19
-lái	PV:	indicates	21			

		dark)		*mén*	N:	door	16
-lyǎu	PV:	indicates ca-pacity for doing something, or for carrying it through to completion	21	*míngbai*	V:	understand (clearly)	18
				míngnyán(MA)	N:	next year	13
				míngtyan(MA)	N:	tomorrow	12
				mǔchin	N:	mother	8
				ná	V:	take hold of; take, carry (smaller articles)	17
lyòu	NU:	six	3				
lyǔgwǎn	N:	hotel	15				
lyù	SV:	be green	24	*náchilai*	V:	pick up	17
ma	P:	(sentence suffix to simple questions)	1	*nà*	SP:	that (in general)	13
				(*nà*) *bú yaujǐn*	IE:	that's nothing! never mind!	13
mǎi	V:	buy	2				
mǎimai	N:	business (buy-sell)	7	*nán-*	N:	male (of persons)	5
mài	V:	sell; sell for	6	*nán*	SV:	be difficult, hard	9
màn	SV:	be slow	16				
máng	SV:	be busy, hurried	1	*nân*	N:	south	23
-máu	M:	dime	6	*nǎr*	N:	where?	10
màudz	N:	hat	8	*ne*	P:	(sentence suffix indicating continuance of action in positive statements)	10
méiyǒu, méiyou	V:	don't have, haven't	3				
méi(*you*)	P:	(verb prefix, negating completion of action)	12		P:	(sentence suffix, indicating suspense in negative statements)	12
méi(*you*) *fádz*	IE:	there's no way out! it can't be helped!	21				
					P:	(suffix to questions)	24
méi shémma!	IE:	don't mention it! it's nothing at all!	12	*něi-*	SP:	which?	4
				nèi-	SP:	that (there); the other	4
méiyisz	SV:	be dull, flat	8				
měi-	NU:	each	18	*nèm*(*ma*)	A:	in that way, to that degree, so	22
Měigwo	N:	America (U.S.A.)	2				
mèimei	N:	younger sister	8	*néng*	AV:	can, be able to	7

nèr	N: there	10		be acquainted		
nǐ	N: you (sing)	1		with		
nǐmen	N: you (pl)	1	rēng	V: throw (away)		24
nín	N: polite for nǐ	5	ròu	N: meat		14
-nyán	M: year	13	rúngyi	SV: be simple, easy		9
nyánnyán	A: year by year	13	sān	NU: three		3
nyàn	V: read aloud; study	9	shān	N: hill, mountain		21
nyànshū	VO: study; go to school	9	shàng	V: ascend, go up on; go to		15
nyǔ-	N: female (of persons)	5	shàngchē	VO: board a train or car		15
nyǔer	N: daughter	9	shàng(ge)(MA)líbai	N: last week		13
pà	V: be afraid of; fear that	21	shàng(ge)(MA)ywè	N: last month		13
pángbyār	N: the side of, flank	23	shàngjyē	VO: to the shopping district		15
pàng	SV: be fat (of persons)	22	shàngkè	VO: go to class		15
pǎu	V: run	16	shànglóu	VO: come or go upstairs		15
péngyou	N: friend	4				
píngcháng	SV: be ordinary, common	20	shàngsywé	VO: go to school		15
			shàngtou	N: above, top		10
-pù	N: -store, -shop	10	shàngwǔ (MA)	N: forenoon		19
pùdz	N: store	10	shǎu	SV: be little in quantity, few		8
pyányi	SV: be inexpensive	8				
-r	P: (diminutive suffix to nouns)	17	sháur	N: spoon		14
			shéi	N: who?		5
Rbǔn	N: Japan	5	shém(ma)	N: what?		5
rdz	N: day; a special day	19	shēngchì	VO: get angry, be angry		18
ràng	CV: (indicates agent) by	24	shǒu	N: hand		17
			shòu	SV: be thin(opp. pàng)		22
rè	SV: be hot	22				
rén	N: man, person	4	shŕ	NU: ten		3
rénrén	N: everyone (subject only)	4	shŕèr	NU: twelve		3
			shŕhou	N: time		13
rènde rènshr	V: know, recognize,	20	shŕyī	NU: eleven		3

shŕ	EV: is, are (equals)	5	
shŕ(ching)	N: affair; under-	7	
	taking		
shŕjyè(shang)	N: the world	22	
shū	N: book	2	
shūfáng	N: study, den (book		
	room)	17	
shūfu	SV: be comfortable	18	
shwěi	N: water	9	
shwèijyàu	VO: sleep, retire	19	
shwō	V: say (that)	4	
shwō gùshr	VO: tell a story	12	
sùng	V: send, deliver	17	
	(things); send,		
	escort, see off		
sùng(gěi)	V: present as a	17	
	gift		
swéibyàn	IE: as one pleases	24	
	(lit. follow		
	convenience)		
-swèi	M: year(s) old	18	
swèishu	N: age (year count)	23	
swóyi	MA: therefore, so	11	
swóyǒude	N: all	22	
syà	V: descend, go down	15	
	from		
syà(ge)lǐbai	(MA)N: next week	13	
syà(ge)ywè	(MA)N: next month	13	
syàtou	N: below, bottom	10	
syàwǔ	(MA)N: afternoon	19	
syān	A: first	14	
syānsheng	N: Mr., sir,	5	
	gentlemen;		
	teacher; polite		
	for husband; you,		
	sir!		
syàndzài	MA: now, at present	7	

syāngsya	N: country (rural)	8	
syǎng	V: think, think	9	
	about; desire		
	AV: consider, plan to;		
	want to		
syáujye	N: Miss; polite for	5	
	daughter		
syǎu	SV: be little, small	4	
syǎusyin	SV: be careful	24	
	V: look out for		
syàu	V: laugh ot smile;	20	
	laugh at		
syàuhwa	N: a joke	20	
	V: make fun of		
-syē	M: quantity of;	9	
	several		
syě	V: write	7	
syèsye	V: thanks, thank	3	
	you		
syī	N: west	23	
syīwang	V: hope that, hope	13	
	for, expect that		
	N: hope, expectation		
syǐ	V: wash	21	
syǐhwan	V: like, be pleased	3	
	with		
	AV: like to, enjoy	8	
syīn	SV: be new	8	
syìn	N: letter, mail	14	
syíng	SV: be satisfactory,	11	
	all right, 'can		
	do'		
sying	N: surname	5	
	EV: be surnamed		
sywé	V: study; learn	8	
	AV: learn to, study		
	how to		

sywésheng	N:	student (learner)	8	*twō*	V:	take off (clothes)	21
sywésyàu	N:	school	10				
sż	NU:	four	3	*-tyān*	M:	day	13
tā	N:	he, she, him, her	1	*tyānchi*	N:	weather, climate	22
				tyāntyān	A:	every day	13
tāmen	N:	they, them	1	*-tyáu*	M:	(measure for rivers, roads, fish, etc.)	22
tài	A:	too, excessively	2				
tàitai	N:	Mrs., madam; polite for wife	5				
				wāigwo	N:	foreign country	9
tán	V:	converse; chat about	16	*wàitou*	N:	outside	10
				-wán	PV:	indicates end or completion of the action	21
tánhwà	VO:	carry on conversation	16				
tāng	N:	soup	14	*wǎn*	SV:	be late	19
táng	N:	sugar, candy	7	*wǎn*	N:	bowl	14
tèbyé	SV:	be special, distinctive	20	*-wǎn*	M:	bowl (of)	14
				wǎnfàn	N:	supper, dinner (late meal)	12
tì	CV:	for (in place of)	14				
				wǎnshang(MA)	N:	evening	12
tīng gùshr	VO:	listen to a story	12	*-wàn*	NU:	ten-thousand	6
				wǎng, wàng	CV:	towards (in direction of)	23
tīngjyan	V:	hear	18				
tīngshwō	IE:	hear(d) it said that	14	*wàng*	V:	forget	18
				wár	V:	play	14
tóu	N:	head	17	*-wèi*	M:	(polite for persons)	9
tóu-	P:	first (see Note 5)	18				
				wèishém(ma)	MA:	Why? (for what reason)	10
tsái	A:	just, merely	23				
	A:	then and only then, not until	24	*wèn*	V:	ask, inquire of or about	5
tsài	N:	vegetables; dish of Chinese food	14	*wèn...hǎu*	IE:	inquire after another's welfare	14
tsūngming	SV:	be intelligent, clever	9				
				wǒ	N:	I, me	1
tsúng	CV:	from	11	*wǒmen*	N:	we, us	1
tsúngchyán	MA:	formerly	18	*wūdz*	N:	room	10
-tsż	M:	a time; occasion	18	*wǔ*	NU:	five	5

wǔfàn	N:	noon meal	19
-yàng	M:	kind, sort, way	22
yàngdz	N:	style, appearance; sample	22
yàu	V:	want; want to	2
	AV:	going to, expect to; shall, will	11
yàuburán	MA:	if not, then; otherwise, or else	24
yàubúshr	MA:	(*yàushr búshr*)	24
yàujǐn	SV:	be important	13
yàushr	MA:	if, in case	19
yě	A:	also, too; (with negative statements) either	3
yěsyǔ	MA:	perhaps, maybe	24
-yè	M:	night	19
yèli	(MA)N:	nighttime, during the night	19
yī	NU:	one	3
yīshang	N:	clothes	21
yídìng	A:	certainly, definitely	11
yígùng	MA:	altogether, in all	6
yíkwàr	A:	together (also as N)	14
yílù-píngān	IE:	a pleasant journey!	20
yíyàng	SV:	be the same, alike, similar	22
	A:	equally, similarly	
yíyè	(MA)N:	a night, the whole night	19
yǐchyán	MA:	previously;	20

		formerly	
...*yǐchyán*	MA:	before..., ...ago	20
yǐdz	N:	chair	4
...*yǐhòu*	MA:	after...	20
yǐhòu	MA:	(t)hereafter	20
yǐjing	A:	already	12
yìdyǎr	N:	a little, a bit; some	6
Yìgwo	N:	Italy	5
yìhwěr	(MA)N:	(in) a moment	16
yìjŕ	A:	straight on, direct	23
yìsz	N:	idea, meaning	8
yìtyān	(MA)N:	a day; a whole day	15
yīnwei	MA:	because (of), for	10
yīngdāng	AV:	ought to, should	15
Yīnggwo	N:	England	5
-yīnglǐ(lù)	M:	an English mile	23
Yīngwén	N:	English language	9
yǒu	V:	have, has	3
	V:	there is or are	8
	CV:	be as much as; be as	22
yǒubìng	VO:	be sick	18
yǒude	N:	some, some of, certain (used only in subject)	4
yǒu(de) shŕhou	MA:	sometimes	13
yǒumíng	SV:	be prominent, well-known	20
yǒuyìsz	SV:	be interesting	8
yǒuyùng	SV:	be useful	14
yòu	A:	again (in past)	17
yòu	N:	right	23

yú	N:	fish	14	*ywǎn*	SV:	be far	23
yùbei	V:	prepare	21	*ywànyi*	AV:	wish to, be	7
yùng	V:	use, employ	14			willing to	
	CV:	with, (using)		₁*ywè*	N:	month	13

INDEX

A

ABLE TO néng A 7
ABOUT (almost) chàbudwō IE 19
ABOVE shàngtou N 10
ACT PART OF dzwò V 7
ACQUAINTED WITH (recognize)rènshr,
  rènde V 20
ADULT dàren N 7
AFFAIR (matter) shrching N 7
AFRAID OF pà V 21
AFRAID THAT kŭngpà V 21
AFTER, in time yìhòu MA 20
AFTERNOON syàwŭ (MA)N 19
AFTERWARDS hòulai MA 15
AGAIN (in past) yòu A 17
AGAIN (still more) hái A 12
AGAIN (in future) dzài A 17
AGE (of life) swèishu N 23
AGO yǐqián MA 20
AIRPLANE fēijī N 11
ALIKE (be the same) yīyàng SV 22
ALL swóyǒude N 22
ALL dōu A 2
ALMOST chàbudwō IE 19
ALREADY yǐjīng A 12
ALLRIGHT (satisfactory) syíng A 12
ALSO (too) yě A 3
ALTOGETHER (in all) yígùng MA 6
ALWAYS (often) cháng(cháng) A 9
ALWAYS (keep on) lǎu A 20
AUTOMOBILE chìchē N 11
AMERICA Měigwo N 2
AND gēn CV 14
ANGRY shēngchì VO/SV 18
APPEARANCE yàngdz N 22
ARRIVE AT (reach) dàu V 13
ASCEND shàng V 15
ASK (inquire) wèn V 5
ASSIST (render aid) bāngmáng VO 17
(be) AT, in, on dzài V 10

B

BACK (behind) hòutou N 10
BAD hwài SV 18
BE AS MUCH AS yǒu SV 22
BECAUSE OF yīnwèi MA 10
BEFORE, in time yǐchyán MA 20

BELOW syàtou N 10
BIG dà SV 4
a BIT yìdyǎr N 6
BLACK hēi SV 19
BLUE lán SV 24
BOARD (to go upon train car) shàng-
  chē VO 15
BOOK shū N 2
BOTH (all) dōu A 2
BOTTOM syàtou N 10
BOWL wǎn N 14
BREAKFAST dzǎufàn N 12
BRIGHT lyàng SV 19
BRING dài V 17
BUILDING fángdz N 10
BUSINESS mǎimai N 7
BUS-STOP chìchējàn N 13
BUSY máng SV 1
BUT kěshr MA 4
BUY mǎi V 2
BY (indicating doer of action)
  jyàu, ràng CV 24

C

CAN (know how to) hwèi AV 7
CAN (may) kéyi AV 7
CAN (able to) néng AV 7
"CAN DO" (be all right) syíng SV 11
CANDY táng N 7
CAR chìchē N 11
CAREFUL syàusyīn SV 24
CARRY (small things) ná V 17
CONVERSE tánhwà VO 16
CARRY OUT (manage) bàn V 21
CENT -fēn M 6
CERTAINLY yídìng A 11
CERTAINLY (indeed) kě A 19
CHARACTER (written symbol) dz̀ N 7
CHAIR yǐdz N 4
CHILD háidz N 5
CHINA Jūnggwo N 2
CHOPSTICKS kwàidz N 14
CITY chéng N 10
CLEAN gānjing SV 21
CLEAR (in meaning) chīngchu SV 18

CLEVER (intelligent) tsūngming SV 9
CLIMATE (weather) tyānchi N 22
CLOCK jūng N 3
CLOSE UP (shut) gwān(shang) V 16
CLOTHES yīshang N 21
CLUMSY bèn SV 21
COLD lěng Sv 22
COME lái V 11
COME BACK (return here) hwéilai V 12
COMFORTABLE shūfu SV 18
COMMON (usual) píngcháng SV 20
COMPARED WITH bǐ SV 22
CONSIDER (plan to) syǎng AV 5
CONSIDER (have opinion that) kàn V 20
CONSIDER (feel that) jywéde V 20
CONVENIENT fāngbyàn SV 22
CONVERSE (chat) tán V 16
CORRECT dwèi SV 4
COUNTRY (rural area) syāngsya N 8
COUNTRY (nation) gwó N 5
COUPLE (two of) lyǎng- NU 4
CROSSOVER (pass over to) gwò V 19
CRY, CRY ABOUT kū V 18

D

DARK hēi Sv 19
DAUGHTER (polite) syáujye N 5
DAUGHTER nyuér N 9
DAY BEFORE YESTERDAY chyántyān (MA)N 20
DAYTIME báityān (MA)N 19
DAY tyān M 13
DAY (special day) rdz N 19
DAY AFTER TOMORROW hòutyān (MA)N 20
DAY (of month) hàu M 13
(one) DAY (once upon a time) yǒu yityān (MA) N 15
DEFINITELY yídìng A 11
DELIVER sùng V 17
DEN (study) shūfáng N 17
(it) DEPENDS ON kàn V 23
DESIRE syǎng V 9
DIFFER BY chà V 19
DIME -máu M 6
DINNER wǎnfàn N 12
DINING ROOM fàntīng N 17
DIRECTLY (straight on to) yìjŕ A 23
DIRTY dzāng SV 21
DISH (of food) tsài N 14
DISTINCTIVE (special) tèbyé SV 20
DO dzwò V 7

DOLLAR -kwài M 6
DON'T (imperative) byé AV 15
DOOR mén N 16
DRAW hwà V 9
DRINK hē V 9
DULL (uninteresting) méiyìsz SV 8
DURING THE DAY báityān (MA)N 19

E

EACH měi- NU 18
EARLY dzǎu SV 19
EAST dūng N 23
EASY (simply) rúngyi SV 9
EAT FOOD chŕ fàn VO 7
EAT chŕ V 7
EIGHT bā- NU 3
EITHER (or) hwòshr Ma 24
ELDER BROTHER gēge N 8
ELEVEN shŕyī- NU 3
EMPLOY (use) yùng V 15
ENGLAND Yīngwo N 5
ENGLISH LANGUAGE Yīngwén N 9
ENJOY syǐhwān AV 8
(that'll be) ENOUGHT Gòule! IE 14
ENOUGHT gòu SV 6
ENTER IN jìn V 16
ESCORT (a person) sùng V 17
EXCEED (pass beyond) gwò V 19
EXCESSIVELY tài A 2
EXCITED jāují SV 24
EXCUSE ME! Dwèibuchǐ! IE 16
EXIT FROM THE HOUSE chūmén V 16
EXPECTATION syīwang N 13
EXPECT THAT syīwang V 13
EXPENSIVE gwèi SV 2
EVEN (including) lyán CV 24
EVEN (still more) gèng A 22
EVENING wǎnshang N 12
EVERYONE rénrén N 4

F

FACE lyǎn N 21
FAIR (in complexion) bái SV 13
FAMILY jyā N 10
FAR ywǎn Sv 23
FAST kwài SV 16
FAT (of person) pàng SV 22
FATHER fùchin N 8
FEAR THAT pà N 21

FEEL THAT jywéde V 20
FEMALE (of persons, prefix) nyǔ-
   N 5
FEW shǎu SV 8
FIERCE lìhai SV 22
FIGHT A WAR dǎjàng VO 20
FIRST (before anything else) syān
   A 14
FIRST (first in order) dìyī P 13
FISH yú N 14
(you) FLATTER ME! bugǎndāng IE 20
FLY fēi V 23
FOOD (cooked rice) fàn N 7
FOOD (prepared dish) tsài N 14
FOOT (Chinese measure) chř M 23
FOR (because of) yīnwèi MA 10
FOR (in place of) tì CV 14
FOR (in benefit of) gěi CV 14
FORENOON shàngwǔ (MA) N 19
FORK chādz N 14
FORMERLY (in the past) yǐchyán MA20
FOUR sz̀ NU 3
FRANCE Fàgwo N 5
FRIEND péngyǒu N 4
FROM (distant from) lí CV 23
FROM tsúng CV 11
FRONT chyántou N 10
FULL (satisfied after eating) bǎu
   SV 21

G

GENTLEMAN syānsheng N 5
GIVE gěi V 3
GO (move, of watches, cars, etc.)
   dzǒu V 23
GO BY (ride on) dzwò CV 16
GO (walk away) dzǒu V 12
GO BY WAY OF dzǒu V 23
GO DOWN (descend) syà V 15
GO UP ON (ascend) shàng V 15
GO INTO CITY jìnchéng VO 16
GO TO CLASS shàngkè VO 15
GO TO SCHOOL (study) nyànshū VO 15
GO TO SCHOOL shàngsywé VO 15
GO TO SHOPPING DISCRICT shàngjyē
   VO 15
GO UPSTAIRS shànglóu VO 15
GO UP (ascend) shàng V 15
GOOD hǎu SV 1

GOOD TO LISTEN TO hǎutīng SV 9
GOODLOOKING hǎukàn SV 2
GREEN lyù SV 24
GUEST kèren N 24

H

HALF -bàn, bàn- NU 6
HAND shǒu N 17
HAPPY gāusyìng SV 18
HAS yǒu V 3
HAT màudz N 8
HAVE yǒu V 3
HAVE TO (must) děi AV 15
HAVEN'T méiyou V 3
HE tā N 1
HEAD tóu N 17
HEAR tīngjyàn V 18
HEARD IT THAT tīngshwō IE 14
HELP (someone) bāng (jù) V 17
(it can't be) HELPED! (no way out!)
   méi(you) fádz! IE 12
HER tā N 1
HERE jèr N 10
HIGH gāu SV 1
HILL shān N 21
HIM tā N 1
HOME jīa N 10
HOPE syīwàng N 13
HOPE THAT/FOR syīwàng V 13
HOT (in temperature) rè SV 22
HOTEL lyúgwǎn N 15
HOUR (on the clock) -dyǎn jūng M 19
HOUR (in duration) N 19 jūngtóu
HOUSE fángdz N 10
HOWEVER kěshr MA 4
HOW (to what degree?) dwō(ma) A 23
HOW'S EVERYTHING? dzěmmayàng? IE 22
HOW ABOUT ...? ... dzěmmayàng IE 22
HOW ABOUT ...? ... hǎubuhǎu IE 6
HOW MANY? (under ten) jǐ- NU 4
HOW MUCH/MANY? (over ten) dūoshǎu NU 6
HUNDRED -bǎi NU 6
HUNGRY è SV 21
HUNT FOR jǎu V 15
HURRIED máng SV 1
HUSBAND syānsheng N 5

I

I wǒ N 1
IDEA yìsz N 8
INDISPOSED (slightly ill) bùshūfu
  SV 18
IF yàushr MA 19
IF NOT yàuburán MA 24
IMMEDIATELY lìke jìu A 18
IMPORTANT yàujǐn SV 13
IN CASE yàushr MA 19
INDEED kě A 19
INEXPENSIVE pyányi SV 8
INFORM (tell) gàusung V 19
INSIDE lǐtou N 10
IN THIS WAY dzèmma A 22
INQUIRE AFTER ... wèn ... hǎu IE
  14
INQUIRE ABOUT wèn V 5
IS shr EV 5
INTELLIGENT tsūngming SV 9
INTERESTING yǒuyìsz SV 8
INTRODUCE jyèshau V 20
INVITE chǐng V 3
ITALY Yìdali, Yìgwo N 5

J

JAPAN rběn N 5
JOKE syàuhwa N 20
(have a pleasant) JOURNEY yílù píng-
  ān IE 20
JUST (merely) tsái A 23
JUST A MOMENT AGO gāngtsái MA 19
JUST IN THE MIDST OF jèng dzài
  A 17
JUST THIS MINUTE gāng(gāng) A 19

K

KEEP ON lǎu A 20
KIND (sort) -yàng M 22
KITCHEN chúfáng N 18
KNIFE dāudz N 14
KNOW (recognize) rènde, rènshr V20
KNOW HOW TO hwèi AV 7
KNOW OF/ABOUT jrdau V 5

L

LATE wǎn SV 19
LACK (differ by) chà V 19
LANGUAGE (speech) hwà N 7
LARGE dà SV 4
LAST MONTH shàngge yùe (MA) N 13
LAST WEEK shàngge syīngchī, shàngge
  lǐbài (MA) N 13
LAST YEAR chyùnyán (MA) N 13
LAUGH/LAUGH AT syàu V 20
LEARN sywé V 8
LEARN TO sywé AV 8
LEAVE (a place) líkāi V 23
LEAVE (go from) dzǒu V 12
LEFT dzwǒ N 23
LEISURE TIME gūngfu N 14
LESSON kè M 15
LET (allow) jyàu CV 16
LET GO OF fàng V 7
LETTER syìn N 14
LIGHT (be bright) lyàng SV 19
LIKE, LIKE TO syǐhwān V 3
LIKE TO (love to) ài AV 7
LIQUOR jyǒu N 9
LISTEN TO A STORY tīng gùshr VO 12
LITTLE (in size) syǎu SV 4
LITTLE (in quantity) shǎu SV 8
LITTLE BIT yidyǎr N 6
LIVE (reside at) jù V 15
LONG (in length or time) cháng SV 22
LONG WHILE bàntyān (MA) N 15
LOOK AT kàn V 2
LOOK FOR jǎu V 15
LOOK OUT FOR (be careful about)
  syǎusyīn V 24
LOST FACE (publicly) dyōulyǎn IE 21
LOSE (missplace) dyōu V 21
LOVE ài V 7
LOW (in elevation) dī Sv 23
LUNCH wǔfàn N 19, jūngfàn N 12

M

MADAM tàitai N 5
MAIL syìn N 14
MAKE dzwò V 7
MAKE FUN OF syàuhwà V 20
MAKE WAR dǎjàng VO 20
MALE (of persons, prefix nán- N 5

MANAGE bàn V 21
MAN (person) rén N 4
MANY (in number) dwō Sv 8
(a good) MANY hǎusyē NU 15
MAY kéyi AV 7
MAYBE yěsyǔ MA 24
ME wǒ N 1
MEANING (idea) yìsz N 8
MEAT ròu N 14
MEET jyàn V 16
(don't) MENTION IT! Méi shémma!
    IE 12
MERELY tsái A 23
METHOD (way) fádz N 21
MILE (English) Yīnglǐ M 23
MILE (Chinese) -lǐ M 23
MINUTE -fēn M 6
MISS syǎujye N 5
MISSPLACE (lose) dyōu V 21
(in a) MOMENT yìhwěr (MA) N 16
MONEY chyán N 3
MONTH ywè N 13
MORNING dzǎushang (MA) N 12
(the) MOST/-EST dzwèi A 9
MOTHER mǔchin N 8
MOUNTAIN shān V 21
MOVE (heavy articles) bān V 17
MOVE (change residence) bān V 16
MOVE ONE'S RESIDENCE bānjyā VO 16
MR. syānsheng N 5
MRS. tàitai N 5
MUST (have to) děi A 15

                  N

NAMED (is called) jyàu EV 5
NATION (state) gwó N 5
NATURALLY (of course) dāngrán M 24
NEED NOT búbì A 15
NEGATIVE PREFIX bù, bú P 1
NERVIOUS bùfàngsyīn SV 24
NEVER MIND (that's nothing) búyàu-
    jǐn IE 13
NEW syīn SV 8
NEWSPAPER bàu N 2
NEXT (week, month, time) syà-
    (MA) N 13
NIGHT (a night) yíyè (MA) N 19
NIGHTTIME (during the night) yèlǐ
    (MA) N 19

NINE jyǒu NU 3
NO USE TO búyùng AV 15
NOON jūngwǔ (MA) N 19
NORTH běi N 23
NOT NECESSARILY bùyídìng A 11
NOT VERY buda A 18
(it's) NOTHING AT ALL méi shémma
    IE 12
(that's) NOTHING (of no importance)
    búyàujǐn IE 13
NOW syàndzài MA 7
NUMBER (of a house, room, etc.)
    hàu M 13

                  O

(much) OBLIGED láujyà IE 17
OCCASION (time occurrence) -tsz M 18
  -hwéi M 18
OF COURSE dāngrán MA 24
OFTEN cháng(cháng) A 9
OLD (in years) lǎu SV 8
OLD (not new) jyòu SV 8
ON dzài N 20
(at) ONCE jyòu A 18
ONE yī NU 3
ONESELF dzìjǐ N 20
ONLY jyòu A 6
OPEN kāi V 15
OPERATE (machinery) kāi V 15
OR hwòshr MA 24
ORDER (tell) jyàu CV 16
ORDINARY (be common) píngcháng SV 20
ORIGINALLY běnlái MA 20
OTHER (person or thing) byéde N 12
OTHER PEOPLE byérén N 12
OTHERWISE yàuburán MA 24
OUGHT TO yīngdāng AV 15
OUT OF ORDER (broken) hwàile V 18
OUTSIDE wàitou N 10

                  P

PAINT (draw) hwà V 9
PAPER jǐ V 6
PARENTS fùmǔ N 8
PARLOR (living room) kètīng N 16
PART (section) -bù M 23
PASS (exceed) gwò V 19
PASS BY jīnggwò V 23

PEN bǐ N 2
PENCIL bǐ N 2
PERHAPS kǔngpà V 21
PERMITTED TO kéyi AV 7
PERSON rén N 4
PICK UP náchilai V 17
PIECE -kwài M 15
PLACE dìfang N 10
PLACE (put) fàng V 17
PLAN TO dǎswàn V 20
PLAN TO (desire to) syǎng AV 9
PLEASED WITH syǐhwān V 3
PLAY wár V 14
(as you) PLEASE swéibyàn IE 24
POCKET kǒudàr N 17
POLITE kèchi SV 7
PERHAPS yésyǔ MA 24
PREPARE yùbei V 21
PRESENT (a gift) sùng V 17
PRETTY GOOD bùhwài SV 18
PREVIOUSLY yǐchyán MA 20
PROBABLY dàgài Ma 24, kǔngpà V 21
PUT (place) fàng V 17
PUT DOWN fàngsya(lai) V 17
PUT ON (clothes) chwān V 21

Q

QUARTER (of an hour) -kè zhōng M 19
QUEER (strange) chígwài SV 21
QUICK (fast) kwài SV 16
QUICKLY (soon) kwài A 16
QUITE A FEW háujǐ- NU 15
QUITE GOOD bútswò SV 14
QUITE (very) hěn A 1

R

RAILROAD STATION hwǒchējàn N 13
READ ALOUD nyàn V 9
REACH (arrive at) dàu V 13
(be) READY (done) hǎule V 18
REALLY (truly) jēn A 7
RECOGNIZE (know) rènde, rènshr V20
RED húng SV 24
REFRESHMENTS (light snacks) dyǎn-
     syīn N 18
REMEMBER jìde V 24
REQUEST chǐng V 3

REST ASSURED fàngsyīn SV 24
RESTAURANT fàngwǎr N 10
RETURN (to) hwéi V 15
RETURN HERE hwéilai V 12
RETURN HOME hwéijyā VO 15
RIDE ON dzwò V 11
RIGHT (correct) dwèi SV 4
(that's) RIGHT! Dwèile! IE 13
RIGHT (opposite of left) yòu N 23
RISE (get up) chǐlai V 19
RIVER hé N 22
ROAD lù N 16
ROOM wūdz N 10
ROUTE lù N 16
RUN pǎu V 16
RUSSIA Ègwo N 5

S

SAMPLE yàngdz N 22
(be) SATISFACTORY sying SV 11
SATISFIED (after eating) chrbǎule
SAY (that) shwō V 4
SCHOOL sywésyàu N 10
SEA hǎi N 23
SECTION (part) -bù M 23
SEE (meet formally) jyàn V 16
SEE (look at) kàn V 11
SEE (and perceive) kànjyan V 18
SEE OFF sùng V 17
SELF (oneself) dzìjǐ N 20
SELL, SELL FOR mài V 6
SEND (deliver) sùng V 17
SENTENCE jyùdz N 14
SEVEN chī NU 3
SEVERAL -cyē M 9
SHE tā N 1
SHORT (in length) dwǎn SV 22
SHORT (not tall) ǎi SV 22
SHOULD yīngdāng A 15
SICK (have an illness) yǒubìng VO 18
SICK (become ill) bìngle V 18
SICKNESS bìng N 18
SIDE (border, part) -byār M 23
SIDE OF pángbyār N 23
SIMILAR yíyàng SV 22
SIMILARLY yíyàng SV 22
SIMPLE (easy) rúngyi SV 9
SING chàng V 7

THOUSAND -chyān NU 6
THROW AWAY rēng V 24
TIME shŕhou N 13
TIME (occasion) -tsz M 18
TIRED lèi SV 1
TO (for the benefit of) gěi CV 14
TO (towards direction of) dàu CV11
TO (facing) dwèi CV 14
TODAY jīntyān N 12
TOGETHER yíkwar A 14
TOMORROW míngtyān (MA) N 12
TOO tài A 2
TOO (also) yě A 3
TOP shàngtou N 10
TOWARDS (the direction of) wàng
   CV 23
TRAIN hwǒchē N 11
TRULY jēn A 7
TWELVE shŕrèr NU 3
TWENTY èrshŕ NU 3
TWO èr NU 3
TWO (couple of) lyǎng- NU 4

U

UNCERTAIN bùyídìng A 11
UNCOMFORTABLE bùshūfu SV 18
UNDERNEATH dǐsyà N 10
UNDERSTAND dǔng V 4
UNDERSTAND CLEARLY míngbai V 18
UNDERSTANDING (as a consequence of
   seeing, hearing etc.) -dǔng PV21
UNEASY (be nervous about) bùfàng-
   syīn SV 24
UNUSUALLY fēicháng S 22
UPSTAIRS lóushang N 10
US wǒmen N 9
USE (employ) yùng V 14
USEFUL yǒuyùng SV 14
USING (with the aid of) yùng CV 14
USUALLY cháng(cháng) A 9

V

VEGETABLES tsài N 14
VEHICLE (wheeled) chē N 11
VERY (to an exagggerated degree)
   -jíle P 16
VERY hěn A 1

VIA jīnggwò V 23
VISIT kàn V 11
VOLUME (books) -běn M 4

W

WAIT, WAIT FOR děng V 16
WALK dzǒu V 12
WANT yàu V 2
WASH syī V 21
WATCH (clock) byǎu N 3
WATER shwěi N 9
WAY (method) fádz N 21
(no) WAY OUT méiyou fádz IE 21
WE wǒmen N 1
WEAR (hat, watch) dài V8
WEAR(clothes) chwān V 21
WEATHER tyānchi N 22
WEEK syīngqī, lǐbài N 13
WELL (be good) hǎu SV 1
(be) WELL ONCE AGAIN hǎule V 18
WELL KNOWN yǒumíng SV 20
WEST syī N 23
WHAT shémma N 5
(in) WHAT WAY dzěmma (MA)   11
WHAT CAN BE DONE ABOUT IT? Dzěmma
   bàn? IE 19
WHAT'S HAPPENED?/ WHAT'S THE MATTER?
   dzěmma le? IE 18
WHERE nǎr N 10
WHETHER hwòshr MA 24
WHICH něi- SP 4
WHICH (of a series) dìjǐ SP 13
(long) WHILE bàntyān (MA) 15
WHITE bái SV 19
WHO shéi, shémma rén N 5
WHY (how is it that?) dzěmma A 18
WHY (for what reason) wèishemma MA 10
WIFE (polite form) tàitai N 5
WILLING TO kěn AV 21
WILLING TO (want to) ywànyi AV 7
WINDOW chwānghu N 16
WILL (shall) yàu AV 11
WINE jyǒu N 9
WISH FOR syīwàng V 13
WISH TO (be willing to) ywànyi AV 7
WITH gēn CV 14
WORD (written character) dz̀ N 7
WORRIED jāují SV 24

WORLD shŕjyè (shàng) N 22
WRITE syě V 7
WRITING INSTRUMENT bǐ N 2
YEAR -nyán M 13
(this) YEAR jīnnyán (MA) N 13
(next) YEAR míngnyán (MA) N 13
YEARS OLD -swèi M 18
YEAR BY YEAR nyánnyán A 13
YELLOW hwáng SV 24
YESTERDAY dzwótyān (MA) N 12
YOU (singular) nǐ N 1
YOU (plural) nǐmen N 1
YOUNGER BROTHER dìdi N 8

           Z

ZERO líng NU 6